# ESSAYS ON MANDEL'ŠTAM

*Harvard Slavic Studies*
*Volume VI*

# ESSAYS ON MANDEL'ŠTAM

Kiril Taranovsky

Harvard University Press
Cambridge, Massachusetts, and London, England   1976

Library of Congress Cataloging in Publication Data

Taranovsky, Kiril.
   Essays on Mandel'štam.

   (Harvard Slavic studies; v. 6)
   Includes index.
   1.   Mandel'shtam, Osip Emil'evich, 1891–1938—
Criticism and interpretation. I.   Title. II.
Series: Harvard Slavic studies (Cambridge, Mass.); v. 6.
PG13.H3 vol. 6 [PG3476.M355] 891.7'1'3 75-20195
ISBN 0-674-26705-2

# FOREWORD

My first serious encounter with Mandel'štam's poetry took place over forty years ago, in Prague, where I was spending the summer of 1931, having just completed my sophomore year at the Law School of Belgràde University. There, in the famous Slavic bookstore in Wenceslaus Square, I happened on the first edition of *Tristia* (1922)—which, strange though it may seem today, had not yet sold out, despite the fact that only three thousand copies had been printed. Until then I was familiar with only a few of Mandel'štam's poems, published in various anthologies; reading *Tristia* prompted me to search out the other two books of his poetry. Thus I discovered his unique poetic world, whose fascination was to remain strong for the rest of my life. Though taken with the "music" of his verse and his exquisite imagery, I was annoyed with my inability to understand the cryptic messages of certain of his poems, to grasp their "deep meaning." Even at that time I believed that there must be one, since the majority of his poems did not present problems in this respect. Later, during my philological studies at Belgrade University (1933–36) and at the Charles University in Prague (1938–39), I became aware of the many "poetic reminiscences" in Mandel'štam's poetry; it was not difficult to recognize at least those from Lermontov and Tjutčev. Subsequently I came to believe that in order to understand his poetic world, one had to acquire Mandel'štam's culture, as far as possible. However, neither in the thirties, nor in the next two decades, did I think of undertaking such a task.

My second major encounter with Mandel'štam occurred after I came to this country (in 1958) and bought the New York edition of Mandel'-štam's *Sobranie sočinenij* (1955). At this time I became primarily interested in his versification, especially when I noticed that his iambic hexameter after 1915 has a most original rhythmic structure, un-precedented in eighteenth- and nineteenth-century Russian poetry. It was then that I decided to make a thorough statistical description of his verse, based on the texts published in *Sobranie sočinenij*. My study "Stixosloženie Osipa Mandel'štama (1908–1925)" appeared in the *International Journal of Slavic Linguistics and Poetics* V, 1962.

While working with Mandel'štam's poetry line by line, I became convinced that his poetic themes and images needed to be studied in the broad context of both his poetry and his prose writings. By this time I was finding many reminiscences from other poets, primarily Russian, which helped me to understand the poetic messages of several poems labeled enigmatic. I was astonished to find him appropriating images from the poetry of Vjačeslav Ivanov, whose poetic world I considered an antipode of Mandel'štam's. Nonetheless, it was in Ivanov's translation of Sappho and in his original poetry that I found the key to the interpretation of two Mandel'štam poems containing ancient Greek images. My first essay to deal with Mandel'štam's poetic themes and imagery, "Pčely i osy v poèzii Mandel'štama" (published in the 1967 Festschrift for Roman Jakobson), also represented my first attempt to analyse his poetry in the double terms I have designated context and subtext.

Exactly at that time several Harvard graduate students who were aware of my current scholarly interests asked me to give a seminar devoted to Mandel'štam's poetry. This seminar took place in the spring of 1968, and proved exceptionally successful. I am very grateful to all its participants for lively discussions and for stimulating questions which helped me to formulate my own views more precisely. Naturally enough, these discussions and questions centered on theoretical problems, particularly the function of "other voices" in his poetry.

The seminar resulted in more than one publishable (and published) paper, and two excellent doctoral dissertations, to whose authors—Omry Ronen, now of the Hebrew University in Jerusalem, and Steven Broyde, of Amherst College—I should like to offer my sincere gratitude. Our intellectual exchanges over work in progress, theirs and my own, were no less valuable than the bibliographical checking they so willingly undertook on my behalf. I am further indebted to Steven Broyde for his translation of those essays of mine that were originally published in Russian.

Since this book is so closely connected both with my research and teaching at Harvard, I am particularly gratified that it should appear in the present series. My warm appreciation extends to the Harvard University Press for undertaking such a complex work, and to my colleague and friend, Donald Fanger, general editor of the Harvard Slavic Studies, for his help in making this publication possible.

The essays here collected and revised have all been previously published: seven of them in various Mouton and Company publications and one in *California Slavic Studies* (see the Author's Note at the end of this book). I would like to thank the Edicom N.V. and the University of California Press for their permission to include them here.

This volume would have been poorer without the generous help of scholars who read some of my essays in manuscript or commented on them after their first publication. I owe a debt of deepest gratitude to my teacher and friend Roman Osipovič Jakobson for friendly criticism and valuable advice. Gratitude of the same order goes to my dear Moscow friends, Mixail Leonovič Gasparov and Jurij Iosifovič Levin, for detailed letters responding to problems raised in my essays, for their helpful and stimulating suggestions, and, finally, for supplying me with some texts and information unavailable to me in this country.

Last, but not least, I am very much indebted to Mrs. Leslie O'Bell of the Harvard Society of Fellows for helping in a variety of ways to prepare the manuscript for publication.

# CONTENTS

**I**  Concert at the Railroad Station  1

**II**  The Hayloft  21

**III**  The Black-Yellow Light  48

**IV**  The Clock-Grasshopper  68

**V**  Bees and Wasps  83

**VI**  The Soil and Destiny  115

Notes  135

Author's Note  173

Indexes  175

# ESSAYS ON MANDEL'ŠTAM

# I

## CONCERT AT THE RAILROAD STATION

*The Problem of Context and Subtext*

On October 22, 1920, Blok wrote in his diary:

Гвоздь вечера — И. Мандельштам, который приехал, побывав во
врангелевской тюрьме. Он очень вырос. Сначала невыносимо
слушать общегумилевское завывание. Постепенно привыкаешь . . .
Виден артист. Его стихи возникают из снов — очень своеобразных,
лежащих в областях искусства только.

It is not completely clear whether Blok's last sentence means that the
main concern of Mandel'štam's poetry is art itself, or that art is the
main source of his inspiration. Whatever Blok may have meant, both
assumptions are true.

> Я получил блаженное наследство –
> *Чужих певцов блуждающие сны;*
> Свое родство и скучное соседство
> Мы презирать заведомо вольны.
> И не одно сокровище, быть может,
> Минуя внуков, к правнукам уйдет,
> И снова скальд *чужую* песню сложит
> И как *свою* ее произнесет.
>
> («Я не слыхал рассказов Оссиана»)

These lines were written by Mandel'štam as early as 1914. In June
1932, the same idea is repeated in the conclusion of his poem dedicated
to Batjuškov:

> Что ж, поднимай удивленные брови,
> Ты, горожанин и друг горожан,
> Вечные сны, как образчики крови,
> Переливай из стакана в стакан.

The idea of pouring eternal dreams from one glass to another is further developed in the poem "K nemeckoj reči," written two months later:

> Чужая речь мне будет оболочкой,
> И много прежде, чем я смел родиться,
> *Я буквой был, был виноградной строчкой,*
> *Я книгой был, которая вам снится.*

The image of the grape line finds its explanation in the poem dedicated to Batjuškov. It is a metaphor for the genuine freshness of poetry:

> И отвечал мне оплакавший Тасса:
> «Я к величаньям еще не привык,
> Только стихов виноградное мясо
> Мне освежило случайно язык».

It should be noted that the metaphor of the grape as poetry was already hinted at in "Grifel'naja oda" (1923), Mandel'štam's most complicated poem about the creative poetic process: "Plod naryval. Zrel vinograd."[1]

The idea of the preexistence of poetry ("... prežde čem ja smel rodit'sja ... ja knigoj byl ...") is expressed on a more abstract level in one of his "Vos'mistišija" (1934). "Lips" in this poem are undoubtedly the "poetic lips" (a favorite image in Mandel'štam's poetry), and the whispering which was born before the lips is poetry itself:

> И Шуберт на воде, и Моцарт в птичьем гаме,
> И Гёте, свищущий на вьющейся тропе,
> И Гамлет, мысливший пугливыми шагами,
> Считали пульс толпы и верили толпе.
> Быть может, прежде губ уже родился шёпот
> И в бездревесности кружилися листы,
> И те, кому мы посвящаем опыт,
> До опыта приобрели черты.[2]

Poetry existed even before humanity became aware of it, Mandel'štam believes. But there were no poets: there were only joyful presentiments:

Поэзия — плуг, взрывающий время так, что глубинные слои времени, его чернозем оказываются сверху. Но бывают такие эпохи, когда человечество, не довольствуясь сегодняшним днем, тоскуя по глубинным слоям времени, как пахарь, жаждет целины времен...

Часто приходится слышать: это хорошо, но это вчерашний день. А я говорю: вчерашний день еще не родился. Его еще не было по-настоящему. Я хочу снова Овидия, Пушкина, Катулла, и меня не удовлетворяют исторический Овидий, Пушкин, Катулл.

Удивительно, в самом деле, что все возятся с поэтами и никак с ними не развяжутся. Казалось бы — прочел и ладно. Преодолел, как теперь говорят. Ничего подобного. Серебряная труба Катулла:

Ad claras Asiae volemus urbes

мучит и тревожит сильнее, чем любая футуристическая загадка. Этого нет по-русски. Но ведь это должно быть по-русски. Я взял латинские стихи потому, что русским читателем они явно воспринимаются, как категория долженствования; императив звучит в них нагляднее. Но это свойство всякой поэзии, поскольку она классична. Она воспринимается как то, что должно быть, а не как то, что уже было.

Итак, ни одного поэта еще не было. Мы свободны от груза воспоминаний. Зато сколько редкостных предчувствий: Пушкин, Овидий, Гомер. Когда любовник в тишине путается в нежных именах и вдруг вспоминает, что это уже было: и слова и волосы, и петух, который прокричал за окном, кричал уже в Овидиевых тристиях, глубокая радость повторенья охватывает его, головокружительная радость:

Словно темную воду, я пью помутившийся воздух,
Время вспахано плугом, и роза землею была.

Так и поэт не боится повторений и легко пьянеет классическим вином.

(«Слово и культура», 1921)

The Old Testament and the Apocalypse, Homer and Sappho, Ovid and Tibullus, Dante and Tasso, Racine and Balzac, Dickens and Edgar Allan Poe, Deržavin, Batjuškov, Puškin, Jazykov, Tjutčev, Lermontov, Fet, Blok, Andrej Belyj, Vjačeslav Ivanov, Gumilev, Axmatova — these are only some of the sources reflected in Mandel'štam's poetry, either as obvious reminiscences or as enciphered subtexts. Needless to say, such reminiscences, and even direct quotations, acquire a new quality in his work. Mandel'štam was not an imitator. This quality of Mandel'-štam's poetry was noted by Benedikt Livšic as early as 1919 (that is, after *Kamen'*, but before *Tristia*):

Не новых слов ищет поэт, но новых сторон в слове, данном как некая завершенная реальность — какой-то новой, доселе не замеченной нами грани, какого-то ребра, которым слово еще не было к нам обращено. Вот почему не только «старыми» словами орудует поэт: в стихах Мандельштама мы встречаем целые строки из других поэтов; и это не досадная случайность, не бессознательное заимствование, но своеобразный прием поэта, положившего себе целью заставить чужие стихи зазвучать по-иному, по-своему.[3]

Mandel'štam might well have applied to himself what he wrote of the poet Annenskij: "Innokentij Annenskij uže javljal primer togo, čem dolžen byt' organičeskij poèt: ves' korabl' skoločen iz čužix dosok, no u nego svoja stat'."[4]

A close friend of Mandel'štam, Nikolaj Ivanovič Xardžiev, told me on one occasion the following story. A short time before his last arrest, Mandel'štam visited him and complained that he had nothing to read. Xardžiev then gave him poems by Xlebnikov, a novel by H. G. Wells, and several recently published French novels. Mandel'štam looked at this pile of books and said: "What can one make of all of this?" ("Čto iz ètogo vsego možno sdelat'?")[5]

The assumption that Mandel'štam considered his reading as potential raw material for his own creative work seems to be fairly reasonable. Not only literature, but architecture, painting, and music, as well as philosophy, history, and even natural sciences, were sources of his inspiration. Jurij Levin called Mandel'štam in a private letter to me "samyj pereliteraturennyj i perekul'turennyj [russkij] poèt." Therefore, Clarence Brown is essentially right when he attributes to Mandel'štam the following thought: "If you would read me, you must have my culture."[6]

Thus, the investigation of all of Mandel'štam's literary and cultural sources becomes a very important prerequisite for a better understanding and fuller appreciation of his poetry. In other words, if an investigator finds a subtitle "Pindaričeskij otryvok" in the first printing of "Našedšij podkovu," it means that he has to reread Pindar's odes. And I would like to emphasize that such reading is fascinating indeed. The reader experiences the genuine joy of recognition, joy of discovery, of which Cvetaeva speaks so persuasively in her memoirs, calling it "nesravnennaja radost' otkrytija v sokrytii."[7]

Sometimes this recognition comes immediately, without further investigation. For example, Mandel'štam's line:

Да будет в старости *печаль моя светла* . . .

contains a simple quotation from Puškin's famous poem:

На холмах Грузии лежит ночная мгла;
Шумит Арагва предо мною.

Мне грустно и легко; *печаль моя светла;*
Печаль моя полна тобою . . .

The problem is more complicated in the first stanza of the poem "10 janvarja 1934," written immediately after the death of Andrej Belyj:

Меня преследуют две-три случайных фразы –
Весь день твержу: *печаль моя жирна,*
О Боже, как черны и синеглазы
*Стрекозы смерти, как лазурь черна.*

In this case, a new poetic reminiscence is projected, as it were, over the Puškinian pattern. It comes from *Slovo o polku Igoreve*: "Pečal' žirna teče sred' zemli ruskyja."[8]

I would like to mention parenthetically that the images of the dragon-flies of death and of the black azure have their source in Belyj's symphony *Kubok metelej* (pp. 131–132):

*Холодные стрекозы* садились на окна и ползали по стеклу . . . Прыснули вверх снега и как линии качались над домами. Обрывались *стеклянеющими стрекозами, стрекозы* садились на окна, смерзались снегом. Стеклянели там *мертвыми лилиями.*

And further (p. 224):

Милое, милое небе сияло — милая, милая *гробная лазурь.*

Moreover, we can find in Belyj's poetry the adjective "black" applied to azure, in his *tanka* "Lazuri" (1916):

Светлы, легки лазури . . .
Они — черны, без дна;
Там — мировые бури.
Там жизни тишина:
Она, как ночь, черна.[9]

It is not surprising that Mandel'štam, mourning the death of his fellow poet, recalls the images from his writings.[10]

As we see, the echoes of Puškin, *Slovo o polku Igoreve*, and of Belyj constitute a *subtext* of the stanza just quoted.

It is not always so easy to find a subtext in the poetry of Mandel'štam. At the end of his article "Slovo i kul'tura" (1921), Mandel'štam has the following statement:

Говорят, что причина революции — *голод в междупланетных пространствах.* Нужно рассыпать *пшеницу по эфиру.*[11]

The same image occurs in his poem "A nebo buduščim beremenno" (1923).[12]

> Итак, готовьтесь жить во времени,
> Где нет ни волка, ни тапира,
> А небо будущим беременно,
> *Пшеницей сытого эфира.*

In my Harvard seminar on Mandel'štam (spring 1968), all the participants were puzzled by this image. The verb *govorjat* indicated that it was a quotation. In June of the same year, during a visit to Moscow, I asked Mandel'štam's widow, Nadežda Jakovlevna, whether she knew the source. Her answer was: "He just wrote it, and I was always angry with him" ("Èto on prosto tak napisal, i ja vsegda na nego serdilas' "). However, Mandel'štam wrote nothing *prosto tak*. Recently, the subtext has been found by one of the participants of the seminar, Omry Ronen. The image comes from the mystical philosophy of G. I. Gurdžiev (Gurdjieff), who believed that organic life on the Earth fed the Moon and other celestial bodies, that wars and revolutions were results of planetary influences, particularly — that they were provoked by the hunger of the Moon.[13]

Mandel'štam liked to dream about the happy life of humanity, its "golden age," past or future. In 1919, during the height of the civil war, he turned to Hesiod's myth of the "holy islands."[14] In the early twenties, facing the threat of a new intervention by the Western allies, Mandel'štam transformed Gurdžiev's fantastic cosmology into a new poetic myth.

All poets have their favorite themes, their favorite images, and even their favorite words. All these recurrent themes and images form inner cycles in the work of a given poet, cycles which very often cannot be placed within exact chronological limits. Moreover, such recurrent themes and images may be characteristic of several poets, often independent of both the so-called poetic schools and even of historical periods. For example, many Russian poets of the twentieth century were fascinated by the image of the ship, including such different poets as Blok, Gumilev, Majakovskij, Mandel'štam, and B. Livšic. An autobiographic image of crucifixion is common to many twentieth-century Russian poets (Belyj, Brjusov, Blok, Xlebnikov, Majakovskij, Esenin, Pasternak, and others). There are hundreds of Russian poems written in trochaic pentameter which deal with a dynamic theme of the road and a static theme of life. All these poems form a "Lermontovian cycle," as I have called it, which begins with Lermontov's "Vyxožu odin ja na dorogu" and leads to Blok's "Vyxožu ja v put' otkrytyj vzoram," to

Majakovskij's "procyganennyj romans" ("Mal'čik šel v zakat glaza ustavja"), or to Pasternak's "Gamlet" ("Gul zatix. Ja vyšel na podmostki").[15]

Needless to say, we receive more poetic information when we put a poem in a broader context and reveal its links with other texts.

At this point I shall analyze Mandel'štam's poem "Koncert na vokzale" (1921) in terms of context and subtext in order to show how this concept works. Before doing so, however, I might ask a question: what would Mandel'štam himself think about such a method? The answer to this question can be found in his article "Barsuč'ja nora" and in his essay "Razgovor o Dante":

Установление литературного генезиса поэта, его литературных источников, его р о д с т в а и происхождения сразу выводит нас на твердую почву. На вопрос, что хотел сказать поэт, критик может и не ответить, но на вопрос, откуда он пришел, отвечать обязан . . .

(«Барсучья нора», 1922)

Конец четвертой песни «Inferno» — настоящая цитатная оргия. Я нахожу здесь чистую и беспримесную демонстрацию упоминательной клавиатуры Данта.

Клавишная прогулка по всему кругозору античности. Какой-то шопеновский полонез, где рядом выступают вооруженный Цезарь с кровавыми глазами грифа и Демокрит, разъявший материю на атомы.

*Цитата не есть выписка. Цитата есть цикада. Неумолкаемость ей свойственна.* Вцепившись в воздух, она его не отпускает.

(«Разговор о Данте», 1933)

Mandel'štam was not a poet of large forms; he did not write long poems or novels. But, as a matter of fact, his entire creative work is one entity, one large form: his unique poetic vision of the world, or — in more modern terms — the genuine poetic model of the world, created by him.

Many themes and images occur both in his poetry and in his prose. This is the case with his poem "Koncert na vokzale." A realistic description of concerts held at Pavlovsk railroad station may be found in *Šum vremeni*, in the chapter "Muzyka v Pavlovske," first published in 1925:

В середине девяностых годов в Павловск, как в некий Элизий, стремился весь Петербург. Свистки паровозов и железнодорожные звонки мешались с патриотической какофонией увертюры двенадцатого года, и особенный запах стоял в огромном вокзале, где царили Чайковский и Рубинштейн. Сыроватый воздух заплесневевших парков, запах гниющих парников и оранжерейных роз и навстречу ему — тяжелые испарения буфета, едкая сигара, вокзальная гарь и косметика многотысячной толпы.

However, in the poem a particular concert is described. The iron world of the station is enchanted, and the music which the poet hears acquires a symbolic meaning.

> Нельзя дышать, и твердь кишит червями,
> И ни одна звезда не говорит,
> Но, видит Бог, есть музыка над нами,
> Дрожит вокзал от пенья аонид,
> И снова, паровозными свистками
> Разорванный, скрипичный воздух слит.
>
> Огромный парк. Вокзала шар стеклянный.
> Железный мир опять заворожен.
> На звучный пир в элизиум туманный
> Торжественно уносится вагон.
> Павлиний крик и рокот фортепьянный –
> Я опоздал. Мне страшно. Это сон.
>
> И я вхожу в стеклянный лес вокзала,
> Скрипичный строй в смятеньи и слезах.
> Ночного хора дикое начало,
> И запах роз в гниющих парниках,
> Где под стеклянным небом ночевала
> Родная тень в кочующих толпах.
>
> И мнится мне: весь в музыке и пене
> Железный мир так нищенски дрожит,
> В стеклянные я упираюсь сени;
> Горячий пар зрачки смычков слепит.
> Куда же ты? На тризне милой тени
> В последний раз нам музыка звучит.

Lidija Ginzburg, in her article "Poètika Osipa Mandel'štama" (*Izvestija AN SSSR*, Serija literatury i jazyka, 1972, no. 4, 314–315) gives her own interpretation of "Koncert na vokzale," a very fine one. I shall quote it *in extenso*:

Архитектоника стихотворения сложна. В нем настоящее встречается с детскими воспоминаниями о знаменитых симфонических концертах в помещении Павловского вокзала. Внутри этой охватывающей антитезы сталкиваются три мира: *мир музыки* (для Мандельштама, как и для Блока, музыка не только искусство, но и высшая символика исторической жизни народов и духовной жизни отдельного человека); *стеклянный* мир вокзального концертного зала и *железный* мир проходящей рядом железной дороги — суровый антимузыкальный мир. Не следует однозначно, аллегорически расшифровывать подобные образы, это полностью противопоказано поэтической системе Мандельштама.

Все переплелось в тесном контексте: вокзал и аониды (музы), паровозные свистки и скрипичный, то есть наполненный звуком скрипок, воздух. Железный мир вовлечен в мир музыки. Достаточно уже слова *торжественно* с его классичностью и удлиненным звучанием, чтобы вагон уподобился атрибутам музыкального «элизиума». Вокзал дрожит от музыки («от пенья аонид») — это метафора традиционная, но в последней строфе она появляется опять в новом и усложненном облике:

> И мнится мне: весь в музыке и пене
> Железный мир так нищенски дрожит.

Теперь дрожит уже железный мир, завороженный, побежденный музыкой. Поэтому он весь в музыке. А в пене он потому, что дрожь вовлекла в этот смысловой круг представление о загнанном, взмыленном коне. Необычайное сочетание музыки и пены придает музыке материальность, а пене символическое значение.

Ассоциативность Мандельштама никоим образом не следует смешивать с заумной нерасчлененностью и тому подобными явлениями, с которыми Мандельштам сознательно боролся. Символистической «музыке» слов он противопоставлял поэтически преображенное значение слова, знакам «непознаваемого» — образ как выражение иногда трудной, но всегда познаваемой интеллектуальной связи вещей.

There is only one point on which I cannot agree with L. Ginzburg. To my best understanding, there is nothing in the poem that would indicate the image of a winded horse in a lather.[16] The trembling of the building at the railroad station (*vokzal*) simply envelops the outside iron world as well, and the adverb *niščenski* indicates only that the *rich, beautiful* world of music is opposed to the *poor*, plain world of the railroad station. For me, the *pena* (foam in the lines quoted above) is a plausible metaphor for white steam from locomotives. This metaphor is explained by Mandel'štam himself in the fourth line of the last stanza:

"Gorjačij par zrački smyčkov slepit."[17] And if we want to look for a symbolic meaning of the *pena*, we may recall the image of the foam from which Aphrodite was born (used by Mandel'štam in his "Silentium," 1910):

> Она еще не родилась,
> Она и музыка и слово . . .
> . . . . . . . . . . . . .
> Останься *пеной*, Афродита,
> И слово в *музыку* вернись . . .

Even the beginning of "Koncert na vokzale," the first impersonal sentence, "Nel'zja dyšat'," is significant for the general mood of the poem. The theme of air and breathing was very prominent throughout Mandel'štam's poetry. It is noteworthy that beginning in the early twenties the images of dense and unclear air and difficulty in breathing predominate. This theme is so complex that it should require a separate study. However, the following quotations will illustrate its complexity:

> *Дыханье вещее* в стихах моих
> Животворящего их духа.
>
> (1909)
>
> За радость тихую *дышать и жить*,
> Кого, скажите, мне благодарить?
> . . . . . . . . . . . . .
> На стекла вечности уже легло
> *Мое дыхание*, мое тепло.
>
> («Дано мне тело», 1909)
>
> Чудак Евгений — бедности стыдится,
> *Бензин вдыхает* и судьбу клянет!
>
> («Петербургские строфы», 1913)
>
> Отравлен хлеб и *воздух выпит*,
> Как трудно раны врачевать!
> Иосиф, проданный в Египет,
> Не мог сильнее тосковать!
>
> (1913)
>
> И *воздух горных стран* — эфир;
> Эфир, которым не сумели,
> Не захотели мы *дышать*.
>
> («Зверинец», 1916)

В Петрополе прозрачном мы умрем,
Где властвует над нами Прозерпина.
*Мы в каждом вздохе смертный воздух пьем,*
И каждый час нам смертная година.

(1916)

О этот *воздух, смутой пьяный*
На черной площади Кремля!

(1916)

И сколько *воздуха* и шелка
И ветра в шепоте твоем . . .

(«Твое чудесное произношенье», 1917)

И, зернами *дыша* рассыпанного мака,
На голову мою надену митру мрака . . .

(«Кто знает», 1918)

Вот неподвижная земля, и вместе с ней
*Я христианства пью холодный горный воздух.*

(«В хрустальном омуте», 1919)

Словно темную воду я пью *помутившийся воздух* . . .

(«Сестры – тяжесть и нежность», 1920)

И розовыми, белыми камнями
*В сухом прозрачном воздухе* сверкаешь.

(«Феодосия», 1920)

Соборы вечные Софии и Петра,
Амбары *воздуха и света* . . .

(«Люблю под сводами», 1921)

*Нельзя дышать*, и твердь кишит червями . . .

(«Концерт на вокзале», 1921)

Приподнять, как *душный* стог,
*Воздух*, что шапкой томит . . .

(«Я не знаю, с каких пор», 1922)

Я *дышал* звезд млечной трухой,
Колтуном пространства *дышал* . . .

(«Я по лесенке приставной», 1922)

*Воздух бывает темным,* как вода, и все живое в нем
плавает как рыба.
. . . . . . . . . . . . . . . . . . . . . . . . . . . .
*Воздух* замешан так же густо, как земля, –
Из него нельзя выйти, а в него трудно войти.
. . . . . . . . . . . . . . . . . . . . . . . . . . . .
Хрупкое летоисчисление нашей эры подходит к концу.
(«Нашедший подкову», 1923)

*Весь воздух выпила* огромная гора . . .
(«Армения», VIII, 1930)

Кто-то чудной меня что-то торопит забыть, –
*Душно,* и все-таки до смерти хочется жить.
(«Колют ресницы», 1931)

Мне с каждым днем *дышать все тяжелее,*
А между тем нельзя повременить –
И рождены для наслажденья бегом
Лишь сердце человека и коня.
(«Сегодня можно . . .», 1931)

Люблю появление ткани,
Когда после двух или трех,
А то четырех *задыханий*
*Придет выпрямительный вздох.*
(«Восьмистишия», I-II, 1933)

Так, чтобы умереть на самом деле,
Тысячу раз на дню лишусь обычной
*Свободы вздоха* и сознанья цели.[18]

(Декабрь, 1933)

*В легком воздухе свирели* раствори жемчужин боль . . .
(«Улыбнись ягненок гневный», 1936)

О, этот медленный, *одышливый простор* –
Я им пресыщен до отказа! –
И *отдышавшийся* распахнут кругозор –
Повязку бы на оба глаза.

(1937)

Я обращался *к воздуху слуге,*
Ждал от него услуги или вести
И собирался в путь, и плавал по дуге
Неначинающихся путешествий.
(«Не сравнивай», 1937)

*Народу нужен* свет и *воздух голубой,*
И нужен хлеб и снег Эльбруса.
(«Я нынче в паутине световой», 1937)

Я в яму, в бородавчатую темь,
Скольжу к обледенелой водокачке,
*И, задыхаясь, мертвый воздух ем,*
И разлетаются грачи в горячке.
(«Куда мне деться», 1937)

Нам союзно лишь то что избыточно,
Впереди не провал, а промер,
И бороться за *воздух прожиточный* –
Это слава другим не в пример.
(«Стихи о неизвестном солдате», 1937)

А грудь стесняется, без языка тиха,
Уже не я пою — *поет мое дыханье* . . .
. . . . . . . . . . . . . . . . . . .
Песнь . . . которую поют . . .
*Держа дыханье вольно и открыто.*
(«Пою, когда гортань сыра», 1937)

Что ж мне под голову другой песок подложен?
Ты — горловой Урал, плечистое Поволжье
Иль этот ровный край — вот все мои права, –
И полной грудью их *вдыхать еще я должен.*
(«Разрывы круглых бухт», 1937)

Если б меня лишили всего в мире –
*Права дышать* и открывать двери
И утверждать, что бытие будет . . .
. . . . . . . . . . . . . . . . . . .
Я не смолчу . . .
(«Если б меня наши враги взяли», 1937)

And, finally, only one quotation from Mandel'štam's prose:

Все произведения мировой литературы я делю на разрешенные и написанные без разрешения. Первые — это мразь, вторые — *ворованный воздух.*

(«Четвертая проза», 1930 – 1931)

I believe that these quotations speak for themselves. Most of them operate within the following semantic fields: happiness, grace, freedom (not only political freedom, of course), poetic creation, as opposed to lack of happiness, lack of freedom and lack (or impossibility) of poetic creation.

The first sentence "Nel'zja dyšat' " becomes even more suggestive in connection with the next two:

Нельзя дышать, и твердь кишит червями,
И ни одна звезда не говорит . . .

The image of the unfriendly sky was familiar to Mandel'štam's early poetry.

. . . неживого небосвода
Всегда смеющийся хрусталь!

(«Сусальным золотом горят», 1908)

Я вижу каменное небо
Над тусклой паутиной вод.
. . . . . . . . . . .
Я понимаю этот ужас
И постигаю эту связь:
И небо падает, не рушась,
И море плещет, не пенясь.

(1910)

Я вижу месяц бездыханный
И небо мертвенней холста.. . . .

(«Слух чуткий парус напрягает», 1910)

Твердь умокла, умерла . . .

(«Скудный луч холодной мерою», 1911)

Небо тусклое с отсветом странным –
Мировая туманная боль . . .

(«Воздух пасмурный влажен и гулок», 1911)

О небо, небо, ты мне будешь сниться!
Не может быть, чтоб ты совсем ослепло . . .

(1911)

But never had his sky been as hostile and frightening as it was in "Koncert na vokzale."

In the first line of this poem, the image of the sky[19] swarming with worms may have been suggested by David Burljuk's poem "Mertvoe nebo" (published in the almanac *Doxlaja luna*, 1913):

«Небо труп!!» не больше!
Звезды — *черви* — пьяные туманом
Усмиряю боль ше-лестом обманом
Небо — смрадный труп!![20]

One could dislike this poem, and I would not blame anybody for doing so. One may well recall the lines by Axmatova:

Когда б вы знали, из какого сора
Растут стихи, не ведая стыда!

If Mandel'štam actually took the image of worms from Burljuk, this fact may be interesting, on the one hand because it contributes to our understanding of his creative process, and on the other as an evidence of his exquisite memory, but such a subtext does not afford a deeper comprehension of his poem.

The second line of the poem contains an overt poetic polemic with Lermontov's lines:[21]

Ночь тиха. Пустыня внемлет Богу,
И звезда с звездою говорит.
В небесах торжественно и чудно . . .

In Mandel'štam, a strong sensation of an impending cataclysm is sharply opposed to Lermontov's sense of cosmic harmony.

Mandel'štam will return to the image of Lermontovian cosmos in "Grifel'naja oda" (1923):

Звезда с звездой могучий стык,
Кремнистый путь из старой песни . . .

and in "Stixi o neizvestnom soldate" (1937):

Научи меня, ласточка хилая,
Разучившаяся летать,
Как мне с этой *воздушной могилою*
*Без руля и крыла* совладать.

> И за Лермонтова Михаила
> Я отдам тебе строгий отчет,
> Как сутулого учит могила
> И *воздушная яма* влечет.

This is again a polemic with Lermontov. *Vozdušnaja jama*, with an obviously negative shade of meaning, is opposed to Lermontov's *vozdušnyj okean:*

> *На воздушном океане*
> *Без руля и без ветрил*
> Тихо плавают в тумане
> Хоры стройные светил.

Lermontov's voice is heard in "Koncert na vokzale" once more, in the last stanza. Mandel'štam's lines:

> *И мнится мне:* весь в музыке и пене
> *Железный мир* так нищенски дрожит . . .

may be compared with those by Lermontov:

> *И снился мне* сияющий огнями
> *Вечерний пир* в родимой стороне . . .

This is a clear case of borrowing *po ritmu i zvučaniju* (in Sergej Bobrov's terms).[22] Nevertheless, we may ask the question: why did this borrowing occur? The probable answer is that the theme of death (and dreaming of death: "Mne strašno. Èto son") is present both in the prophetic "Son" and in the apocalyptic "Koncert na vokzale."

There is, indeed, an apocalyptic mood in the image of a sky that swarms with worms, where all the stars are silent. There is also an apocalyptic purport in the pointed conclusion of the poem:

> *Куда же ты?* На тризне милой тени
> *В последний раз нам музыка звучит.*

This conclusion echoes the fifth and the sixth line of the following poem by Tjutčev:

> Я лютеран люблю богослуженье,
> Обряд их строгий, важный и простой –
> Сих голых стен, сей храмины пустой
> Понятно мне высокое ученье.
>
> *Не видите ль?* Собравшися в дорогу,
> *В последний раз вам вера предстоит:*[23]
> Еще она не перешла порогу,
> Но дом ее уж пуст и гол стоит, –

Еще она не перешла порогу,
Еще за ней не затворилась дверь . . .
Но час настал, пробил . . . Молитесь Богу,
*В последний раз вы молитесь теперъ.*

The mood here is apocalyptic, just as it is in Mandel'štam's poem.[24]
Against the background of this subtext the music in "Koncert na
vokzale" acquires a higher meaning: it becomes a kind of religious rite.

The theme of death and music appears in Mandel'štam's poetry as
early as 1912 in the poem "Pešexod." Here, as in "Koncert na vokzale,"
the poet is frightened by "mysterious heights," listening to the sound of
a snowball which is on its way to becoming an avalanche, and will
destroy him (and probably not only him). He is aware that music
cannot rescue him from the abyss, despite the fact that his whole soul
is "in the bells":

Действительно, лавина есть в горах!
И вся моя душа — в колоколах,
Но музыка от бездны не спасет!

The last line of the poem may suggest a polemic with Skrjabin's belief
that the power of music can save humanity.[25]

There is one puzzling image in the last stanza of "Koncert na vokzale"
—*trizna miloj teni*— which should be explained. One can guess that the
poet is mourning a Russia which is gone forever, and primarily her cultural past. The reader who recalls another of Tjutčev's poems, "Duša
moja—Ēlizium tenej," will be assured that his guess is correct. It should
be recalled that the image of Elysium appears both in Mandel'štam's
prosaic description of the concert and in the poem.

Душа моя — Элизиум теней,
Теней безмолвных, светлых и прекрасных,
Ни помыслам годины буйной сей,
Ни радостям, ни горю не причастных.
Душа моя, Элизиум теней,
Что общего меж жизнью и тобою!
Меж вами, *призраки минувших, лучших дней,*
И сей бесчувственной толпою? . .

I believe that the first subtext by Lermontov and both subtexts by
Tjutčev contribute to a better understanding of the very message of
Mandel'štam's poem.[26] They are important, and their function is entirely
different from that of Burljuk's subtext, which may be ignored.

A remarkable note has been found among Mandel'štam's papers. It
deals with the idea of reading one poet and hearing the voice of another.

2 мая 31 г. Чтенье Некрасова. «Влас» и «Жил на свете рыцарь бедный».

Некрасов

Говорят, ему видение
Все мерещилось в бреду:
Видел света преставление,
Видел грешников в аду.

Пушкин

Он имел одно виденье,
Недоступное уму,
И глубоко впечатленье
В сердце врезалось ему.

«С той поры» — и дальше как бы слышится второй потаенный голос:

Lumen coelum, Sancta Rosa . . .

Та же фигура стихотворная, та же тема отозвания и подвига.

If we define the context as a set of texts which contain the same or a similar image, the subtext may be defined as an already existing text (or texts) reflected in a new one.

There are four kinds of subtexts: (1) that which serves as a simple impulse for the creation of an image; (2) *zaimstvovanie po ritmu i zvučaniju* (borrowing of a rhythmic figure and the sounds contained therein); (3) the text which supports or reveals the poetic message of a later text; (4) the text which is treated polemically by the poet. The first two do not necessarily contribute to our better understanding of a given poem. However, (2) may be combined with (3) and/or (4), and (3) and (4) may, in their turn, be blended.

It is self-evident that the concept of context and subtext may overlap in cases of self-quotations and autoreminiscences. This happens often in Mandel'štam's poetry. For example, in the poem "Čto pojut časy-kuznečik" (1917) there is an image of a sinking bark:

. . . зубами мыши точат
Жизни тоненькое дно . . .
. . . ласточка и дочка[27]
Отвязала мой челнок . . .
Но черемуха услышит
*И на дне морском: прости.*
. . . смерть невинна . . .

This bidding farewell to life and its simple beauty[28] is repeated in the poem "Telefon" (1918):

> В высоком строгом кабинете
> Самоубийцы — телефон . . .
> Звонок — и закружились сферы:
> Самоубийство решено . . .
> Молчи, проклятая шкатулка!
> *На дне морском цветет: прости!*

For a person who does not know the first poem the image may be surprising, even enigmatic.

It goes without saying that the majority of Mandel'štam's poems are not written in a cryptic code. They reveal clearly enough, though not completely, Mandel'štam's model of the world. There are many readers, and literary critics, too, who would prefer not to decipher the concealed meaning of Mandel'štam's "difficult" poems. They have a right to enjoy the "verse music" of his poems for its own sake, for example, the elegiac tone of "Solominka" or the oratorical solemnity of "Grifel'naja oda," to be fascinated by the "music" of his images—always original, unusual, fresh, colorful.

With respect to Mandel'štam's cryptic poems, the following lines from his "My naprjažennogo molčan'ja ne vynosim" (1912) are often cited:[29]

> (Кошмарный человек читает «Улялюм».)
> Значенье — суета, и слово — только шум,
> Когда фонетика — служанка серафима.

However, those who cite these lines forget that the "horrible man" ("košmarnyj čelovek") might have read Edgar Allan Poe's poem "Ulalume" in English, that is, in a language that Mandel'štam did not understand.[30]

Mandel'štam is often compared to Puškin, and they both are praised for their "Mozartism." However, from Puškin's drafts, we know with what effort his "Mozartian lightness" was achieved. Mandel'štam composed his poems in his head, working for days. Mrs. Mandel'štam tells in her memoirs how hard it was for him to find the exact epithet in the phrase *"sovestnyj* degot' truda." It would be appropriate, I believe, to end this chapter with the following quotation from Mandel'štam's essay "O prirode slova":

На место романтика, идеалиста, аристократического мечтателя о чистом символе, об отвлеченной эстетике слова, на место символизма, футуризма и имажинизма пришла живая поэзия слова-предмета, и ее творец не идеалист-мечтатель Моцарт, а суровый и строгий ремесленник мастер Сальери, протягивающий руку мастеру вещей и материальных ценностей, строителю и производителю вещественного мира.

# II

## THE HAYLOFT

*The "Closed" and "Open" Interpretation of a Poetic Text*

One can examine any work of poetry as an isolated aesthetic fact and interpret it by restricting oneself to the semantics of the given text. To a certain extent such a "closed" analysis of single poems limits the possibilities of revealing the figurative (analogous, metaphoric, symbolic) meanings of a word, insofar as these are unusual and the key to their deciphering is not given in the poem itself. An "open" analysis of a poetic text, which considers a broad context of the poet's work and at times the work of other poets (present as obvious or veiled reminiscences), helps us decipher these figurative meanings and brings us closer to a deeper understanding of the imagery in the given poem. It goes without saying that these two approaches are not mutually exclusive; on the contrary, they complement each other.

To illustrate this theoretical proposition I shall offer an interpretation of the following two "twin-poems" by Mandel'štam, written in 1922:

### I

| | | |
|---|---|---|
| I | 1 | Я не знаю, с каких пор |
| | 2 | Эта песенка началась – |
| | 3 | Не по ней ли шуршит вор, |
| | 4 | Комариный звенит князь? |
| | | |
| II | 5 | Я хотел бы ни о чем |
| | 6 | Еще раз поговорить, |
| | 7 | Прошуршать спичкой, плечом |
| | 8 | Растолкать ночь — разбудить. |
| | | |
| III | 9 | Приподнять, как душный стог, |
| | 10 | Воздух, что шапкой томит. |
| | 11 | Перетряхнуть мешок, |
| | 12 | В котором тмин зашит, |

| IV | 13 | Чтобы розовой крови связь, |
|----|----|---------------------------|
|    | 14 | Этих сухоньких трав звон, |
|    | 15 | Уворованная нашлась |
|    | 16 | Через век, сеновал, сон. |

## II

| I | 1 | Я по лесенке приставной |
|---|---|------------------------|
|   | 2 | Лез на всклоченный сеновал, – |
|   | 3 | Я дышал звезд млечных трухой, |
|   | 4 | Колтуном пространства дышал. |

| II | 5 | И подумал: зачем будить |
|----|---|------------------------|
|    | 6 | Удлиненных звучаний рой, |
|    | 7 | В этой вечной склоке ловить |
|    | 8 | Эолийский чудесный строй? |

| III | 9 | Звезд в ковше Медведицы семь. |
|-----|----|------------------------------|
|     | 10 | Добрых чувств на земле пять. |
|     | 11 | Набухает, звенит темь, |
|     | 12 | И растет и звенит опять. |

| IV | 13 | Распряженный огромный воз |
|----|----|--------------------------|
|    | 14 | Поперек вселенной торчит, |
|    | 15 | Сеновала древний хаос |
|    | 16 | Защекочет, запорошит. |

| V | 17 | Не своей чешуей шуршим, |
|---|----|------------------------|
|   | 18 | Против шерсти мира поем, |
|   | 19 | Лиру строим, словно спешим |
|   | 20 | Обрасти косматым руном. |

| VI | 21 | Из гнезда упавших щеглов |
|----|----|-------------------------|
|    | 22 | Косари приносят назад, – |
|    | 23 | Из горящих вырвусь рядов |
|    | 24 | И вернусь в родной звукоряд, |

| VII | 25 | Чтобы розовой крови связь |
|-----|----|--------------------------|
|     | 26 | И травы сухорукий звон |
|     | 27 | Распростились: одна скрепясь, |
|     | 28 | А другая — в заумный сон. |

The "plot" of these two poems is rather simple: the poet is spending the night in a hayloft and meditating on poetic creation.[1] Their "scenario" can be traced to Fet's well-known poem, written in 1857:

На *стоге сена ночью* южной
Лицом ко тверди я лежал,
И хор светил, живой и дружный,
Кругом раскинувшись, дрожал.

Земля, как смутный *сон* немая,
Безвестно уносилась прочь,
И я, как первый житель рая,
Один в лицо увидел *ночь*.

Я ль несся к бездне полуночной,
Иль сонмы *звезд* ко мне неслись?
Казалось, будто в длани мощной
Над этой бездной я повис.

И с замираньем и смятеньем
Я взором мерил глубину,
В которой с каждым я мгновеньем
Всё невозвратнее тону.

There are a few word-signals common to both poets: *stog sena* (*stog, senoval*), *son*, *noč'*, and *zvezdy*. However, Mandel'štam's feeling for the cosmos is quite different. To Fet's cosmic harmony Mandel'štam opposes, as we shall see later, the Tjutčevian chaos.

The lexical stock of Mandel'štam's two "Hayloft" poems divides naturally into three semantic fields: (1) *Nature* (landscape, cosmos), (2) *Poetry* (poetic creation), (3) *I* (lyric subject). Two small fields can be added to these: (4) *Things*, and (5) *People*. The first field consists mainly of substantives and one distinctive adjective, *komarinyj*. In the second field, along with substantives (*pesenka, stroj, lira*), verbs play an important role (*pet'*, [liru] *stroit'*). The third field is characterized, in the first place, by the personal pronoun *ja*, as well as by the two nouns (*plečo, krov'*). The fourth and fifth fields contain only nouns.

On the basis of the primary meanings of the words, we can assign the nouns from the first "Hayloft" poem to the following five fields:[2]

| (1) *Nature* | (2) *Poetry* | (3) *I* | (4) *Things* | (5) *People* |
|---|---|---|---|---|
| noč', stog, vozdux, tmin, travy | pesenka | plečo, krov' | spička, šapka, mešok | vor, knjaz' |

In the first "Hayloft" poem the field *Nature* turns out to be the largest and *Poetry* the smallest. The nouns *knjaz'* and *vor* are clearly used figuratively: *komarinyj knjaz'* is a mosquito, but he is also a thief, as we shall see later. All the remaining nouns are seemingly used according to their literal meanings; two of them ("stack," "cap") figure as the second part of a simile. But as we draw upon a larger context from Mandel'štam's poetry and prose, these fields will begin to "regroup."

Jurij Tynjanov wrote about Mandel'štam's "Hayloft" as early as 1925, in his essay "Promežutok" (*Arxaisty i novatory*, pp. 568–573). In this essay, Tynjanov formulated a thesis which is very important theoretically: verse, as a system, generates specific shades of meaning peculiar to the system as such. Tynjanov's idea proved to be fruitful. Such concepts as "poetical shades of meaning" and "the mutual contamination of word-meanings in the compressed verse line" (or line sequence) became common property in Mandel'štam scholarship, as well as in contemporary Russian structural poetics in general.

But let us look at Tynjanov's own text:

[Стих как] строй имеет окрашивающее свойство, *свою* собственную силу; он рождает *свои*, стиховые оттенки (р. 569).

Смысловой строй у Мандельштама таков, что решающую роль приобретает для целого стихотворения *один* образ, один словарный ряд и незаметно окрашивает все другие, — это ключ для всей иерархии образов:

    . . . Как я ненавижу *пахучие*, древние *срубы*,
    . . . Зубчатыми *пилами* в стены *врезаются* крепко . . .
    . . . Еще в *древесину* горячий топор не *врезался* . . .
    . . . Прозрачной слезой на *стенах* проступила *смола*,
    И чувствует город свои *деревянные ребра* . . .
    . . . И падают стрелы сухим *деревянным дождем*
    И стрелы другие растут на земле *как орешник*.

Этот ключ перестраивает и образ крови:

    . . . Никак не уляжется *крови сухая возня* . . .
    . . . Но хлынула к *лестницам кровь* и на приступ пошла.

Еще заметнее ключ там, где Мандельштам меняет «удлиненную» мелодию на короткий строй:

            Я не знаю, с каких пор
            Эта *песенка* началась –
            Не по ней ли *шуршит вор*
            *Комариный звенит князь.*
            . . . *Прошуршать спичкой*, плечом
            *Растолкать* ночь — разбудить.

*Приподнять, как душный стог,*
*Воздух, что шапкой томит,*
*Перетряхнуть мешок,*
*. . .* Чтобы розовой крови связь,
Этих *сухоньких трав звон,*
*Уворованная* нашлась
Через *век, сеновал, сон.*

Век, сеновал, сон — стали очень близки в этом шуршаньи стиха, обросли особыми оттенками. А ключ находим в следующем стихотворении:

Я по лесенке приставной
Лез на *всклоченный сеновал,* –
Я дышал *звезд* млечной *трухой,*
*Колтуном пространства* дышал.

Но и ключ не нужен: «уворованная связь» всегда находится у Мандельштама. Она создается *от стиха к стиху*; оттенок, окраска слова в каждом стихе не теряется, она сгущается в последующем (pp. 570-572).

Tynjanov only outlines the method and limits of semantic analysis but does not carry out the analysis itself.[3] Unfortunately, he does not even define the particular shades of meaning which the members of the triad "vek, senoval, son" acquire. Tynjanov very likely considered the first and third members of the triad to be correlated with the semantic field *Dry, Rustling* (*Suxoe, šuršaščee, zvenjaščee*). In that case, the middle member of the triad extends its shades of meaning over the other two.[4]

When we read Mandel'štam's poem with Tynjanov's "key," that is, when we direct our attention to "one" basic, central image and to the grouping of words into semantic fields connected with it, we can begin to grasp Mandel'štam's "magic of the word" quite consciously. In other words, the aesthetic information which we receive from the given text increases.

Let us note how Tynjanov quotes the first "Hayloft." He simply omits those lines which he probably does not consider to be connected with the central image (lines 5–6, 12). He apparently would not have needed them for a semantic analysis. But it is precisely these lines ("*Ja xotel by ni o čem / Ešče raz pogovorit'* " and "*Peretrjaxnut' mešok, / V kotorom tmin zašit'*") which are intimately connected with the two basic themes of the poem: (1) *I, my life,* and (2) *poetry, poetic creation.*

These omitted lines are essential for interpreting the poetic message of the poem.[5]

In her article, "Poètika Osipa Mandel'štama" (*Izvestija AN SSSR Serija literatury i jazyka*, 1972, no. 4, 309–327), Lidija Ginzburg broadens the analytical framework sketched by Tynjanov. On the basis of the two Tynjanov examples ("Za to, čto ja ruki tvoi ne sumel uderžat' " and "Senoval"), Ginzburg points to the "pervasive symbolism" (*skvoznaja simvolika*) of the semantic field *Dry* (*Suxoe*) which runs through a large number of poems from 1915–1922. In other words, Ginzburg draws on a broader context in her analysis of this "symbolism":

Мандельштамовская концепция человека, его силы и его слабости, имеет свою исходную символику, разветвляющуюся рядами производных образов. В 1915 г. Мандельштам объявил о перемене материала. Он написал:

> Уничтожает пламень
> *Сухую* жизнь мою,
> И ныне я не камень,
> А *дерево* пою.

Но тогда речь еще шла «О деревянном рае, где вещи так легки». Позднее тема *сухости* — и связанная с ней тема дерева — приобретает для Мандельштама все большее значение. Сухость становится знаком жизненной недостаточности, ущербности. В стихотворении «За то, что я руки твои не сумел удержать...» человек заключен в деревянном мире (срубы, пилы, древесина, топор, смола на стенах, деревянные ребра города, деревянный дождь стрел, стрелы — как орешник...), и это возмездие за жизненное бессилие, за сухость.

> За то, что я руки твои не сумел удержать,
> За то, что я предал соленые нежные губы,
> Я должен рассвета в дремучем акрополе ждать.
> Как я ненавижу пахучие древние срубы!

Другое ключевое слово стихотворения — *кровь*. Кровь — жизненная сила: «Но хлынула к лестницам кровь и на приступ пошла...». Но крови угрожает сухость — «Никак не уляжется крови сухая возня...». Так оправдано необычайное сцепление сухости и крови.

Значение образов Мандельштама определяется в конкретных связях контекста. Но оно бывает очень устойчивым, из стихотворения в стихотворение переходящим. Сухость — это неудача, подмененная кровь. Эти значения окончательно прояснены стихотворением того же 1920 г. В нем любовная тема предстает на этот раз без античного покрова:

> Я наравне с другими
> Хочу тебе служить,
> От ревности *сухими*
> Губами ворожить.

> Не утоляет слово
> Мне *пересохших* уст,
> И без тебя мне снова
> Дремучий воздух пуст . . .

> . . . Тебя не назову я
> Ни радость, ни любовь.
> На дикую, чужую
> Мне подменили *кровь*.

А в стихотворении «Как растет хлебов опара . . .» тема сухости поворачивается своей, так сказать, исторической гранью:

> И свое находит место
> *Черствый* пасынок веков –
> *Усыхающий* довесок
> Прежде вынутых хлебов.

В двух стихотворениях 1922 г. «Я не знаю, с каких пор . . .» и «Я по лесенке приставной . . .» (вариации одной темы) — уже не сухость дерева, а душная сухость сена, сеновала. Отсюда ряд вторичных образов — *душного стога, шуршания, мешка с тмином, сухой травы, трухи, колтуна, склоки*, наконец. Знаменательно, что и здесь присутствует образ крови. Поэту нужно освободить кровь от сухости: « . . . Чтобы розовой крови связь И травы сухорукий звон Распростились . . .». Стихи, таким образом, дают друг к другу смысловой ключ. Каждое из них обладает целостностью, и в то же время они связаны сквозной, проходящей через поэзию Мандельштама символикой (pp. 319–320).

First, the subtlety and exactitude of Lidija Ginzburg's observations should be given due credit. Her analysis of the motifs "wood" (*derevo*) and "dryness" (*suxost'*) in the poems from 1915–1920 is very convincing. All that Ginzburg says about the semantics of the "Hayloft" is likewise true. However, her assertion that "dryness is . . . substituted blood" ("suxost' — èto . . . podmenennaja krov' ") seems too categorical to me.

Mandel'štam himself calls his "substituted blood" only "wild and foreign" (*dikaja, čužaja*). Lidija Ginzburg's interpretation of the last stanza of the second "Hayloft" poem is also doubtful: "Poètu nužno osvobodit' krov' ot suxosti:... Čtoby rozovoj krovi svjaz' I travy suxorukij zvon Rasprostilis'..." The quotation is broken off at the most important point. In his two "Hayloft" poems, Mandel'štam foresees two different "solutions to the dilemma." As a matter of fact, Ginzburg does not comment at all on the poetic message of the first poem. In the first "Hayloft," however, the poet equates his blood with the "ringing of the grasses" (*zvon suxon'kix trav* is an absolute nominal attribute to the subject clause *svjaz' rozovoj krovi*, and therefore the predicate clause *našlas' uvorovannaja* agrees in gender and number with the noun *svjaz'*). The poet expresses the wish that the stolen "bond of the rose-colored blood" (which is simultaneously the "ringing of the dry grasses") be found in a century, that is, that it be preserved. In the second "Hayloft" the wish is different: the poet wants the "bond of the blood" and the "ringing of the grasses" to part; "one" (blood) must "gird itself up," "take control of itself" ("skrepit'sja") and the "other" (grass) go off "to a transsense dream." The verb *skrepit'sja* in this text means "restrain oneself, conquer within oneself any feelings, subdue their external manifestation." One might assume that the images of the "blood that is held in check" and the "dry blood" are not really so far removed from each other.[6] In attempting to decipher the poetic imagery of both "Hayloft" poems, we must do more than explain the "pervasive imagery" (*skvoznaja obraznost'*) of the semantic field *Dry* in its broader context. For example, it is necessary to incorporate the entire context of "dry grasses" in Mandel'štam's poetry and prose since it clearly reveals the figurative meaning of this image as well. Georgij Margvelašvili obviously knew this context when he asserted that the image of "dry grass" in the "Hayloft" "personifies poetry" ("Ob Osipe Mandel'-štame," *Literaturnaja Gruzija*, 1966, no. 3, 82). But even this explanation is insufficient; it is also necessary to define in what sense Mandel'-štam uses the adjective "transsense" and the noun "dream."

Let us also quote Lidija Ginzburg's statements on the meaning of a broad context in poetry in general:

Художественный контекст, определяющий значение слова, имеет самые разные объемы, и он может выходить далеко за пределы одного произведения. И целым литературным направлениям, и отдельным поэтическим системам присущи разные типы контекста. Поэзия Блока, например, не может быть понята вне его больших циклов, в конечном счете сливающихся в единый контекст «трилогии вочеловечения», как Блок сам называл три тома своих стихов. У раннего Пастернака стихи несутся стремительно, переступая через свои границы и образуя единый лирический поток. Мандельштам, напротив того, поэт контекстов разграниченных (хотя и взаимосвязанных) (p. 313).

Everything in this quotation is essentially true, and very precisely formulated. The "lyric stream" of early Pasternak can in no way be equated with Mandel'štam's recurring and recrossing motifs. There is, of course, an essential difference between the symbol of the "Beautiful Lady" or the symbol of the "blizzard" in Blok's poetry and the repeated motif of "air and breathing" in Mandel'štam's. In Blok, single poems (and whole cycles and *poèmy*, as well) reveal various aspects of a symbol, and only the totality of all aspects gives a symbol its complex figurative meaning, which does not lend itself to exact paraphrase. In Mandel'štam, however, the motif of air and breathing varies within rather narrow limits: freedom / non-freedom, creativity / absence of creativity (see Chapter One, pp. 10–14). Studying a broad context in Mandel'štam's work explains much — both in the analysis of "recurring motifs" and "key words" in the poetry of a specific period ("salt and stars", for example, in the poetry of 1921–23) and in the analysis of a basic, "central" image of one single poem. But this is not enough. It is essential to go beyond the bounds of the text in deciphering particular, "peripheral" images in a given poem.[7]

At this point we may begin a detailed analysis of such images in "Hayloft, I–II." We shall start with the "mosquito prince." As shown in my note, "Komarinyj knjaz'" (*IJSLP* XII, 167–169), this image most likely derives from Deržavin's humorous ode "Poxvala komaru." In Deržavin, this mosquito looks like a Tatar prince because of his whiskers ("po usam — ordynskij knjaz' "), but is like a "celestial spirit in his flight" ("po letu — dux nebesnyj"). He not only impels people to work, but inspires poetic creativity. He is a precursor of such singers as skylarks and nightingales. Through his poetic imagination, Deržavin puts "the Mosquito" on a par with "spirits who soar in eternity" and expresses his wish to become a celestial Mosquito:

> Но большую коль с меньшой
> Сравним вещь между собой,
> То поэзии пареньем
> Нам нельзя ль воображеньем
> Комаров равнять душам,

> Кои в *вечности* витают,
> Мириадами летают
> По полям и по лесам;
> В плоти светлой и прозрачной
> Воспевая век свой злачный,
> Не кусают, — нет там жал.
> О! когда бы я, в восторге
> Песни в райском пев чертоге,
> Комаром небесным стал!

Deržavin concludes his "ode" with a humorous *pointe*:

> *Мои песни вечно будут*
> *Эхом звучным Комара.*

But in Mandel'štam's *Egipetskaja marka* there is another image of the "ringing mosquito" which is clearly part of the semantic field "I":[8]

*Комарик звенел:*
— Глядите, что сталось со мной: я *последний* египтянин — я пла-кальщик, пестун, пластун — я маленький *князь-раскоряка* — я *нищий* Рамзес-кровопийца — *я на севере стал ничем* — от меня так мало осталось — *извиняюсь!* . . .
— *Я князь невезенья* — коллежский асессор из города Фив . . . Все такой же — *ничуть не изменился* — ой, страшно мне здесь — *извиняюсь* . . .
— *Я безделица. Я —* ничего. Вот попрошу от холерных гранитов на копейку — египетской кашки, на копейку — девической шейки.
— Я ничего — заплачу́ — *извиняюсь.*

The theme of steadfastness, closely connected with other themes such as the motif of the downtrodden outcast, the motif of isolation, bad luck, and some imagined fault for which the poet must ask forgiveness, began to appear in Mandel'štam's poetry from the early twenties and gained even more strength in the thirties. The "refrain" from the just-quoted excerpt, "I apologize," will be heard in a 1930 poem too:

> Еще далеко мне до патриарха,
> Еще на мне полупочтенный возраст,
> Еще меня ругают за глаза
> На языке трамвайных перебранок,
> В котором нет ни смысла ни аза:
> — Такой, сякой! — *Ну, чтож, я извиняюсь,*
> *Но в глубине ничуть не изменяюсь.*

When Mandel'štam was writing about the ringing little mosquito, the prince of ill-fortune, certainly he recalled his 1922 "mosquito-prince" and the ringing "mosquito trifle," the "splinter in the azure" from 1923.[9]

As we see, against the background of this broad context, the image of the "mosquito prince" does not belong just to the semantic field *Nature*; it also borders on the field *Poetry* and perhaps even the field *I*.

A conversation about nothing in particular — that is, about little nothings and trifles (like matches, a sack in which caraway seeds are sewn up, dry grass: "the dear Egypt of [little] things") is the age-old content of that kind of poetry which, in Puškin's witty words, "must, God forgive me, be a little bit silly." Actually, this chatting about nothing will turn out to be about what is the most important.

Lighting a match in a hayloft is not a wise thing to do. The second, figurative sense of this match is revealed by a subtext from Mandel'štam's own poem, also written in 1922, "Komu zima — arak i punš goluboglazyj":

> Немного *теплого* куриного помета
> И бестолкового овечьего *тепла*;
> Я все отдам за жизнь — мне так нужна *забота* –
> И *спичка серная* меня б *согреть* могла.

In this context, the care (that is, heartfelt warmth) borders on the semantic field *Warmth*, and the sulphur match becomes an analogue of the human sympathy so badly needed by the freezing poet. I believe that the other match, which the poet wants to strike, can thus be correlated with the semantic field *I*.

The "night" in the second stanza which the poet wants to shove with his shoulder, to awake, is, if not personified, then clearly animated. It recalls the motif of night from "Rakovina" (1911) and "Grifel'naja oda" (1923):

> (1)  Быть может, я тебе не нужен,
> *Ночь*; из пучины мировой,
> Как раковина без жемчужин,
> Я выброшен на берег твой.
>
> Ты равнодушно волны пенишь
> И несговорчиво поешь;
> Но ты полюбишь, ты оценишь
> Ненужной раковины ложь.
>
> Ты на песок с ней рядом ляжешь,
> Оденешь ризою своей,
> И неразрывно с нею свяжешь
> Огромный колокол зыбей;

И хрупкой раковины стены,
Как нежилого сердца дом,
Наполнишь шёпотами пены,
Туманом, ветром и дождем.[10]

(2)    Как мертвый шершень, возле сот,
День пестрый выметен с позором.
И *ночь*-коршунница несет
Горящий мел и грифель кормит.

In both examples, night appears as "an older, teaching force," a "creative time which subordinates the creator to itself, watches over him" (D. M. Segal, *Russian Literature* 2, 83, 87). Segal posits two meanings for the Russian *grifel'* in Mandel'štam's ode — the slate pencil and the slate used for writing (p. 86), and deciphers "nursing the slate" as creation at night (p. 92). While writing his "Grifel'naja oda," Mandel'štam had in mind the fact that Deržavin wrote his famous "Reka vremen" on a slate. In Mandel'štam's "Grifel'naja oda," just as in Tjutčev, creative night is counterposed to motley day. We have in mind in the first place the following two early Tjutčev poems (written in 1829 or the beginning of the thirties):

(1)    «Видение»
Есть некий час, в ночи, всемирного молчанья,
И в оный час явлений и чудес
Живая колесница мирозданья
Открыто катится в святилище небес.

Тогда густеет ночь, как хаос на водах,
Беспамятство, как Атлас, давит сушу;
*Лишь Музы девственную душу*
*В пророческих тревожат боги снах!*

(2)    Ты зрел его в кругу большого света –
То своенравно-весел, то угрюм,
Рассеян, дик иль полон тайных дум,
Таков поэт — и ты презрел поэта!

На месяц взглянь: весь *день*, как облак тощий,
Он в небесах едва не изнемог, –
Настала *ночь* — и, светозарный бог,
Сияет он над усыпленной рощей!

(3)    «Silentium!»
   I   Молчи, скрывайся и таи

И чувства и мечты свои –
Пускай в душевной глубине
Встают и заходят оне
Безмолвно, *как звезды в ночи*, –
Любуйся ими и молчи!

. . . . . . . . . . . . . .

III Лишь жить в себе самом умей –
Есть целый мир в душе твоей
Таинственно-волшебных дум;
Их оглушит наружный шум, –
*Дневные* разгонят *лучи*, –
Внимай их пенью — и молчи![11]

In these poems Tjutčev's night is "positive"; it is to be distinguished
from a different Tjutčev night — terrible, frightening, exposing the
abyss with its fears and mists (for example, in "Den' i noč," written in
the late thirties, and other poems). The essential difference between
Tjutčev's and Mandel'štam's night should be emphasized: in Tjutčev,
night is only a time of creation, but in Mandel'štam, as stated, it is a
higher creative force. It is not without interest that "motley" (*pestryj*),
as an epithet for "day," also appears in Tjutčev, in his "Motiv Gejne":

Если смерть есть ночь, если жизнь есть день –
Ах, умаял он, *пестрый день*, меня![12]

The theme of air in general and the theme of difficulty in breathing in
particular run like a leitmotif through all of Mandel'štam's poetry of the
twenties and thirties, on the one hand touching the semantic fields
*Freedom / Non-freedom*, on the other, *Poetic Creation / Absence of Creation* (see Chapter One above, pp. 10–14). "To lift, like a stuffy haystack,
the air, which stifles like a cap" means to breathe in with one's whole
chest. We might recall the lines from *Kamen'* written in 1913 ("Otravlen
xleb i vozdux vypit"):

Под звездным небом бедуины,
Закрыв глаза и на коне,
*Слагают вольные былины*
*О смутно пережитом дне.*

Немного нужно для *наитий*:
Кто потерял в песке колчан,
Кто выменял коня — событий
Рассеивается туман;

И если *подлинно поется*
И *полной грудью* — наконец
Всё исчезает: остается
Пространство, звезды и *певец!*

We should also note in passing that a lost quiver and a bartered horse are also subjects for a "conversation about nothing," like the match or the sack with caraway seeds in the "Hayloft."

The image of the sack in which the caraway is sewn is much more puzzling than the image of the match or night. Mandel'štam writes in *Šum vremeni* ("Knižnyj škap"):

Как крошка мускуса наполнит весь дом, так малейшее влияние юдаизма переполняет целую жизнь. О, какой это сильный запах! Разве я мог не заметить, что в настоящих еврейских домах пахнет иначе, чем в арийских. И это пахнет не только кухня, но люди, вещи и одежда. До сих пор помню, как меня обдало этим приторным еврейским запахом в деревянном доме на Ключевой улице, в немецкой Риге, у дедушки и бабушки.

And in *Egipetskaja marka* Mandel'štam directly calls this smell the "native caraway air" (*rodnoj tminnyj vozdux*) which "Parnok's morning coat ... not long ... for a couple of hours smelled of" in the apartment of Mervis the tailor.

At this point I would like to apologize to the reader for the long digression which follows. My intention is to show how the image of the "sack" (*mešok*) works among Mandel'štam's other analogues of poetry and poetic creation.

In *Egipetskaja marka* there is a remarkable passage where the author's own voice is clearly heard:

Страшно подумать, что наша жизнь — это повесть без фабулы и героя, сделанная из пустоты и стекла, из горячего лепета одних отступлений, из петербургского инфлуэнционного бреда.

Розовоперстая Аврора обломала свои цветные карандаши. Теперь они валяются как птенчики, с пустыми разинутыми клювами. Между тем, во всем решительно *мне* чудится задаток любимого *прозаического бреда.*

Знакомо ли вам это состояние? Когда у всех вещей словно жар; когда все они радостно возбуждены и больны: рогатки на улице, шелушенье афиш, рояли, толпящиеся в депо, как умное стадо без вожака, рожденное для сонатных беспамятств и кипяченой воды.

Тогда, признаться, *я* не выдерживаю карантина и *смело шагаю,* разбив термометры, по заразному лабиринту, *обвешанный придаточными предложениями,* как веселыми случайными покупками ... и летят *в подставленный мешок поджаристые жаворонки,* наивные как пластика первых веков христианства, и *калач,* обыкновенный *калач,* уже не скрывает от меня, что он задуман пекарем, как *российская лира из безгласного теста.*

All the striking images in this passage are connected with the process of poetic creation. Thus, the broken "colored pencils" ( = "instruments of production"), scattered about like nestlings with empty gaping beaks, echo the slate and bird imagery in "Grifel'naja oda":

> И ночь-коршунница несет
> Горящий мел и грифель кормит.
> . . . . . . . . . .
>
> На изумленной крутизне
> Я слышу грифельные визги.
> Твои ли, память, голоса
> Учительствуют, ночь ломая,
> Бросая грифели лесам,
> Из птичьих клювов вырывая?

Specifically characteristic of Mandel'štam, too, is the "pastry imagery" in the last paragraph of the excerpt quoted. The *podžaristye žavoronki* (not birds, of course, but "buns shaped like birds," nonetheless remaining part of the bird imagery of the second paragraph) and the *kalač,* conceived by the baker as a Russian lyre of voiceless dough, are analogues of works of art and poetic creation.

As early as 1922 Mandel'štam developed this "bread imagery" in the following poem:

> Как растет хлебов опара,
> По началу хороша,
> И беснуется от жару
> Домовитая душа.
>
> Словно хлебные Софии
> С херувимского стола
> Круглым жаром налитые
> Подымают купола.
>
> Чтобы силой или лаской
> Чудный выманить припек,

> Время — царственный подпасок –
> Ловит слово-колобок.
>
> И свое находит место
> Черствый пасынок веков –
> Усыхающий довесок
> Прежде вынутых хлебов.

The key to the figurative level of the poem is given by the poet in the image of the "word-small-round-loaf" (*slovo-kolobok*), which comes from a folktale in Afanas'ev's collection. The folkloric *kolobok*, baked of remains of meal and grain scraped from the meal-bin and swept up from the granary floor (cf. the "usyxajuščij dovesok prežde vynutyx xlebov") is saved by the song ("Ja po korobu skreben / Po suseku meten," and so on) from the cross-eyed rabbit, the gray wolf, the pigeon-toed bear, and falls into the mouth of the fox.

Highly characteristic of Mandel'štam is the architectural image of the "bread Sophias" (*xlebnye Sofii*). The "voiceless dough" from which these bread cathedrals are baked might be compared to Mandel'štam's explanation of the stone in Tjutčev's "Problème." In "Utro akmeizma" (1913) Mandel'štam wrote:

(1) *Булыжник* под руками зодчего превращается в субстанцию . . .

(2) . . . камень Тютчева, что «с горы скатившись лег в долине, сорвавшись сам собой или низвергнут мыслящей рукой» — есть *слово*. Голос материи в этом неожиданном паденьи звучит, как членораздельная речь. На этот вызов можно ответить только архитектурой. Акмеисты с благоговением поднимают таинственный тютчевский камень и кладут его в основу своего здания.

(3) Строить значит бороться с пустотой, гипнотизировать пространство. Хорошая стрела готической колокольни — злая, — потому что весь её смысл уколоть небо, попрекнуть его тем, что оно *пусто*.

Compare his 1912 poem:

> Паденье — неизменный спутник страха,
> И самый страх есть чувство *пустоты.*
> Кто камни нам бросает с высоты –
> И камень отрицает иго праха?
> . . . . . . . . . . .
> *Булыжники* и грубые мечты –
> В них жажда смерти и тоска размаха . . .

E. Toddes accurately formulated the "compositional principle" of the first *Kamen'* as "the juxtaposition of two lyric levels — the I, its Being in an empty world and the filling of this emptiness by verbal building, the analogue of architectural and other historical-cultural values" (*IJSLP* XVII, 78). We should not forget that the first edition of *Kamen'* closed with a stanza from "Notre Dame":

> Но чем внимательней, твердыня Notre Dame,
> Я изучал твои чудовищные ребра, –
> Тем чаще думал я: *из тяжести недоброй*
> И я когда-нибудь прекрасное создам.[13]

In the voiceless dough there is no "evil heaviness" as there is in the stone. The "bread Sophias," raising their cupolas from a *cherubic* table, become part of the Christian symbolism of spiritual bread. The epithet "cherubic" most probably is suggested by the church hymn "Iže xeruvimy," which is sung when the holy offerings are carried out from the altar. The *čerstvyj pasynok vekov* is obviously a precursor of the *nepriznannyj brat, otščepenec v narodnoj sem'e* of 1931 ("Soxrani moju reč' ").

In the excerpt from *Egipetskaja marka* quoted above there are no "moving lips," Mandel'štam's favorite metaphor for poetic creation, but there is a "daring step" over the "contagious labyrinth." As Mandel'štam wrote in *Razgovor o Dante*:

Мне не на шутку приходит в голову вопрос, сколько подметок, сколько воловьих подошв, сколько сандалий износил Алигьери за время своей поэтической работы, путешествуя по козьим тропам Италии.

Inferno и в особенности Purgatorio прославляют человеческую походку, размер и ритм шагов, ступню и ее форму. Шаг, сопряженный с дыханьем и насыщенный мыслью, Дант понимает как начало просодии. Для обозначения ходьбы он употребляет множество разнообразных и прелестных оборотов.

У Данта философия и поэзия всегда на ходу, всегда на ногах. Даже остановка — разновидность накопленного движения: площадка для разговора создается альпийскими усилиями. Стопа стихов — вдох и выдох — шаг. Шаг — умозаключающий, бодрствующий, силлогизирующий.

In reading these lines, one cannot but recall "Baratynskij's soles," disturbing the dust of the ages ("Dajte Tjutčevu strekozu," May 1932), Goethe, whistling on the winding path, and Hamlet, reflecting with frightened steps ("I Šubert na vode," January 1934); also these lines about Belyj:

> Он дирижировал кавказскими горами
> И машучи вступал на тесных Альп тропы,
> И озираючись, *пугливыми шагами*
> Шел через разговор бесчисленной толпы, –

and Belyj's "seeing foot climbing the steep choir galleries of mountains of sound" (January 1934); and, finally, Mandel'štam's Voronezh poem about Tiflis (February 1937):

> Еще он помнит башмаков *износ* –
> *Моих подметок* стертое величье.

Therefore, the "proferred sack" into which "crisp pastry birds" fall (finished fragments of works or images already formed?) becomes part of the author's "poetic baggage." Mandel'štam was to return to the image of the "poetic sack" in *Razgovor o Dante*:

> ... вместо того, чтобы взгромоздить свою скульптуру на цоколь, как сделал бы, например, Гюго, Дант обволакивает ее сурдинкой, окутывает сизым сумраком, упрятывает на самое дно туманного *звукового мешка.*

Thus, the poet wants to chat about nothing, to awaken night the inspirer, to lift the cap of air and to shake the sack in which the caraway is sewn (recollections of childhood, the Jewish theme in his poetry of 1916–20, or both?), in order that the bond of his blood (which is also the "ringing of the dry grass") be found stolen in "a century, a hayloft, a dream" (*čerez vek, senoval, son*). In this triad, three different kinds of space are represented: time space (*vek*), physical space (*senoval*) and psychological space (*son*). However, *senoval*, meaning the real hayloft, might also refer to the poems *about* the hayloft. Possibly, the third member of the triad also approaches the semantic field *Poetry*. As we will see later, in the *pointe* of the second "Hayloft" *son* is a metaphor for poetry.

Mandel'štam himself deciphered the image of the "dry grass" in his 1922 article "O prirode slova":

> Неспособность Анненского служить каким бы то ни было влияниям, быть посредником, переводчиком, прямо поразительна. Оригиналь-нейшей хваткой он когтил чужое, и еще в воздухе, на большой высоте, надменно выпускал из когтей добычу, позволяя ей упасть

самой. И орел его поэзии, когтивший Еврипида, Малларме, Леконта
де Лиля, ничего не приносил нам в своих лапах, *кроме горсти
сухих трав,* —

> Поймите, к вам стучится сумасшедший,
> Бог знает где и с кем всю ночь проведший,
> Блуждает взор, и речь его дика,
> И камешков полна его рука.
> Того гляди, другую опростает,
> Вас листьями сухими закидает.[14]

Гумилев назвал Анненского великим европейским поэтом. . . . При-
касаясь к мировым богатствам, он сохранил для себя только
*жалкую горсточку,* вернее, поднял горсточку праха и бросил ее
обратно в пылающую сокровищницу Запада. . . . [Он] долгие ночи
боролся с Еврипидом, впитывал в себя змеиный яд мудрой эллинской речи, *готовил настой таких горьких, полынно-крепких
стихов,* каких никто ни до, ни после его не писал.

Mandel'štam returned to the image of grasses in his elegy "1 janvarja
1924":

> Какая боль — искать потерянное слово,
> Больные веки поднимать,
> *И с известью в крови,* для племени чужого
> *Ночные травы* собирать.

These lines recall the 1920 poem "Ja slovo pozabyl," where the "forgotten
word" is the poetic word. The epithet *nočnye* is, of course, connected
with Mandel'štam's creative night.

Blood, as a token of the poet's personality, his physical existence, is
frequently found in Mandel'štam's lyric poetry. Some characteristic
examples:

> Душу от внешних условий
> Освободить я умею,
> Пенье-кипенье крови
> Слышу и быстро хмелею.
>
> (1911)

> На дикую, чужую
> Мне подменили кровь.
>
> («Я наравне с другими», 1920)

А ведь раньше лучше было,
И пожалуй не сравнишь,
Как ты прежде шелестила,
Кровь, как нынче шелестишь.

(«Холодок щекочет темя», 1922)

Век. Известковый слой в крови больного сына
Твердеет . . .

.   .   .   .   .   .   .   .   .   .   .   .   .

И известковый слой в крови больного сына
Растает, и блаженный брызнет смех . . .

(«1 января 1924»)

И крови моей не волнуя,
Как детский рисунок просты,
Здесь жены проходят, даруя
От львиной своей красоты.

(«Армения» II, 1930)

But in Mandel'štam's work there is also another kind of blood, the
collective blood, the blood on which Russia stands ("Zasnula čern',"
1913: "Rossija, ty na kamne i krovi"), "blood the builder" (*krov'-
stroitel'nica*, in "Vek," 1923), blood which "will freeze like the dawn at
the mutual, peaceful judgment" ("A nebo buduščim beremenno," 1923).[15]
There is also in Mandel'štam the blood of heroic sacrifice, both individual
and collective ("Vek"):

Век мой, зверь мой, кто сумеет
Заглянуть в твои зрачки
И своею кровью склеит
Двух столетий позвонки?
Кровь-строительница хлещет
Горлом из земных вещей,
Захребетник лишь трепещет
На пороге новых дней.

Since the meaning of the noun "bond" is not completely clear, it is
difficult to decide to what kind of blood the "rose-colored blood" refers.
Naturally, the question arises: if it is the poet's own blood, then what
kind of "bond" is being talked of in the first "Hayloft"? Is it the bond of
his blood with life in general, with his past, his time? Or is it the bond of
blood with blood, that is, the bond of one person's blood with the blood
of other people, a mutual guarantee of blood?

Georgij Margvelašvili obviously understands the image of the "rose-
colored blood" as the collective blood, since he thinks that this image

"personifies time." Margvelašvili writes ("Ob Osipe Mandel'štame," p. 82): "V poèzii Mandel'štama v 1922 godu načinajut mel'kat' obrazy 'rozovoj krovi' i 'suxoj travy,' olicetvorjajuščie obrazy vremeni i poèzii, o vosstanovlenii narušennoj vzaimosvjazi kotoryx mečtaet poèt" — and then he quotes the last stanza of the first "Hayloft." I would say that it is difficult to agree with this explanation. There is no social theme in the first "Hayloft" (it appears only in the second), but the personal theme is, on the contrary, very strong. I therefore lean toward another interpretation of the image (while not claiming that this explanation is totally correct or the only one possible).

Proceeding from the principle of contiguity, I will define the "bond of blood" in the first "Hayloft" as the personal principle, the poet's bond with his past and his poetic work (with the sack in which the caraway is sewn). We should remember that the poet equates his life and his poetry: "the ringing of the dry grass" is an absolute nominal attribute to the subject clause "bond of the rose-colored blood." We might assume, then, that the poet is expressing the following wish: that his poetry (reflecting his life and personality) be preserved, that the stolen bond be found — in a century, a hayloft, a dream. But another question arises here: why must the bond be "stolen?" This participle is associated with the noun "thief" from the first stanza, where the subjects "mosquito prince" and "thief" clearly relate to one and the same agent. As early as 1913 Mandel'štam wrote:

> У вечности ворует всякий,
> А вечность — как морской песок . . .
>                    («В таверне воровская шайка»)

and at the very beginning of his poetic career (1909, "Dano mne telo") he proclaimed:

> На стекла вечности уже легло
> Мое дыхание, мое тепло.

Even then, Mandel'štam believed in the permanent value of his poetry.[16] Finally, in 1930 or 1931 he wrote these bitter lines: "Vse proizvedenija mirovoj literatury ja delju na razrešennye i napisannye bez razrešenija. Pervye — èto mraz', vtorye — *vorovannyj vozdux*" ("Četvertaja proza"). The poet's wish came true: his stolen poetry was found not in a century but a quarter century after his death.

The second "Hayloft" begins with a realistic description explaining the "plot" of the first:

> Я по лесенке приставной
> Лез на всклоченный сеновал . . .

But immediately after this the realistic level seems to disappear: the hay-dust in the air becomes the "hay-dust of the milky stars"; the hay in the hayloft "the matted hair [plica] of space." The hayloft expands to fill the whole cosmos.

In the second stanza the poet returns to the theme of poetry. And while in the first "Hayloft" he wanted to *awaken* the creative night, in the second one he asks, as if wondering whether poetry is needed: "Why *awaken* the swarm of lengthened sounds?" The image of the "eternal conflict" (*večnaja skloka*) in this stanza cannot be explained straightforwardly. It is probably connected both with the universe ("the plica of space," the "ancient chaos of the hayloft") and with the current epoch — the "burning ranks" and the poets who tune their lyre and sing in defiance of the world order.[17] Be that as it may, an "Aeolian harmony" is hidden in this conflict (Horace: "ex humili potens / Princeps *Aeolium carmen* ad Italos / Deduxisse modos"). Mandel'štam, of course, does not have in mind Alcaic and Sapphic stanzas,[18] but the wonderful harmony of Hellenism, so dear to the poet's heart. In the same year that the "Hayloft" was written, Mandel'štam wrote the essay "O prirode slova":

Русский язык — язык эллинистический. В силу целого ряда исторических условий, живые силы эллинской культуры, уступив Запад латинским влияниям и не надолго загащиваясь в бездетной Византии, устремились в лоно русской речи, сообщив ей самоуверенную тайну эллинистического мировоззрения, тайну свободного воплощения, и *поэтому русский язык стал именно звучащей и говорящей плотью.*

The "swarm of lengthened sounds" becomes understandable precisely in connection with the "Aeolian harmony." In 1914, Mandel'štam wrote:

> Есть иволги в лесах, и гласных долгота
> В тонических[19] стихах единственная мера.
> Но только раз в году бывает разлита
> В природе длительность, как в метрике Гомера.
>
> Как бы цезурою зияет этот день:
> Уже с утра покой и трудные длинноты;
> Волы на пастбище, и золотая лень
> Из тростника извлечь богатство целой ноты.

The "swarm of lengthened sounds" is echoed, too, in one of Mandel'štam's octets from 1933:

Люблю появление ткани,
Когда после двух или трех,
А то четырех задыханий
Придет выпрямляющий вздох –
И так хорошо мне и тяжко,
Когда приближается миг –
И вдруг *дуговая растяжка*
*Звучит в бормотаньях моих.*

We need not doubt that this poem as well deals with poetic creation.
So, the poet asks if poetry is necessary when all seems so clear and
simple:

Звезд в ковше Медведицы семь.
Добрых чувств на земле пять.

These are irrefutable truths, like two times two is four. And nonetheless:

*Набухает, звенит темь,*
И *растет и звенит* опять.

One is strongly tempted to explain the "ringing darkness" as a
synonym for the night which the poet shoved with his shoulder, awak-
ened. Poetry is seemingly being born against the poet's will. To the
reader such a straightforward explanation was naturally suggested
when immediately after the third stanza there followed in many
editions:

Не своей чешуей шуршим,
Против шерсти мира поем.
Лиру строим . . .

Situated between the "wonderful harmony," "singing" and "lyre," the
"sounding darkness" was naturally included in the semantic field
*Poetic Creation.*[20] But Mandel'štam restored a middle stanza in the poem:

Распряженный огромный воз[21]
Поперек вселенной торчит,
Сеновала *древний хаос*
Защекочет, запорошит.

In this stanza the image of the hayloft acquires cosmic dimensions and
apocalyptic meaning. It is easy to recognize in the "ancient chaos"
Tjutčev's chaos, connected with night that exposes the abyss. In
Tjutčev's "Son na more" we find a parallel to Mandel'štam's *tem'*:

Я в хаосе звуков лежал оглушен,
Над хаосом звуков носился мой сон.
Болезненно-яркий, волшебно-немой,
Он веял легко над *гремящею тьмой* . . .

However, the second meaning of "ringing darkness" (night chaos) does
not cancel the first meaning (night — creative element).

The fifth stanza, as was said, continues the theme of the poetic
creation of a whole group of poets:

Не своей чешуей шуршим,
Против шерсти мира *поем*.
*Лиру строим*, словно спешим
Обрасти косматым руном.

The first person plural present tense appears in this stanza. The "I" of
the previous text seemingly merges with a new, implied "we" (Ja ne
znaju . . . / Ja xotel by . . . / Ja . . . lez . . . na senoval . . . / I podumal
. . . — [My] šuršim . . . [my] poem . . . [my] liru stroim). This stanza is
marked by contradictory statements reflecting, however, the inner con-
tradictions of the age. If the first line hints at compulsion (*"ne svoej
češuej šuršim"*), then the second line speaks of creative activity in
defiance of the world order (*"Protiv šersti mira poem"*). The last two
lines introduce two new motifs: reverting to savagery and self-protection.

Mandel'štam concludes his sketch "V ne po činu barstvennoj šube"
(in *Šum vremeni*) with the images of the deep winter of the Russian
nineteenth century and the literature-beast with its fur hide:

Оглядываясь на весь девятнадцатый век русской культуры, . . . я
. . . вижу в нем единство непомерной стужи, спаявшей десятилетия
в один денек, в одну ночку, в глубокую зиму, где страшная госу-
дарственность, как печь, пышущая льдом. И в этот зимний период
русской истории литература в целом и в общем представляется
мне, как нечто барственное, смущающее меня: с трепетом при-
поднимаю пленку вощеной бумаги над зимней шапкой писателя.
*Нельзя зверю стыдиться пушной своей шкуры. Ночь его опушила.
Зима его одела. Литература — зверь.* Скорняк — ночь и зима.

Mandel'štam's image of the freezing poet who has grown a fur hide is
probably suggested by his reading of Ovid's *Tristia*. Echoes from the
elegy "Cum subit illius tristissima noctis imago" ("Tristium liber
primus," III) are heard in Mandel'štam's 1918 elegy "Tristia" ("prostovolosye žaloby nočnye," and so on; see Victor Terras, "Classical
Motives in the Poetry of Osip Mandel'štam," pp. 259–260). In his

article "Slovo i kul'tura," Mandel'štam quotes the beginning of this Ovid elegy immediately after the Puškin lines about the exile who had the "gift of wondrous songs":

> Не понимал он ничего
> И слаб и робок был, как дети,
> Чужие люди для него
> Зверей и рыб ловили в сети.

Mandel'štam probably remembered these lines of Ovid's (I, III, 89–90):

> Egredior, sive illud erat sine funere ferri,
> Squalidus imissis hirta per ora comis.[22]

In his essay "O prirode slova" (1922) Mandel'štam talks of Annenskij, who tenderly, as befits a Russian poet, put "the animal hide on the still freezing Ovid," and somewhat later he again returns to the image of the Roman poet in Puškin's *Cygany:*

Эллинизм — это . . . всякая одежда, возлагаемая на плечи людям, и с тем же самым чувством священной дрожи, с каким

> Как мерзла быстрая река
> И зимни вихри бушевали,
> Пушистой кожей прикрывали
> Они святого старика.

It is worth mentioning that in the same essay Mandel'štam quotes the last two lines from Annenskij's translation of Verlaine's poem "Pensée du soir":

> На темный жребий мой я больше не в обиде:
> И наг и немощен был некогда Овидий.

Lastly, one should remember Villon's "animal hide": "Villon žil v Pariže, *kak belka v kolese,* ne znaja ni minuty pokoja. On ljubil v sebe xiščnogo, suxoparogo *zver'ka* i dorožil svojej potrepannoj *škurkoj*" ("Fransua Villon," 1910).[23]

The motif of return to the nest appears in the sixth stanza of the second "Hayloft." In this stanza a nest is compared to the "native musical mode" (*rodnoj zvukorjad*): "[Kak] kosari prinosjat nazad ščeglov, upavšix iz gnezda, [tak i ja] vyrvus' iz gorjaščix rjadov i vernus' v rodnoj zvukorjad." The first person singular verbs (*vyrvus', vernus'*) are in sharp contrast to the plural of the previous stanza. A return to the native mode involves a break with the collective, with the "burning ranks."

The image of the "burning ranks" is difficult to interpret: it obviously contains something left intentionally unsaid. Of course, it is clear that these are ranks of fighters, but one can only guess as to what kind of fighters. Is it Majakovskij's "attacking class" in general, or is it ranks of singers, singing in defiance of the world order? It is difficult to decide. Georgij Margvelašvili, in his article referred to above, seems to favor the first interpretation. He thinks that the last three stanzas of the "Hayloft" reflect a "mood close to Esenin's": "Otdam vsju dušu oktjabrju i maju, no tol'ko liry miloj ne otdam." Be that as it may, leaving the "burning ranks" is equivalent to complete artistic isolation.

The poet wishes to return to the "native mode" (which is related to the "swarm of lengthened sounds" and the "wonderful Aeolian harmony") in order that the "bond of the rose-colored blood and the ringing of arm-like dry grasses finally part":[24] "odna [krov'] skrepjas', a drugaja [trava] — [ujdja, prevrativšis'] v zaumnyj son." If in the first "Hayloft" life and poetic creation are equated, then in the second the possibility of their separation is foreseen: life is supressed, and art acquires a new expression, a new "form."

In Mandel'štam's essays we find two statements about transsense poetry. The first ("Zametki o poèzii," 1923) relates to Xlebnikov:

Он наметил пути развития языка, переходные, промежуточные, и этот исторически небывший путь российской речевой судьбы, осуществленный только в Хлебникове, закрепился в его *зауми*, которая есть не что иное, как переходные формы, не успевшие затянуться смысловой корой *правильно и праведно развивающегося языка.*[25]

Ten years later, in *Razgovor o Dante*, Mandel'štam wrote:

Когда понадобилось начертить окружность времени, для которого тысячелетие меньше, чем мигание ресницы, Дант вводит *детскую заумь в свой астрономический, концертный, глубоко публичный, проповеднический словарь.*

In both instances it is a question of a new poetic language. Might Mandel'štam not have had in mind the new stage in the development of his own poetics which received its most colorful expression in the "elevated transsense" of "Grifel'naja oda"? Obviously, in the phrase "zaumnyj son," the noun is also a metaphor for poetry. Let us recall, for instance, these lines from "Ja ne slyxal rasskazov Ossiana" (1914):

Я получил блаженное наследство –
*Чужих певцов блуждающие сны . . .*

As Margvelašvili noted, in the first and second "Hayloft" Mandel'-štam offers two different "solutions to the dilemma." The second solution turned out to be unrealizable: the poet's breath and the breath of his time are unfailingly present in Mandel'štam's post-1922 poetry; the "bond of the rose-colored blood" and the "ringing of the grass" did not part.

With this we shall conclude our commentary on the "Hayloft."

We have observed the "regrouping" of particular semantic fields. Some words and phrases have not only acquired new shades of meaning but have been endowed with a new figurative sense as well, without, however, losing their ties to the basic semantic field (thus "dry grasses," while remaining grasses, simultaneously become an analogue of poetry, and so on). We hope that after our analysis the polysemantic quality of the texts concerned has become more evident.

# III

## THE BLACK-YELLOW LIGHT

### *The Jewish Theme in Mandel'štam's Poetry*

It has been stated on many occasions that the spiritual and emotional problematics of Mandel'štam's *Kamen'* and *Tristia* revolved predominantly around Christianity, while the subject of Judaism was broached only in three poems of *Tristia*: "Èta noč' nepopravima" (1916), "Sredi svjaščennikov levitom molodym" (1917), and "Vernis' v smesitel'noe lono" (1920); the latter two poems have often been called enigmatic.[1] It is also well known that in *Kamen'* the poet was more concerned with Catholicism (Protestantism plays only a marginal role in this collection), while in *Tristia* he turned to Orthodoxy, although Catholic Rome was not forgotten. In the last poem in *Tristia* he makes no distinction between St. Sophia in Constantinople and St. Peter's in Rome:

> Соборы вечные Софии и Петра,
> Амбары воздуха и света,
> Зернохранилища вселенского добра
> И риги Нового Завета.

In *Kamen'* and *Tristia* the themes of Catholicism and Orthodoxy are paralleled by the poetic vision of ancient Rome and ancient Hellas. One may say that the Hellenic-Christian spirit determined Mandel'štam's intellectual and emotional outlook and perspective in the period of *Tristia*. As compared to *Kamen'*, the poet's model of the world in his second book, *Tristia*, has undergone a considerable change. The themes of Christianity and Hellenism in *Tristia* are in harmony with each other, while the Judaic theme is strongly antithetic, if not even antagonistic to both of them.

The best commentary on all three themes is found, as usual, in Mandel'štam's prose: in *Šum vremeni* (particularly in the sketch "Xaos iudejskij"), in his essays "Slovo i kul'tura" and "O prirode slova," and in the preserved fragments of his essay, "Puškin i Skrjabin" (the complete text of which has been lost).

We shall juxtapose the following quotations which offer us a key, I believe, to understanding the mutual relation between the three poetic themes mentioned above:

(1) Весь стройный мираж Петербурга был только сон, блистательный покров, накинутый над бездной, а кругом простирался *хаос иудейства*, не родина, не дом, *не очаг*, а именно хаос, незнакомый *утробный мир*, откуда я вышел, которого я боялся, о котором смутно догадывался и бежал, всегда бежал.

Иудейский хаос пробивался во все щели каменной петербургской квартиры, угрозой разрушенья, шапкой в комнате провинциального гостя, крючками шрифта нечитаемых книг «Бытия», заброшенных в пыль на книжную полку шкафа, ниже Гёте и Шиллера, и *клочками черно-желтого ритуала*.[2]

Крепкий румяный русский год катился по календарю с крашеными яйцами, елками, стальными финляндскими коньками, декабрем, вейками и дачей. А тут же путался призрак — новый год в сентябре и невеселые странные праздники, терзавшие слух дикими именами: Рош-Гашана и Иом-кипур.

(*Шум времени*, «Бунты и француженки»)

(2) Эллинизм — это *печной горшок*, ухват, *крынка с молоком*, это *домашняя утварь*, посуда, все окружение тела; эллинизм — это *тепло очага*, ощущаемое, как священное, всякая собственность, преобщающая часть внешнего мира к человеку, всякая одежда, возлагаемая на плечи, и с тем же самым чувством священной дрожи, с каким

Как мерзла быстрая река
И зимни вихри бушевали,
Пушистой кожей прикрывали
Они святого старика.[3]

Эллинизм — это сознательное окружение человека утварью, вместо безразличных предметов, превращение этих предметов в утварь, очеловечение окружающего мира, согревание его *тончайшим телеологическим теплом*. Эллинизм — это всякая *печка*, около которой сидит человек и ценит ее тепло, как родственное его внутреннему теплу.

(«О природе слова»)

(3)   Наконец мы обрели *внутреннюю свободу,* настоящее *внутрен-
нее веселье. Воду в глиняных кувшинах* пьем как вино, а солнцу
больше нравится в монастырской столовой, чем в ресторане. Яблоки,
хлеб, картофель — отныне утоляют не только физический, но и
духовный голод. Христианин, а теперь всякий культурный человек
— христианин, не знает только физического голода, только духовной пищи. Для него и слово плоть и простой хлеб — веселье и
тайна.

(«Слово и культура»)

(4)   Вся наша двухтысячелетняя культура, благодаря чудесной
милости христианства, есть *отпущение мира на свободу* для игры,
для духовного *веселья,* для свободного «подражания Христу».

(«Пушкин и Скрябин»)

I would like to call the reader's attention to the image of the hearth
(*očag*), which the poet found not in Jewish, but in Hellenic tradition.[4]
What is more, the Hellenic "household utensils" (*domašnjaja utvar'*)
are clearly opposed to the Judaic scraps of "black-yellow ritual." The
water in "the earthenware jug" in the third quotation (*voda v glinjanom
kuvšine*) echoes the "earthenware pot of milk" (*krynka s molokom*) and
the "stove pot" (*pečnoj goršok*) from the second. All three objects are
*domašnjaja utvar'*. The third and the fourth quotations share the motif
of inner freedom and spiritual joy.[5] In Mandel'štam's poetry this theme
is reflected in the famous poem (1920) describing the Orthodox Eucharist:

> Вот дароносица, как солнце золотое,
> Повисла в воздухе — великолепный миг,
> Здесь должен прозвучать лишь греческий язык:
> Взять в руки целый мир, как яблоко простое.
>
> Богослужения торжественный зенит,
> Свет в круглой храмине под куполом в июле,
> Чтоб полной грудью мы вне времени вздохнули
> О луговине той, где время не бежит.
>
> И Евхаристия как вечный полдень длится –
> Все причащаются, играют и поют,
> И на виду у всех божественный сосуд
> Неисчерпаемым веселием струится.

As was pointed out in Chapter Two, in *Kamen'* Mandel'štam was
juxtaposing "two lyric levels — the 'I,' its Being in an empty world
and the filling of the emptiness by verbal building, the analogue of

architectural and other historical-cultural values." But in the same book, in the poem "I ponyne na Afone" (1915), he already affirms that the word is pure joy and deliverance from anguish:

> Слово — чистое веселье,
> Исцеленье от тоски!

From that time on, the main concern of his poetry and philosophy has been to strive for the preservation of inner freedom, of spiritual joy and "teleological warmth" in our cold world.

Until now it has been generally accepted that the Judaic theme appeared for the first time in Mandel'štam's poetry in the poem describing his mother's funeral ("Èta noč' nepopravima"). Recently Omry Ronen made a good point (in his article on Mandel'štam, *Encyclopedia Judaica: Yearbook 1972*) when he maintained that the poet's Jewish family background is reflected in his poetry as early as 1910, in the following "twin-poems":

### I

> Из омута злого и вязкого
> Я вырос, тростинкой шурша,
> И страстно, и томно, и ласково
> Запретною жизнью дыша.
>
> И никну, никем не замеченный,
> В холодный и топкий приют,
> Приветственным шелестом встреченный
> Коротких осенних минут.
>
> Я счастлив жестокой обидою
> И в жизни, похожей на сон,
> Я каждому тайно завидую
> И в каждого тайно влюблен.

### II

> В огромном омуте прозрачно и темно,
> И томное окно белеет;
> А сердце — отчего так медленно оно
> И так упорно тяжелеет?
>
> То всею тяжестью оно идет ко дну,
> Соскучившись по милом иле,
> То, как соломинка, минуя глубину,
> Наверх всплывает без усилий.

С притворной нежностью у изголовья стой
И сам себя всю жизнь баюкай,
Как небылицею, своей томись тоской
И ласков будь с надменной скукой.

The central image of these twin-poems is the evil and viscid, translucent and dark, huge pool; and their dominant theme is existence on the border of reality and dream, of being and non-being. The figurative meaning of *omut* rests on a lexical metaphor in Russian (compare the English "slough"), and as such is very often used in poetry (Puškin uses the word *omut* twice, only with metaphorical meaning). Both poems follow the same asymmetric compositional model: in the first two quatrains they contain a visual image of the pool; the last quatrain is not directly connected with this image; it is a kind of lyrical afterword to the first two. According to Ronen, the image of the "evil and viscid pool" is a metaphor for the "Judaic chaos," for the atmosphere of the Jewish way of life cherished by Mandel'štam's grandparents from Riga and, in his own family, particularly preserved by his father.

If we read the first poem keeping in mind the fragment from *Šum vremeni* quoted above, then the image of the "forbidden life" becomes completely clear: the poet feels that he has no inherent right to become an equal participant in Russian life. In light of this, the motif of the brutal offense and of secret envy becomes equally transparent. However, the poet's attitude toward the *omut* is ambivalent: in the second stanza he calls it "the cold and boggy shelter" (*xolodnyj i topkij prijut*). The noun *prijut* obviously belongs to the positive semantic field, while the epithets, *xolodnyj* and *topkij*, are rather negative.

The *trostinka* (thin reed) from the first quatrain is none other than Pascal's *roseau pensant*, but the source of Mandel'štam's image was probably Tjutčev's poem, "Pevučest' est' v morskix volnax":

Певучесть есть в морских волнах,
Гармония в стихийных спорах,
И стройный мусикийский шорох
Струится в зыбких камышах.

Невозмутимый строй во всем,
Созвучье полное в природе, –
Лишь в нашей призрачной свободе
Разлад мы с нею сознаем.

Откуда, как разлад возник?
И отчего же в общем хоре

Душа не то поет, что море,
И ропщет мыслящий тростник?

И от земли до крайних звезд
Всё безответен и поныне
Глас вопиющего в пустыне,
Души отчаянной протест?

Mandel'štam's and Tjutčev's poems have two motifs in common —
rustling and water. Mandel'štam's rustling of the reed ("Ja vyros
trostinkoj *šurša*"), as well as the rustle of the short, autumnal minutes
("*šelest* korotkix osennix minut") recalls Tjutčev's "musikijskij *šorox*."
But the motif of water is differently treated by Mandel'štam: his *omut*
is clearly opposed to Tjutčev's *more*. It is worth mentioning that in
Mandel'štam's essay "Puškin i Skrjabin" the reference to Tjutčev's
poem is even more direct: "Čto-to slučilos' s muzykoj; kakoj-to veter
slomal s naletu *musikijskie kamyši*, suxie i zvonkie. My trebuem xora,
nam naskučil ropot *mysljaščego trostnika*."

The dreamlike life ("žizn', poxožaja na son") in the third stanza
recalls the first sentence from the fragment from *Šum vremeni* cited
above: "Ves' strojnyj *miraž* Peterburga byl tol'ko *son*, blistatel'nyj
pokrov, nakinutyj nad bezdnoj." Incidentally, the "pokrov nakinutyj
nad bezdnoj" is an exact quotation from Tjutčev's poem "Svjataja noč'
na nebosklon vzošla" (compare also "pokrov zlatotkannyj" in Tjutčev's
poem "Den' i noč' ").

Mandel'štam's first poem ends, as it were, on a conciliatory note:
the poet is happy with the brutal offense (what a striking oxymoron!),
and despite his secret envy he is in love with everyone (presumably
anyone who does not belong to the "evil and viscid pool"). This conciliatory note sounds in contrast to Tjutčev's "protest of the desperate
soul" from the last line of his poem. However, in its first publication,
Mandel'štam's poem had an additional fourth quatrain. In it, the poet
calls his life a torture and introduces the new motif of revenge. Thus,
the *pointe* of the poem is climactic:

Ни сладости в пытке не ведаю,
Ни смысла я в ней не ищу;
Но близкой, последней победою,
Быть может, за все отомщу.

The main theme of the second poem is the oscillation of the poet's
heart between the bottom and the surface of the pool. The heart is
compared to a straw (*solominka*), which echoes the reed (*trostinka*)

of the first poem. It should be noted that the poet's heart at times misses
the "beloved ooze" and returns to it. This ooze (*il*), with the positive
epithet "beloved" (*milyj*), recalls the "cold and boggy shelter," where
it is the noun (*prijut*) which has a positive value. The *pointe* of the
second poem is anticlimactic ("I laskov bud' s nadmennoj skukoj"),
similar to the one in Puškin's "Pamjatnik" — "I ne osporivaj glupca."[6]

Mandel'štam's poem describing his mother's funeral reflects a somber
mood and has a tragic tone:

> Эта ночь непоправима,
> А у вас еще светло.
> У ворот Ерусалима
> Солнце черное взошло.[7]
>
> Солнце желтое страшнее –
> Баю баюшки баю –
> В светлом храме иудеи
> Хоронили мать мою.
>
> Благодати не имея
> И священства лишены,
> В светлом храме иудеи
> Отпевали прах жены.
>
> И над матерью звенели
> Голоса израильтян.
> Я проснулся в колыбели,
> Черным солнцем осиян.

The imagery of this poem does not require much detailed comment.
The black sun in the first and last quatrains is an apocalyptic image
("The Revelation of Saint John" 6.12; compare also "The Book of
Joel" 2.10, 3.15; Matthew 24.29; Mark 13.24). In the Church Slavonic
and Russian texts of the Apocalypse the sun is not "black" but "dark":
(1) ". . . i solnce *mračno* byst' jako vretišče vlasjano, i luna byst' jako
krov' "; (2) ". . . i solnce stalo *mračno* kak vlasjanica, i luna sdelalas'
kak krov'." In all probability, Mandel'štam did not take the epithet
"black" from the Greek or French text of the Apocalypse, but from the
then sensational *Salomé* of Oscar Wilde: "En ce jour-la le soleil deviendra
*noir* comme un sac de poil, et la lune deviendra comme du sang." Nor is
there any yellow sun in the Bible. Obviously, it is a metaphor for the
light illuminating the temple where his mother's funeral is held. This yellow sun turns out to be even more frightening than the black sun which

shines on the poet in his cradle.[8] The word *kolybel'* is evidently used in its common figurative meaning; it refers to the poet's Jewish family background. In the poem quoted above ("Vot daronosica"), the "golden sun" of the Orthodox Eucharist clearly belongs to the positive semantic field and functions as a sharp contrast to the "yellow sun" of the Jewish temple. There is no "golden sun" in Holy Scripture, either, but "golden" is the most common positive epithet of the sun in poetry.

After Nadežda Mandel'štam's comments in *Vtoraja kniga* (p. 130), the poem "Sredi svjaščennikov" (1917) is no longer at all enigmatic. Mrs. Mandel'štam believes that the "young levite" is the poet himself who predicts the "destruction of the city":

> Среди священников левитом молодым
> На страже утренней он долго оставался.
> Ночь иудейская сгущалася над ним
> И храм разрушенный угрюмо созидался.
>
> Он говорил: небес тревожна желтизна.
> Уж над Ефратом ночь, бегите, иереи!
> А старцы думали: не наша в том вина;
> Се черножелтый свет, се радость Иудеи.
>
> Он с нами был, когда на берегу ручья
> Мы в драгоценный лен Субботу пеленали
> И семисвещником тяжелым освещали
> Ерусалима ночь и чад небытия.

The disturbing yellow color of the sky and the night over the Euphrates are perceived by the priests as colors of the "black-and-yellow ritual," the "joy of Judea," but the poet understands the eschatological meaning of the "black-yellow light." Since the Sabbath swathed with precious linen is, as Mrs. Mandel'štam has shown, the image of the dead Christ, the "gloomy rebuilding of the destroyed temple" should be explained as a metaphor for the time between Friday night and Sunday morning, the three days in which Christ has promised to rebuild the temple destroyed by Him (Matthew 26.61).[9]

The image of the cross appeared for the first time in Mandel'štam in the poem "Kogda mozaik niknut travy," written in Lugano in 1910:

> Когда мозаик никнут травы
> И церковь гулкая пуста,
> Я в темноте, как змей лукавый,
> Влачусь к подножию Креста.

И пью монашескую нежность
В сосредоточенных сердцах,
Как кипариса безнадежность
В неумолимых высотах.

Люблю изогнутые брови
И краску на лице святых,
И пятна золота и крови
На теле статуй восковых.

Быть может, только призрак плоти
Обманывает нас в мечтах,
Просвечивает меж лохмотий
И дышит в роковых страстях.

This poem by no means reflects a pious religious mood, since in it the poet compares himself to the subtle serpent. The first quatrain calls to my mind Blok's early poem, "Ljublju vysokie sobory" (1902), particularly the following lines:

В своей молитве суеверной
Ищу защиты у Христа,
Но из-под маски лицемерной
Смеются лживые уста.

The hero of Mandel'štam's poem is more attracted by the figures on the mosaics and by statues of saints, and his mind is occupied with reflections on human flesh and fatal passions. The *"kiparisa beznadežnost' v neumolimyx vysotax"* reminds us of his 1913 statement in "Utro akmeizma": "Xorošaja strela gotičeskoj kolokol'ni — zlaja, — potomu čto ves' ee smysl ukolot' nebo, popreknut' ego tem, čto ono *pusto*."

The image of Christ's crucifixion remains central in the Mandel'štam poem of 1915:

Неутолимые слова . . .
Окаменела Иудея,
И, с каждым мигом тяжелея,
Его поникла голова.
Стояли воины кругом
На страже стынущего тела;
Как венчик, голова висела
На стебле тонком и чужом.
И царствовал и никнул Он,
Как лилия, в родимый омут,
И глубина, где стебли тонут,
Торжествовала свой закон.

The sinking into the water is a common image for dying. But here we are again confronted with the metaphor "the native pool" (*rodimyj omut*). If it is a symbol for Judaism, as Omry Ronen suggests, then the "law" in the *pointe* of the poem might be interpreted as the usual Christian metaphor for the *Old Testament* (John 1.17). Since his school years, Mandel'štam must have known Ilarion's "Slovo o zakone i blagodati." In any case, the foretokening of the resurrection is not mentioned in "Neutolimye slova." It becomes a distinct motif in "Sredi svjaščennikov" in the line: "I xram razrušennyj ugrjumo sozidalsja."

As we see, Mandel'štam's attitude toward the Sabbath of the 1917 poem is quite different. He sees himself as Christ's servant, the young levite who participated in Christ's burial. In a poem written in May 1933 ("Ne iskušaj čužix narečij"), he will even identify himself with Christ:

И в наказанье за гордыню, неисправимый звуколюб,
Получишь *уксусную губку* ты для изменнических губ.

There is a quite different black-yellow coloration in Mandel'štam's poem "Dvorcovaja ploščad'," written in 1915. Here the black and yellow are the colors of the Russian emperor's standard:

Императорский виссон
И моторов колесницы, –
В черном омуте столицы
Столпник-ангел вознесен.
В темной арке, как пловцы,
Исчезают пешеходы,
И на площади, как воды,
Глухо плещутся торцы.
Только там, где твердь светла,
Черно-желтый лоскут злится,
Словно в воздухе струится
Желчь двуглавого орла.

Moreover, Mandel'štam's attitude toward these colors of the standard is negative. The black slough of the capital is opposed to the bright sky. The black-and-yellow cloth is unfriendly; it seems to belch the bile of the two-headed eagle into the air. The black and yellow colors connected with St. Petersburg had for Mandel'štam eschatological implications as well, as Mrs. Mandel'štam has pointed out (*Vtoraja kniga*, p. 130), with credit to the editors of *Sobranie sočinenij* (see their note, "Černoe solnce," in vol. III): "Te že černo-želtye cveta, kak pravil'no zametili komentatory, Mandel'štam videl v obrečennom Peterburge — vplot' do stixotvorenija tridcatogo goda: 'k zloveščemu degtju podmešen želtok'."

In *Tristia*, the poem predicting the destruction of Jerusalem, "Sredi svjaščennikov," is followed by a 1918 poem describing the death of Petersburg:

> На страшной высоте блуждающий огонь,
> Но разве так звезда мерцает?
> Прозрачная звезда, блуждающий огонь,
> Твой брат, Петрополь, умирает.

One should not forget, however, that Petersburg's frightening black and yellow coloration has its own tradition in Russian twentieth-century poetry. It goes back to Annenskij and Blok.

Annenskij, "Peterburg" (published in *Apollon*, 1910):

> *Желтый* пар петербургской зимы
> *Желтый* снег, облипающий плиты . . .
> . . . . . . . . . . . . . . .
> Только камни нам дал чародей
> Да Неву *буро-желтого* цвета,
> Да пустыни *немых площадей,*
> *Где казнили людей до рассвета.*
>
> А что было у нас на земле,
> Чем вознесся орел наш двуглавый,
> *В темных* лаврах гигант на скале, –
> Завтра станет ребячьей забавой.

Blok (1909):

> В эти *желтые дни* меж домами
> Мы встречаемся только на миг.
> Ты меня обжигаешь глазами
> И скрываешься в *темный* тупик.

Blok, "Uniženie" (1911):

> *В черных* сучьях дерев обнаженных
> *Желтый* зимний закат за окном.
> (К эшафоту на казнь осужденных
> Поведут на закате таком).

The first and third examples are linked by the image of execution. In the light of Mandel'štam's black-yellow coloration of 1917, even the *"želtizna* pravitel'stvennyx zdanij" from the 1913 poem "Peterburgskie strofy" acquires a new quality. As for the "*černaja* Neva" in "Solominka," it always had clearly negative connotations. Compare also: "No, kak meduza nevskaja volna / Mne otvraščen'e legkoe vnušaet" (in "Mne xolodno," 1916), "Prozračnaja vesna nad *černoju* Nevoj" ("Na strašnoj vysote," 1918), and in *Egipetskaja marka*: "Ved' i deržus' ja odnim Peterburgom — koncertnym, *želtym*, *zloveščim*, *naxoxlennym*, zimnim."

In the early thirties, Mandel'štam's "*želč'* peterburgskogo dnja" ("Ja p'ju za voennye astry," 1931) clearly echoes the "*želč'* dvuglavogo orla" from "Dvorcovaja ploščad'," and in his "Leningrad" (December 1930) the eschatological black-and-yellow coloration is reflected in the following image:

> Узнавай же скорее декабрьский денек,
> Где к зловещему *дегтю* подмешен *желток*.

In this context, even the adjective *černyj* in the idiom *černaja lestnica* (the backstairs) from the sixth couplet seems to recover its primary meaning:[10]

> Я на лестнице *черной* живу, и в висок
> Ударяет мне вырванный с мясом звонок.

The "black-yellow light, joy of Judea" appears as the "yellow dusk" in Mandel'štam's poem about the incestuous daughter:

> Вернись в смесительное лоно,
> Откуда, Лия, ты пришла,
> За то, что солнцу Илиона
> Ты желтый сумрак предпочла.
>
> Иди, никто тебя не тронет,
> На грудь отца в глухую ночь
> Пускай главу свою уронит
> Кровосмесительница-дочь.
>
> Но роковая перемена
> В тебе исполниться должна:
> Ты будешь Лия — не Елена, –
> Не потому наречена,
>
> Что царской крови тяжелее
> Струиться в жилах, чем другой –
> Нет, ты полюбишь иудея,
> Исчезнешь в нем — и бог с тобой.

"Vernis' v smesitel'noe lono" was written in the Crimea, where Mandel'-
štam had moved alone after his brief sojourn in Kiev. He left behind
Mrs. Mandel'štam (Miss Xazina at that time), with whom he had a
liaison in May 1919 ("Svoej datoj my sčitali pervoe maja devjatnad-
catogo goda, xotja potom nam prišlos' žyt' v razluke poltora goda,"
*Vtoraja kniga*, p. 20). In this book, Mrs. Mandel'štam identifies herself
with the daughter from "Vernis' " (pp. 262–263). Indeed, Mandel'štam
cherished a kind of fatherly feeling for his bride. In a letter from Theodosia, dated December 5, 1919, he addresses her: "Ditja moe miloe!", and
further in the text he calls her *"dočka moja*, sestra moja." However, the
poet, as Mrs. Mandel'štam states, was not aware that he subconsciously
identified her with Leah at the time he was composing the poem.
"[Pozže] on mne priznalsja, čto, napisav èti stixi, on sam ne srazu ponjal,
o kom oni. Kak-to noč'ju, dumaja obo mne, on vdrug uvidel, čto ja
dolžna prijti k nemu. Tak byvaet, čto smysl stixov, založennaja v nix
poètičeskaja mysl', ne srazu doxodit do togo, kto ix sočinil" (*Vtoraja
kniga*, p. 263). The final observation is very well taken. Paul Valéry
might have had such facts in mind when he stated that literary criticism
should attempt to explain even those poetic ideas which are not completely clear to the poet himself.

Since the intimate and personal explanation of the poem was distinctly
formulated only later, we may ask whether the poem had another,
deeper level of meaning when it was in process of creation.

The motif of incest, which is so striking in the poem (*smesitel'noe lono*,
*krovosmesitel'nica-doč*), is also explained by Mrs. Mandel'štam. In a
private conversation, in June 1968, Mrs. Mandel'štam told me that her
husband used to say that all Jews are related by blood, and that all
marriages between Jews are incestuous (see also *Vtoraja kniga*, p. 262:
"Evreev on oščuščal kak odnu sem'ju — otsjuda tema krovosmesitel'-
stva"; and p. 262: "On, kak okazalos', okrestil Liej doč' Lota"). The
"incestuous bosom" from "Vernis' " will become the "womb world"
(*utrobnyj mir*) in *Šum vremeni* (as quoted at the beginning of this chapter).
The "kingly blood" (*carskaja krov'*) in the last stanza is undoubtedly the
blood of the sons of King David. The lines "carskoj krovi tjaželee /
Struit'sja v žilax, čem drugoj" mean that in our civilized age it is harder
to be a Jew than a Hellene. This supposition is supported by a remark
of Mandel'štam's in "Četvertaja proza":

Я настаиваю на том, что писательство в том виде, как оно сложилось
в Европе и в особенности в России, несовместимо с почетным
званием иудея, которым я горжусь. *Моя кровъ, отягощенная*

*наследством овцеводов, патриархов и царей,* бунтует против воро-
ватой циганщины писательского племени.

Since the *Iliad* was the first great product of ancient Greek culture,
we may read the "sun of Ilium" as a symbol for Hellenism, for the
Hellenic spirit. The "yellow dusk" (*želtyj sumrak*) is, of course, the
symbol of Judaism, a paraphrase of the "black-yellow light, joy of
Judea" from the 1917 poem. After 1916, Mandel'štam's poetry gravitated
toward the "sun of Ilium," rejecting the "yellow dusk." A comparison
of the 1916 and 1917 "Jewish poems," for example, with the Hellenic
one, "Na kamennyx otrogax Pièrii" (1919), would clearly reveal how
strongly opposed these two themes are. Mandel'štam must have been
aware that the historical-philosophical problem of Judaism versus
Hellenism, which is the main theme of the poem, was not a dilemma for
the gay, insouciant, and light-hearted young girl, a member of a Kiev
artists' circle ("kievskij tabunok," which was "levee levogo" and
deeply fascinated by Majakovskij's "Levyj marš," *Vtoraja kniga*,
pp. 19–20). The dilemma was his own; it was the problem of his thinking,
of his poetry, of *his Muse.*[11] Bearing this fact in mind, may we assume
that Mandel'štam identified his bride with one of the possible hypostases
of his Muse? Such an assumption is supported by the fact that he
attributed a physical feature of Miss Xazina (the salient brow) to the
Muses in "Na kamennyx otrogax Pièrii" — that is, in the poem which
Mrs. Mandel'štam calls "our wedding verses" (*Vtoraja kniga*, p. 129).
Compare the lines: "I xolodkom povejalo vysokim / Ot *vypuklo-
devičeskogo lba*" with the letter of December 5, 1919: "Daj lobik tvoj
pocelovat' — *vypuklyj* detskij lobik."[12]
I believe that Mandel'štam must have known that the names of Lot's
daughters are not mentioned in the Bible. Did not Mandel'štam have
in mind the famous biblical Leah, as well?[13] And do not the two biblical
women, Lot's daughter and Jacob's first wife, merge in Mandel'štam's
poetic vision into one image? In the biblical legend, Jacob's first wife is
clearly contrasted to her younger sister, the beautiful Rachel, the only
woman whom Jacob desired and for whom he paid such a high price:
fourteen years of hard work for her father. In Mandel'štam's "Vernis',"
the biblical incestuous daughter who willingly comes to her father is
opposed in the same way to the Trojan Helen, the ideal beauty, for
whom men have to fight.[14] Such an image of Helen appears several
times in Mandel'štam's poetry. She is mentioned for the first time in
"Bessonnica. Gomer. Tugie parusa" in a direct address to the Achean
men:

Куда плывете вы? Когда бы не Елена,
Что Троя вам одна, ахейские мужи?

This "not-Helen" is also mentioned in "Zolotistogo meda struja iz butylki tekla" (1917):

Помнишь в греческом доме: любимая всеми жена –
Не Елена — другая — как долго она вышивала?

The Achean men fighting for Helen are the principal "actors" in the poem "Za to, čto ja ruki tvoi ne sumel uderžat' " (1920), which Lidija Ginzburg appraises as "one of the best love poems in Russian poetry of the 20th century" ("Poètika Osipa Mandel'štama", *Izvestija AN SSSR, Serija jazyka i literatury*, 1972, no. 4, 313). Mrs. Mandel'štam must also have had in mind this poem (and "Ja naravne s drugimi", as well), when she wrote in *Vtoraja kniga* (p. 280): "Gruppa stixov Arbeninoj posvjaščena konkurencii 'mužej' i revnosti, estestvennoj v ètoj situacii."

In 1931, Mandel'štam returned to the image of Helen, who eludes him:

Я скажу тебе с последней
Прямотой:
Все лишь бредни, шерри-бренди,
Ангел мой!

. . . . . . . . . . . . . . . . . .

Греки сбондили Елену
По волнам,
Ну, а мне соленой пеной
По губам!

. . . . . . . . . . . . . . . . . .

Ой-ли, так ли, — дуй ли, вей ли, –
Все равно –
Ангел Мэри, пей коктейли,
Дуй вино!

Here, the ideal, unattainable Helen is once again opposed to the earthly, submissive woman, in this instance to Mary from Puškin's "Pir vo vremja čumy." Mrs. Mandel'štam comments on this poem as follows (*Vtoraja kniga*, p. 278): "V stixotvorenii 'Vse liš' bredni, šerri-brendi, angel moj' mne, kak ja dumaju (my ob ètom nikogda ne govorili), predostavlena rol' angela Mèri (slučajnaja ženščina, legkaja utexa!), a Ol'ga [Ol'ga Vaksel' with whom Mandel'štam had a love affair in 1925] — Elena, kotoruju sbondili greki. Ono napisano na ljudjax, kogda ja veselo pila s tolpoj prijatelej kisloe kavkazskoe vino, a on rasxažival i

bormotal, iskosa pogljadyvaja na nas . . ." Such a prosaic explanation
simplifies, of course, the image of Helen in Mandel'štam's poetry. In the
context of the four poems quoted above, the meaning of this image is
more general. I shall also cite Lidija Ginzburg's comment on our third
example: "Počemu, naprimer, — 'Ne Elena, drugaja . . .'? Potomu čto
imja Eleny Prekrasnoj vyvodit na poverxnost' zatajennuju ličnuju temu
(usilennuju ètim 'Pomniš'. . .'). Ona tak i ostaetsja nepodxvačennoj,
nedoskazannoj, no ot nee po vsemu stixotvoreniju proxodit tok liričeskoj
trevogi" ("Poètika O. Mandel'štama," p. 313). In any case, both Leah
and Mary, as compared to Helen, are the poet's second choice. He has no
regrets, predicting to the incestuous Leah her future: "You shall fall in
love with a Jew, you shall disappear in him — *and so be it.*"[15] If my
assumption is valid, and the incestuous daughter is Mandel'štam's
Muse, then the poem seemingly says that the victory of the Judaic
element in his philosophy and his poetry would lead the poet to silence.
This is, I strongly believe, the "deep meaning" of the poem.

In calling his poetry "daughter," perhaps Mandel'štam recalled
Mallarmé's poem "Don du poème," "Dar poèmy" in Annenskij's
translation:

О не казни ее за то, что Идумеи
На ней клеймом горит таинственная ночь:
Крыло ее в крови, а волосы как змеи,
Но это *дочь моя*, пойми: *родная дочь.*

In Annenskij's very free translation, the image of the "daughter"
merges with the image of the "bird": "Krylo ee [dočeri] v krovi" (in the
original of Mallarmé, "l'aile sanglante" is the dawn's wing). A similar
merging of these two images ("daughter" and "swallow") is found in
Mandel'štam's poem "Čto pojut časy-kuznečik" (see Chapter Four,
pp. 75–78). Both in Mallarmé's original and in Annenskij's translation,
Palestinian and ancient Greek images are opposed to each other as light
to dark: "*noč'* Idumeii" ("*nuit* d'Idumée") — "*belaja* Sivilla" ("*blancheur*
sibylline"); compare: "*želtyj sumrak*" — "*solnce* Iliona". Mandel'štam
could not have forgotten the "night of Idumea" which burns like a
stigma on poetry (Mallarmé does not have "stigma"). This night from
Annenskij's translation has parallels in Mandel'štam's "iudejskaja noč' "
and "Erusalima noč' i čad nebytija" (from "Sredi svjaščennikov levitom
molodym").

After having been explored in his prose in the twenties, the Christian
and Judaic themes almost disappear from Mandel'štam's poetry in the
thirties. True, his "Tajnaja večerja" (1937) should be considered as an

addition to his early poems about Christ's passion and death. However, the Hellenic theme seems to be more prominent in the thirties. In the first place, there are the three poems written in March and April of 1937 ("Kuvšin", "Gončarami velik ostrov sinij," and "Flejty grečeskoj tèta i jota").[16] The Hellenic theme of that period merges, as it were, with Mandel'štam's Italian theme into a broader concept of the Mediterranean, and even into the broadest concept of a single European culture.[17] We shall cite a few lines from Mandel'štam's "Ariost":

> На языке цикад пленительная смесь
> Из грусти пушкинской и средиземной спеси.
> . . . . . . . . . . . . . . . . . . . .
> Любезный Ариост, быть может, век пройдет –
> В одно широкое и братское лазорье
> Сольем твою лазурь и наше черноморье.
> И мы бывали там. И мы там пили мед.[18]

Mandel'štam's fascination with Dante in this period is very well known. His longing for spiritual values shared by all humanity is clearly expressed in the last stanza of his poem: "Ne sravnivaj: živuščij ne sravnim" written in Voronezh, in January 1937:

> Где больше неба мне — там я бродить готов –
> И ясная тоска меня не отпускает
> От молодых еще воронежских холмов
> *К всечеловеческим — яснеющим в Тоскане.*

"Mandel'štam ubeždal menja, čto tjaga na jug u nego v krovi. On čuvstvoval sebja prišlecom s juga, voleju slučaja zakinutym v xolod i mrak severnyx širot" (N. Mandel'štam, *Vtoraja kniga*, p. 562). This "pull toward the South" is also reflected in his love and longing for the Crimea, the ancient Taurida, the only territory of ancient Greece on which he had set foot.

The same yearning for the South finds expression in Mandel'štam's poems written during his visit to Armenia, and immediately afterwards. In "Kancona" (May 1931) he voices a wish to leave the "land of the Hyperboreans":

> Я покину край гипербореев,
> Чтобы зреньем напитать судьбы развязку,
> Я скажу «села» начальнику евреев[19]
> За его малиновую ласку.

In a poem written in June of the same year, Mandel'štam mentions his enforced return to "Buddhist Moscow":

В год тридцать первый от рожденья века
Я возвратился, нет — читай: насильно
Был возвращен в буддийскую Москву,
А перед тем я все-таки увидел
Библейской скатертью богатый Арарат
И двести дней провел в стране субботней,
Которую Арменией зовут.
Захочешь пить — там есть вода такая
Из курдского источника Арзни –
Хорошая, колючая, сухая
И самая правдивая вода.

It should be noted that "Buddhism" and "Buddhist" have strongly negative connotations for Mandel'štam; his concept of Buddhism is explained in the essay "Devjatnadcatyj vek" (1922).

In *Vtoraja kniga* (in the chapter "Načal'nik evreev") Mrs. Mandel'-štam compares these two poems ("Kancona" and "V god tridcat' pervyj"): "Kogda Mandel'štam pisal 'Kanconu,' on ne perestaval mečtat' ob Armenii, kotoruju nazval 'stranoj subbotnej.' Uže čerez odin Ararat ona svjazyvaetsja s Bibliej i s praotcami: čem ne mladšaja sestra 'zemli iudejskoj'?" (p. 617); "V 'Kancone' Mandel'štam nazval stranu, kuda on rvalsja. On ždal vstreči s 'načal'nikom evreev.' Sledovatel'no, umozritel'noe putešestvie soveršaetsja v obetovannuju stranu" (p. 618). Mrs. Mandel'štam supposes that the poet identified his "head of the Jews" with the father of the prodigal son from Rembrandt's painting in the Hermitage, a figure which impressed the poet strongly.[20] Therefore, she assumes that the impulse for Mandel'štam's return to the paternal home was the Christian parable. "V xristiansko-iudejskom mire, skrestivšemsja s èllinskoj kul'turoj, on vidit sredizem-nomor'e, k kotoromu vsegda stremilsja. K iudejstvu, k 'načal'niku evreev,' on rvetsja ne po zovu krovi, a kak k istoku evropejskix myslej i predstavlenij, v kotoryx čerpala silu poèzija" (p. 622).

We should not forget, however, that in the same year that "Kancona" was written, Mandel'štam made his proud statement in "Četvertaja proza" about the blood of shepherds, patriarchs, and kings flowing in his veins. The following excerpt from Mrs. Mandel'štam's *Vtoraja kniga* (pp. 563–564) provides the best comment on that statement:

Мандельштам и по метрике Осип, а не Иосиф, никогда не забывал, что он еврей, но «память крови» была у него своеобразная. Она восходила к праотцам и к Испании, к средиземноморью, а скиталь-ческий путь отцов через центральную Европу он начисто позабыл.

Иначе говоря, он ощущал связь с пастухами и царями Библии, с александрийскими и испанскими евреями, поэтами и философами, и даже подобрал себе среди них родственника: испанского поэта, которого инквизиция держала на цепи в подземелье. «У меня есть от него хоть кровинка», — сказал Мандельштам, прочтя в Воронеже биографию испанского еврея. Узник непрерывно сочинял сонеты («губ шевелящихся отнять вы не могли») и, выйдя на короткий срок, записал их. Затем он снова был посажен на цепь (повторный арест!) и опять сочинил груду сонетов.[21]

We might add that Mandel'štam's interest in Central Europe is different. The Germanic-Russian theme was elaborated in "Dekabrist" (1917): "Rossija, Leta, Loreleja," in "Zverinec" (1916), where it merges with the Italian theme:

> А я пою вино времен –
> Источник речи итальянской
> И в колыбели праарийской
> Славянский и германский лен . . .

and in the 1932 poem "K nemeckoj reči."[22] Nor should Mandel'štam's French theme be omitted, at least not these lines written in 1937 in Voronezh:

> Я прошу, как жалости и милости,
> Франция, твоей земли и жимолости.

They echo his longing for the blue hills of Tuscany.

There is one more poem of Mandel'štam's in which the Jewish theme is reflected. It is one of his "Vos'mistišija," written in November 1933:

> Скажи мне, чертежник пустыни,
> Сыпучих песков геометр,
> Ужели безудержность линий
> Сильнее, чем дующий ветр?
> — Меня не касается трепет
> Его иудейских забот –
> Он опыт из лепета лепит
> И лепет из опыта пьет.

As I understand the poem, it describes the endeavor of the Jews in Palestine to conquer the desert. The poet wonders whether the impetuous lines of the draftsman's project can contain the blowing wind. Possibly he recalled the two verses from Ecclesiastes: "Kružitsja, kružitsja na xodu svoem veter, i na krugi svoi vozvraščaetsja veter" (1.6) and "Nikto ne vlasten nad vetrom, čtoby uderžat' veter . . ." (8.8). However, the poet, although skeptical, looks sympathetically on the efforts of the Jewish people. The nouns *trepet* and *lepet* could be interpreted as metaphors for an excitement and enthusiasm which would seem a childish one (*lepet*). I do not think that *lepet* in this context has a negative shade of meaning. In *Razgovor o Dante*, also written in 1933, Mandel'štam praises the "infantile babbling" of Italian phonetics and the "childish transsense language" of Dante.[23] On the one hand, the draftsman's experiment (or experience?) flows from his childish enthusiasm, but, on the other, it becomes a source of ever-new excitement. Despite the poet's claim that the Judaic concerns of the geometer of shifting sands are none of his affair, the poem reflects, I believe, Mandel'štam's new interest in the fate and destiny of the Jewish people.[24]

# IV

## THE CLOCK-GRASSHOPPER

*An Analysis of a "Transsense" Poem*

The poem "Čto pojut časy-kuznečik" (1917) has been called "transsense."[1] Such a characterization of this poem is explained, in the first place, by its complicated syntactic structure; secondly, by its extremely complex metaphoric imagery — both of which make comprehension difficult. The poem is intended for a "penetrating reader" ("dogadlivyj čitatel' "):

| I | 1. | Что поют часы-кузнечик, |
|---|----|-------------------------|
|   | 2. | Лихорадка шелестит, |
|   | 3. | И шуршит сухая печка, – |
|   | 4. | Это красный шелк горит. |
| II | 5. | Что зубами мыши точат |
|   | 6. | Жизни тоненькое дно, |
|   | 7. | Это ласточка и дочка |
|   | 8. | Отвязала мой челнок. |
| III | 9. | Что на крыше дождь бормочет, – |
|   | 10. | Это черный шелк горит, |
|   | 11. | Но черемуха услышит |
|   | 12. | И на дне морском: прости. |
| IV | 13. | Потому что смерть невинна |
|   | 14. | И ничем нельзя помочь, |
|   | 15. | Что в горячке соловьиной |
|   | 16. | Сердце теплое еще. |

Judging by Axmatova's memoirs, "Čto pojut časy-kuznečik" forms part of a cycle of poems written at the end of 1917 and addressed to her:

Особенно часто я встречалась с Мандельштамом в 1917–18 гг. . . .
Мандельштам часто заходил за мной и мы ездили на извозчике

по невероятным ухабам революционной зимы, среди знаменитых
костров, которые горели чуть не до мая, слушая неизвестно откуда
несущуюся ружейную трескотню. Так мы ездили на выступления в
Академию Художеств, где происходили вечера в пользу раненых и
где мы оба несколько раз выступали. Был со мной Осип Эмильевич
и на концерте Бутомо-Незвановой в консерватории, где она пела
Шуберта (см. «Нам пели Шуберта...»). К этому времени относятся
все обращенные ко мне стихи.[2] «Я не искал в цветущие мгновенья»
(декабрь 1917 г.), «Твое чудесное произношенье»; ко мне относится
странное отчасти сбывшееся предсказание:

> Когда-нибудь в столице шалой,
> На диком празднике у берега Невы,
> Под звуки омерзительного бала
> Сорвут платок с прекрасной головы...

А следующее — «Что поют часы, кузнечик» (это мы вместе топим
печку; у меня жар — я мерю температуру)...

После некоторых колебаний, решаюсь вспомнить в этих записках,
что мне пришлось объяснить Осипу, что нам не следует так часто
встречаться, что может дать людям материал для превратного
толкования характера наших отношений. После этого, примерно, в
марте, Мандельштам исчез. Тогда все исчезали и появлялись и
никто этому не удивлялся.[3]

Axmatova's reminiscences tell us only about the external facts which
served as the initial impulse for writing this poem. There is no feminine
image present in it (except possibly metaphorically, as an addressee of
the imperative "prosti" — "čeremuxa"). By close reading, one can
easily make out the "plot" of the poem: the poet is sitting in a room,
*he* has a fever, the clock is ticking and a fire is burning in the stove
(lines 1–4); it is raining outside (lines 9–10), and the poet is reflecting on
life and death (lines 5–8, 11–16). In terms of its plot structure, the poem
divides into two unequal parts: primarily descriptive (1–4, 9–10) and
primarily meditative, speculative (5–8, 11–16).[4]

Mandel'štam's poem is as if superimposed on certain word-signals and
images of the following poem by Blok (October 1913):

> 1.   Милый друг, и в этом тихом доме
> 2.       *Лихорадка* бьет меня.
> 3.   Не найти мне места в тихом доме
> 4.       Возле мирного *огня*!

5.    *Голоса поют, взывает вьюга,*
6.        Страшен мне уют . . .
7.    Даже за плечом твоим, подруга,
8.        Чьи-то очи стерегут!

9.    За твоими тихими плечами
10.        Слышу трепет крыл . . .
11.    Бьет в меня светящими очами
12.        Ангел бури — Азраил![5]

Aside from the coincidence of the basic plot, one can deduce as well many particular correspondences. For example, "fever" (*lixoradka*) is mentioned in the second line of both poems, the image of fire is given in the fourth line (*mirnyj ogon'* in Blok's poem and the metaphoric *krasnyj šelk* in Mandel'štam's). Blok's poem has the symbol of the beseeching snowstorm (line 5: "vzyvaet v'juga") which intensifies the tragic tension of the experience. In Mandel'štam's poem the rain mumbles on the roof (line 9: "na kryše dožd' bormočet") and pertains to the quiet, thoughtful mood. These two images correspond to each other. If in Mandel'štam's poem the clock sings ("*pojut* časy"), then naturally in Blok's poem mysterious voices sing. Finally, in Mandel'štam's poem death is called by name in the last stanza; in Blok's, death is personified by Azrail (the Muslim angel of death), popularized in Russian poetry by Lermontov.

In his poem, Mandel'štam creatively reworks not only some of Blok's imagery but some of Bal'mont's as well (from "Dožd'," May 1901). The elements of basic "plot" common to both of these poems are obvious: there is rain outside, the poet is sitting in a room and listening to the rustle of mice and the ticking of a clock:

В углу *шуршали мыши,*
Весь дом застыл во сне,
*Шел дождъ,* — и капли *с крыши*
Стекали по стене.

*Шел дождъ,* ленивый, вялый,
*И маятник стучал.*
И я душой усталой
Себя не различал.

Я слился с этой сонной
Тяжелой тишиной.
Забытый, обделенный,
Я весь был *тъмой ночной.*

The "rustling" of the stove in Mandel'štam's poem reminds us of the mice which rustle in Bal'mont's. In Bal'mont's poem the mice are primarily real; in Mandel'štam's they are only metaphoric. Mandel'štam's "časy-kuznečik" ("clock-insect") recalls Bal'mont's image of the "insect-clock" that reminds the poet about death:

А бодрый, как могильщик,
Во мне тревожа мрак,
В стене *жучок-точильщик*
*Твердил: «Тик-так. Тик-так».*

Равняя звуки точкам,
Началу всех начал,
Он тонким молоточком
Стучал, стучал, стучал.

И атомы напева,
Сплетаясь в тишине,
Спокойно и без гнева
«*Умри*» твердили мне.

As will be shown later, the singing of the clock in Mandel'štam's poem is also the "music of dying." Finally, in the third stanza of Mandel'štam's poem, the imperative *prosti* corresponds to the analogous form in Bal'mont's poem, *umri*. One of the basic themes of both poems is the premonition of death.[6]

The poem "Čto pojut časy-kuznečik" is notable for its symmetrical and strict compositional structure. The odd stanzas (I–III) are sharply opposed to the even ones (II–IV), and the outer stanzas (I–IV) — to the inner, central ones (II–III).

The first and third stanzas are connected to each other by repetition of the noun *šelk* and the verb *gorit* (that is, by the image of the burning red / black silk) and also by rhymes in stressed /i/ in all even lines. Auditory imagery is characteristic for the odd stanzas (*pojut, šelestit, šuršit — bormočet, uslyšit: prosti*). In the second and fourth stanzas there is no auditory imagery, and there are rhymes in stressed /o/ in all of the even lines of these stanzas. The even stanzas are tied together by "bird imagery" (*lastočka, solov'inaja gorjačka*) as well as the theme of life and death (the only two abstract nouns in the poem [*žizn'* and *smert'*] are found in these stanzas).

The outer stanzas (I–IV) are distinguished by the theme of warmth (*lixoradka — gorjačka, gorjaščaja pečka — teploe serdce*), while the theme of moisture (*more, dožd'*) is characteristic of the inner stanzas (II–III).

The two inner stanzas contain the central image of the poem, the image of the sinking bark. They are connected as well by the repetition of the noun *dno*. In the second stanza this noun evokes the visual image of the surface of water. In the third stanza the prepositional case *na dne morskom* effectively underlines the sharp change of the vertical perspective. Finally, the central stanzas have the only two perfective verbs in the indicative mood, both followed by direct objects ([lastočka-dočka] *otvjazala* čelnok — [čeremuxa] *uslyšit*: prosti). As a result of the juxtaposition of past tense to future and the repetition of the noun "bottom" (once in the accusative, once in the prepositional case), lines 11 and 12, which we placed in the meditative part of the "plot," closely join with lines 5–10. Together they form a compact whole. Because of the compactness of the two central stanzas, the compositional-thematic division of the poem becomes clear-cut; introduction (stanza I), dramatic conflict (stanzas II, III), message (conclusion, stanza IV). In this way, the nonsymmetrical division of the "plot" into a descriptive and meditative part is completely concealed.

I have already mentioned the complicated syntactical structure of Mandel'štam's poem. Three complex sentences (in the first three stanzas) are built according to the pattern *čto — èto*. The subordinate clauses which open the stanzas are introduced by the subordinating conjunction *čto* (*štə*), while the main clauses which follow in these three stanzas begin with the anaphoric pronoun *èto*. This pronoun establishes a close association by contiguity and similarity between the apodosis and the protasis: "[tot fakt], čto pojut časy, šelestit lixoradka i šuršit pečka – èto [značit, čto] gorit krasnyj šelk (or, in other words: penie časov, šelest lixoradki i šuršanie pečki – èto [i est'] gorenie krasnogo šelka); [tot fakt], čto myši točat dno – èto [značit, čto] lastočka-dočka[7] [uže] otvjazala moj čelnok; [tot fakt] čto na kryše bormočet dožd' – èto [značit, čto] gorit černyj šelk (that is, bormotanie doždja – èto [i est'] gorenie černogo šelka)."[8] The third stanza is a compound sentence. It has two main clauses, the first of which is preceded by a subordinate clause. The main clauses are joined by the adversative conjunction *no*: "šelk gorit, no [odnako, vse-taki] čeremuxa uslyšit i [=daže] na dne morskom [proiznesennoe]: prosti."[9] The fourth stanza consists of two causative subordinate clauses which begin with the conjunction *potomu čto*. Stylistically (and rhetorically) they appear to be an afterthought: "čeremyxa uslyšit 'prosti,' potomu čto smert' nevinna [nevinovata] i [potomu čto] ničem nel'zja pomoč' [tomu faktu = ničego nel'zja podelat' s tem faktom], čto moe ešče teploe serdce [naxoditsja, prebyvaet] v solov'inoj gorjačke."

We will assume that the syntactical analysis given above has defined sufficiently clearly the formal ties between the sentences and their parts. Nevertheless, the logical connection between them remains insufficiently elucidated. Therefore, a semantic analysis of the lexical material should be undertaken.

We shall look now at the lexical stock of the text. It contains twenty nouns (two of them — *šelk* and *dno* — are repeated). This figure exceeds the sum of all the adjectives (8) and verbs (11, of which one, *gorit*, is repeated). There are only two abstract substantives in the text (*žizn'* and *smert'*); all the others are concrete. They include: the names of things (*časy, pečka, šelk, dno, čelnok, kryša*) and of natural phenomena (*dožd'*), the names of vegetable and animal organisms (*čeremuxa; kuznečik, myši, lastočka*) and their organs (*zuby, serdce*), a kinship term (*dočka*) and, finally, names of biological processes (*gorjačka, lixoradka*). In terms of the choice of nouns, this poem is very acmeistic; it is completely of this earth.

Of twenty nouns, only seven are used with their concrete meaning:[10] *časy, lixoradka, pečka* (in the first stanza), *žizn'* (in the second), *kryša* and *dožd'* (in the third), and *smert'* (in the fourth). One of the abstract nouns, "life," is seemingly materialized (it has a bottom), while the other, death, is slightly personified (it is guiltless).

Of the eight adjectives, only two are descriptive: "*morskoe* dno" and "*solov'inaja* gorjačka." The remaining six are qualitative: "*suxaja* pečka" (that is, the dry logs in the stove), "*krasnyj* šelk," "*tonen'koe* dno," "*černyj* šelk," "smert' *nevinna*," "*teploe* serdce." Of these six, five are particularly characteristic: those which designate "properties and qualities which are directly perceived by sensory organs." They are all used attributively. Their aesthetic function is to bring the described world closer to the reader, to make it concretely perceptible. Two color attributes, "*krasnyj* šelk" and "*černyj* šelk," are clearly contrasted. I will return to an analysis of them later. In connection with the adjectives, it should be stated that there is only one possessive pronoun, *moj*. It indicates that the author himself is the hero of the poem.

Of the eleven verbs in the text, six are in the "descriptive" part of the "plot." These are all imperfective verbs, third person, present tense (*pojut, šelestit, šuršit, gorit, bormočet, gorit*). This part of the poem is static. In the meditative part of the poem, along with the present tense, there are also past and future tenses (of perfective verbs). There is clearly a certain bond between them: "lastočka-dočka *otvjazala* čelnok," but "čeremuxa *uslyšit:* prosti." Thus, the meditative part of the plot is dynamic.

Of the seven nouns in the descriptive part of the poem, four (*časy, pečka, dožd' na kryše*) seem to create an atmosphere of coziness and comfort, while only one (*lixoradka*) introduces a note of trouble. But after deeper analysis, the comfort will turn out to be illusory. Throughout this part, auditory images are associated with visual ones. In the first stanza, the ticking of a clock (which resembles the singing of a grasshopper), the rustle of fever, and the rustling of the stove (*lixoradka šelestit, šuršit pečka*) are juxtaposed to fire (*krasnyj šelk*). Of the auditory images, the second (*lixoradka šelestit*) is the most unexpected. It is as if the poet hears the biological process going on within his body. However, this "listening to his own organism" is characteristic of Mandel'štam. As early as 1911, he wrote:

> Душу от внешних условий
> Освободить я умею,
> Пенье-кипенье крови
> *Слышу* и быстро хмелею.

The second line ("lixoradka šelestit") should be compared to the third line in the 1922 poem, "Xolodok ščekočet temja," which is thematically close to the text under consideration in other respects as well (and to which we will refer later):

> А ведь раньше лучше было,
> И пожалуй не сравнишь,
> Как ты прежде *шелестила*,
> Кровь, как нынче *шелестишь*.[11]

The ticking of the clock, the rustling of fever and of the stove (to which the poet listens) — all this is the "music" of dying, destruction, annihilation. They are equated with fire, with its destructive power. As early as 1914, Mandel'štam wrote about fire:

> Уничтожает пламень
> Сухую жизнь мою.

In the third stanza (lines 9–10) the mumbling of the rain is equated with the burning of the black silk, that is, with the sparkling (wet) darkness of the night. Unlike in the fourth line, the verb *goret'* is used in the tenth line with a figurative meaning (to sparkle, glitter). By contrast with the auditory images in the first stanza, the mumbling of the rain may be perceived, rather, as the "music" of life. Very effective from an aesthetic point of view is the relationship between the epithets of the noun "silk." It contradicts the usual symbolism associated with these colors (red — the color of life, black — of death).[12]

The motif of the slow, but persistent, destructive work of time is continued in the second stanza. Here, the image of mice gnawing at the very foundation of life, its bottom, is used.[13] It is completely obvious that the bottom of the bark which has been untied is in fact the bottom of life. Being afloat on the sea of life is an ancient poetic motif. An original variation on this motif is found in a poem written by Mandel'-štam in his "symbolist period" (1909):

> Ни о чем не нужно говорить,
> Ничему не следует учить,
> И печальна так и хороша
> Темная звериная душа.

> Ничему не хочет научить,
> Не умеет вовсе говорить
> И плывет дельфином молодым
> *По седым пучинам мировым.*

The images of a bark, a lone sail, as a refuge from life go back, in Russian poetry, to Puškin and Lermontov. We may recall, for example, "Nas bylo mnogo na čelne," "Beleet parus odinokij," or Blok's line "Beri svoj čeln, plyvi na dal'nij poljus" ("Vse na zemle umret," 1909). As has already been mentioned, in Mandel'štam's poem, we find the image of a sinking bark. In line 12, this metaphoric bark is already on the sea-bottom, and from the bottom of the sea the poet says farewell to life. The loss of the bark is caused, of course, by the destructive work of the mice gnawing at its bottom. But, in its turn, the work of the mice is made dependent on the fact that the swallow-daughter has untied the bark. Therefore, the swallow-daughter is the one guilty of its loss.

Strictly speaking, there are only two cryptic images in the whole poem: "lastočka-dočka" and "čeremuxa." In order to decipher these two metaphors, we must draw upon a larger context out of Mandel'štam's poetic heritage.

It was shown in the preceding chapter that Mandel'štam called his Muse "daughter" in the poem written in 1920, "Vernis' v smesitel'noe lono." It often happens in Mandel'štam that an earlier cryptic image is elaborated and even explained in poems written much later, and even in his prose. Therefore, we shall assume that *lastočka-dočka* is his Muse, as well. But why is she called a swallow?

The swallow is the central image of Mandel'štam's "twin-poems" from 1920, "Kogda Psixeja-žizn' spuskaetsja k tenjam," and "Ja slovo pozabyl, čto ja xotel skazat'." The "poetic space" of both poems is ancient Greek Hades, "poluprozračnyj les," "čertog tenej":

1. Когда Психея-жизнь спускается к теням
2. В полупрозрачный лес, вослед за Персефоной,
3. Слепая ласточка бросается к ногам
4. С стигийской нежностью и веткою зеленой.

5. Навстречу беженке спешит толпа теней,
6. Товарку новую встречая причитаньем,
7. И руки слабые ломают перед ней
8. С недоумением и робким упованьем.

9. Кто держит зеркало, кто баночку духов –
10. Душа ведь женщина, — ей нравятся безделки,
11. И лес безлиственный прозрачных голосов
12. Сухие жалобы кропят, как дождик мелкий.

13. И в нежной сутолке не зная, что начать,
14. Душа не узнает прозрачные дубравы;
15. Дохнет на зеркало, и медлит передать
16. Лепешку медную с туманной переправы.

## II

1. Я слово позабыл, что я хотел сказать.
2. Слепая ласточка в чертог теней вернется,
3. На крыльях срезанных, с прозрачными играть.
4. В беспамятстве ночная песнь поется.

5. Не слышно птиц. Бессмертник не цветет.
6. Прозрачны гривы табуна ночного.
7. В сухой реке пустой челнок плывет.
8. Среди кузнечиков беспамятствует слово.

9. И медленно растет, как бы шатер иль храм,
10. То вдруг прокинется безумной Антигоной,
11. То мертвой ласточкой бросается к ногам
12. С стигийской нежностью и веткою зеленой.

13. О если бы вернуть и зрячих пальцев стыд,
14. И выпуклую радость узнаванья.
15. Я так боюсь рыданья Аонид,
16. Тумана, звона и зиянья.

17. А смертным власть дана любить и узнавать,
18. Для них и звук в персты прольется,
19. Но я забыл, что я хочу сказать,
20. И мысль бесплотная в чертог теней вернется.

21. Все не о том прозрачная твердит,
22. Все ласточка, подружка, Антигона . . .
23. А на губах как черный лед горит
24. Стигийского воспоминанье звона.

The theme of contact with the nether world appeared in Mandel'štam's poetry as early as 1917:

Еще далеко асфоделей
Прозрачно-серая весна,
Пока еще на самом деле
Шуршит песок, кипит волна.
Но здесь душа моя вступает,
Как Персефона, в легкий круг,
И в царстве мертвых не бывает.
Прелестных загорелых рук.

The poet knows that death is still far away. He transports himself to the kingdom of the dead only in his imagination, in order, like Persephone, to return to the earth.[14]

The "plot" of the first of these two poems from 1920 is the soul's entry into the nether world, and its "hero" is the "Psyche-life" ("Psixeja-žizn'") who descends into the realm of shadows like Persephone.[15] In the first stanza "Psyche-life" is identified as a blind swallow (*slepaja lastočka*):

Когда *Психея-жизнь* спускается к теням,
В полупрозрачный лес, вослед за Персефоной,
[Это] *слепая ласточка* бросается к ногам
С стигийской нежностью и веткою зеленой.

In the second stanza "Psyche-life" is called a fugitive, a comrade (*beženka, tovarka*). Finally, in the last two stanzas her real identity is revealed: she is a soul (*duša*).

There can be no discussion of the plot of the second poem, for none exists. Its "hero" is the "forgotten word" (*zabytoe slovo — slepaja lastočka — mysl' besplotnaja — prozračnaja [ten'] — lastočka — podružka — Antigona*). Two images, "lastočka: Psixeja-žizn'" and "lastočka: slovo-mysl'," although they do not merge into one complex image, nonetheless are closely connected; they constantly cross.[16] However, in Mandel'štam's work, life and poetry are inseparable, and for him the *word* is also a *soul*: "*Slovo Psixeja. Živoe slovo ne oboznačaet predmeta, a svobodno vybiraet, kak by dlja žil'ja, tu ili inuju predmetnuju znači-most', veščnost', miloe telo. I vokrug vešči slovo bluždaet svobodno, kak duša vokrug brošennogo, no ne zabytogo tela.*"[17]

There can be no doubt that Mandel'štam's "forgotten word" is the poetic word. Adjacent images evidence this: "V bespamjatstve nočnaja pesn' poetsja" (II, 4), "sredi kuznečikov bespamjatstvuet slovo" (II, 8), and "rydan'e Aonid" (II, 15). As Jurij Levin subtly observed (in an as yet unpublished article on Mandel'štam), the "poetic space" of the first poem undergoes a change in the second: "[čertog tenej] stanovitsja dvojstvennym: soxranjaja svoi mifologičeskie čerty, on, stav arenoj priključenij takoj psixologičeskoj real'nosti, kak zabytoe slovo, psixologiziruetsja, obrazuja čto-to vrode 'psixologičeskogo prostranstva,' v kotorom razvertyvajutsja psixologičeskie processy, glavnym obrazom, podsoznatel'nye." These processes (oblivion, forgetfulness or frenzy: recognition, recollection) are connected, of course, with poetic creation. Despite these differences, these twin-poems from 1920 are nonetheless united into a whole by the common motif *memento mori*. This motif is clearly formulated at the end of the second poem in the image of the recollection of the Stygian ringing which burns like black ice on the lips (perhaps of the "swallow, companion, Antigone," or perhaps of the poet himself who forgot the word — whosever the lips, it is essentially the same).[18]

As we see, for Mandel'štam, "swallow" and "daughter" are images correlated with poetic creation. If the "swallow-daughter" untied the poet's bark, then the image is not simply "sailing on the sea of life stirred up by a storm of misfortunes" (plavanie po "žitejskomu morju, vozdvizaemomu napastej bureju"), but poetic sailing, too. Life and poetry, as I have already said, are inseparable for Mandel'štam.

When it is a question of poetic sailing, naturally one again recalls Puškin: the image of the ship in his poem "Osen'" ("Kuda ž nam plyt'?"), his lines published in the foreword to *Otryvki iz putešestvija Onegina*:

> Пора: перо покоя просит;
> Я девять песен написал;
> На берег радостный выносит
> Мою ладью девятый вал.

and his translation from André Chénier:

> На море жизненном, где бури так жестоко
> Преследуют во мгле мой парус одинокий,
> . . . без отзыва утешно я пою
> И тайные стихи обдумывать люблю.

Thus, in "Čto pojut časy-kuznečik" the theme of *death as the penalty for poetic creation* makes its appearance. This theme will be even more distinctly expressed in "Xolodok ščekočet temja."

If we accept the explanation that both *lastočka-dočka* and the sinking bark are images connected with poetry and poetic creation, we may also ask this question: is not the "black silk" from the third stanza also the metaphor for creative night from "Rakovina," "Senoval," and "Grifel'-naja oda" which was discussed in Chapter Two above (pp. 31–33)? In "Rakovina" the night is the creative force which fills the shell (that is, the poet) with impressions of the outer world, with the whispering of the foam, with mist, wind, and rain:

> И [ты, ночь,] хрупкой раковины стены,
> Как нежилого сердца дом,
> Наполнишь шепотами пены,
> Туманом, ветром и *дождем* . . .

In "Čto pojut časy-kuznečik" there is a similar relation. The sparkling darkness of the night is equated with the mumbling of the rain:

> Что на крыше *дождь* бормочет, –
> Это черный шелк горит.

Later, we will see that the "nightingale fever" (*solov'inaja gorjačka*) is also a metaphor for poetic creation.

What, now, does the image of the bird-cherry (*čeremuxa*), to which the poet says farewell and from which he asks pardon, mean?

In 1925, Mandel'štam wrote a poem about a bird-cherry from which I will quote the first three tercets:

> Я буду метаться по табору улицы темной
> За *веткой черемухи* в черной рессорной карете,[19]
> За *капором снега*, за вечным, за мельничным шумом.
>
> Я только запомнил *каштановых прядей осечки*,
> Придымленных горечью, нет — с муравьиной кислинкой;
> От них на губах остается янтарная сухость.
>
> В такие минуты и воздух мне кажется карим,
> И кольца зрачков одеваются выпушкой светлой,
> И то, что я знаю *о яблочной розовой коже* . . .

In "Svjatoj kolodec" (*Novyj mir*, 1965, no. 5) Valentin Kataev tells, in a very colorful way, how this poem was conceived. He and Oleša "kidnaped" Mandel'štam's wife and were taking her to a beer-house where gypsies were singing. Mandel'štam ran after the carriage, trying to overtake them. They did not go to hear gypsies, but went to a Georgian restaurant, and as soon as they were brought a bottle of *teliani*, Mandel'-

štam appeared and began reading his new verses, "Ja budu metat'sja po taboru ulicy temnoj ..."[20] Thus, the image of the bird-cherry in this poem was evoked by a woman. She is present only metonymically: "kapor snega" (a cap covered with snow), "vetka čeremuxi" (a metaphor for this cap), "kaštanovye prjadi," "jabločnaja, rozovaja koža." Mandel'štam's "vetka čeremuxi" invites comparison with Pasternak's "sirenevaja vetv'." In his poem "Devočka," the branch running into the mirror from the garden is metonymic (a girl with a branch). In the poem which comes after "Devočka" (in *Sestra moja – žizn'*) it becomes a metaphoric image (for, let us say, the girl whom he loved):

> Ты в ветре, веткой пробующем,
> Не время ль птицам петь,
> Намокшая воробышком
> Сиреневая ветвь![21]

Similarly, I understand Mandel'štam's bird-cherry branch both as a metonymy and as a metaphor.

We will assume that in "Čto pojut časy-kuznečik" the image of bird-cherry is evoked by the woman to whom it is written. In that case, this image finds its place in a whole series of popular images of tree-woman (or girl) — metaphors, allegories, similes, as, for example, the palm in Tjutčev's translation from Heine, Nekrasov's weeping willow, or Esenin's girl birches. Nevertheless, it would be imprudent to insist on such a direct and factual interpretation of the image of the "bird-cherry." A skeptical reader might be offered a more generalized explanation. There is no doubt that the bird-cherry — blossoming in spring, white, fragrant, and gladdening the sense of both sight and smell — should be included in the positive semantic field. We may recall, too, that for Russians the simple fragrant flowers of the bird-cherry are associated with the beauty of everyday life, its poetry. It is not accidental that Pantelejmon Romanov entitled a story which recounts a coarse, physical encounter between a young man and girl, "Without Bird-Cherry" ("Bez čeremuxi," published 1926). Nevertheless, the fact that the poet not only says farewell to the bird-cherry but asks its forgiveness as well, somehow speaks in favor of my first explanation.

The "sea-bottom" in the fourth line of the third stanza is a metaphor for extreme danger, the last minutes of life. Mandel'štam used this image with the same meaning in his "Telefon" (1918):

> В высоком строгом кабинете
> Самоубийцы — телефон ...
> Звонок — и закружились сферы:

Самоубийство решено . . .
Молчи, проклятая шкатулка!
*На дне морском цветет: прости!*

The poem "Čto pojut časy-kuznečik" helps us to understand the imagery of the last line of the given quotation.

The "nightingale fever" (*solov'inaja gorjačka*) in the fourth stanza (which recalls the fever, *lixoradka*, in the first) is an obvious metaphor for poetic inspiration, the arduous creative process. The comparison of the poet to a nightingale is common in both Eastern (Persian) and European poetry. In Russian poetry it goes back to "Slovo o polku Igoreve": "O, Bojane, soloviju starago vremeni!" Shortly before Mandel'štam, Blok wrote lines about the "unknown melody, ringing in the nightingale garden" ("neizvestnyj napev, zvenjaščij v solov'inom sadu"), and Pasternak defined poetry as a "duel between two nightingales" ("dvux solov'ev poedinok").[22]

The last stanza, the poem's message, consists of two causative subordinate clauses which motivate the poet's farewell to the bird-cherry: ". . . čeremuxa uslyšit 'prosti,' potomu čto smert' nevinna, i [potomu čto] ničem nel'zja pomoč' [tomu faktu], čto [moe] ešče teploe serdce – v solov'inoj gorjačke." The first clause contains an oblique admission of guilt: "death is not guilty" (but the swallow-daughter is the guilty one). The second clause affirms that the "nightingale fever" will not leave the poet even during his last minutes of life. In "Čto pojut časy-kuznečik" we thus see for the first time the Mandel'štamian theme of *death as the penalty for poetic creation*.[23]

In 1922 Mandel'štam wrote, in the same trochaic tetrameter, the poem "Xolodok ščekočet temja," which treats of the same theme, but in a different poetic key. The poetics of this second poem are more traditional and do not need to be deciphered.[24] It is obviously addressed to the poet's wife:

Холодок щекочет темя,
И нельзя признаться вдруг, –
И меня срезает время,
Как скосило твой каблук.

Жизнь себя перемогает,
Понемногу тает звук,
Все чего-то нехватает,
Что-то вспомнить недосуг.

А ведь раньше лучше было,
И пожалуй не сравнишь,

Как ты прежде шелестила,
Кровь, как нынче шелестишь.

Видно, даром не проходит
Шевеленье этих губ,
И вершина колобродит,
Обреченная на сруб.

In the first stanza we again meet the image of time the destroyer (compare "Našedšij podkovu," from the same year: "Vremja srezaet menja, kak monetu, / I mne už ne xvataet samogo sebja"). The second and third stanzas introduce a new motif, the motif of fatigue, weakening of poetic ("Ponemnogu taet zvuk") and life energy ("šelest krovi" — before and now). The basic message of the poem is contained in the last stanza. "The movement of lips" is one of Mandel'štam's favorite metaphors for poetic creation.[25] The motif of doom is very clearly formulated in the last stanza: in 1923 the poet already clearly realized that he would have to pay for his poetry by his death: "nepopravimoj gibel'ju poslednej," "by irreparable final ruin."[26]

# V

## BEES AND WASPS

*Mandel'štam and Vjačeslav Ivanov*

We know very little about Mandel'štam's personal relations with
Vjačeslav Ivanov. At the very beginning of his poetic career, Mandel'-
štam was undoubtedly close to Ivanov, visited him in his Tower, wrote
him letters. Axmatova writes about these times in her memoirs ("Listki
iz dnevnika," *Sočinenija* 2, 1968):

Недавно найдены письма Осипа Эмильевича к Вячеславу Иванову
(1909). Это письма участника Проакадемии (по Башне). Это Мандельштам — символист. Следов того, что Вячеслав Иванов ему
отвечал пока нет. Их писал мальчик 18 лет, но можно поклясться,
что автору этих писем 40 лет. Там же множество стихов. Они хороши,
но в них нет того, что мы называем Мандельштамом.[1]

Воспоминания сестры Аделаиды Герцык утверждают, что
Вячеслав Иванов не признавал нас всех. В 1911 году никакого
пиэтета к Вячеславу Иванову в Мандельштаме не было.

The last statement should be taken with considerable reservation.
Mandel'štam himself indicated Vjačeslav Ivanov's role in the shaping
of Acmeism as a school:

Не идеи, а вкусы акмеистов оказались убийственны для символизма.
Идеи оказались отчасти перенятыми у символистов, и сам Вячеслав
Иванов много способствовал построению акмеистической теории.

(«О природе слова»)

After 1911, Mandel'štam carefully read Vjačeslav Ivanov's books, *Cor
ardens* (1911), *Nežnaja tajna* (1912), and *Alkej i Safo* (1914); he derived
inspiration from them and even "enciphered" lines from Ivanov in his
masterpieces of 1919–20, "Na kamennyx otrogax Pièrii" and "Voz'mi
na radost' iz moix ladonej." This chapter is primarily devoted to an
analysis of these two poems.

The poem "Na kamennyx otrogax Pièrii" was written in May 1919, in Kiev,[2] during the height of the civil war, and was first published in that year in the Kiev "Annual of Art and Humanities," *Germes*. Ryszard Przybylski devoted a long article to this poem, "Arcadia Osipa Mandelsztama" (*Slavia Orientalis* XIII.3, 243–262;[3] the title itself gives an interpretation of the basic theme of Mandel'štam's poem: the longing for a golden age of humanity, now irretrievably lost:[4]

На каменных отрогах Пиэрии
Водили музы первый хоровод,
Чтобы, как пчелы, лирники слепые
Нам подарили ионийский мед.
И холодком повеяло высоким
От выпукло-девического лба,
Чтобы раскрылись правнукам далеким
Архипелага нежные гроба.

Бежит весна топтать луга Эллады,
Обула Сафо пестрый сапожок,
И молоточками куют цикады,
Как в песенке поется, перстенек.
Высокий дом построил плотник дюжий,
На свадьбу всех передушили кур,
И растянул сапожник неуклюжий
На башмаки все пять воловьих шкур.

Нерасторопна черепаха-лира,
Едва-едва беспалая ползет,
Лежит себе на солнышке Эпира,
Тихонько грея золотой живот.
Ну, кто ее такую приласкает,
Кто спящую ее перевернет? –
Она во сне Терпандра ожидает,
Сухих перстов предчувствуя налет.

Поит дубы холодная криница,
Простоволосая шумит трава,
На радость осам пахнет медуница.
О где же вы, святые острова,
Где не едят надломленного хлеба,
Где только мед, вино и молоко,
Скрипучий труд не омрачает неба,
И колесо вращается легко.

The poem is written in octets. The first three each breaks up into two quatrains; thematic unity binds them into a stanzaic whole of a higher order [4 + 4]. Each quatrain represents a complex rhythmic-syntactical entity which invariably concludes on the fourth and eighth lines with a cadence (*intonation calmante* in Karcevskij's terms), always marked in punctuation by a period. The final, fourth, stanza displays another kind of intonational division [3 + 5]. Here it is not the fourth, but the third line which is marked by a strong intonational break, that is, by a cadence, infringing upon the intonational pattern which has become habitual. This infringement of the intonational pattern in the last stanza is not accidental; as we will see subsequently, it plays a substantial role in the thematic segmentation of the poem.

Przybylski was the first to notice the fact that two fragments of Sappho are "enciphered" in the second stanza of Mandel'štam's poem: in the lines about the motley boot and about the shoemaker who stretched "all five oxhides to cobble a pair of shoes." Przybylski quotes the first fragment in Greek and in the Polish translation of Brzostowska; the second fragment is quoted only in Polish translation. According to Močul'skij (*Vstreča* 2, 1945, 30), Mandel'štam never "mastered Greek"; therefore, it is natural to assume that Mandel'štam's sources were Russian translations of Sappho.

Two such translations appeared almost simultaneously in the second decade of this century: Vjačeslav Ivanov's (*Alkej i Safo*, 1914) and V. V. Veresaev's (*Safo, stixotvorenija i fragmenty*, 1915). Had Przybylski familiarized himself with these translations, he would have come to the conclusion that Mandel'štam thoroughly utilized Ivanov's book. If he had gone still further and had studied Ivanov's original poetry instead of contrasting *a priori* Mandel'štam's Hellenism with Ivanov's, and instead of indiscriminately censuring the Hellenic elements in Ivanov's poetry as "typical Alexandrian hack work" ("*typowa aleksandryjska fuszerka*"), he would have become convinced how much the images of Hellas recreated by Mandel'štam owe to Ivanov. About a dozen of Ivanov's lines and images (from *Alkej i Safo*, *Prozračnost'*, *Nežnaja tajna*, and, perhaps, *Cor ardens*) are enciphered in the poem "Na kamennyx otrogax Pièrii."[5]

The thematic range of Mandel'štam's poem is not limited to an idyllic picture of Hellas. The poem begins with the theme of the significance which the Hellenic heritage has for us, its distant descendents: a heritage embodied primarily in the antique poetry of blind rhapsodists — in Ionian honey. Thanks to this poetry, to the cool breeze which blew from the spurs of Pieria, the Hellenic heritage is revealed to us as completely

as possible.[6] Commenting on the first stanza, Przybylski pointed out
that the image of the Muses' circular chorus for the first time treading
the stony heights has its source in Hesiod's *Theogony*, which, in Veresaev's translation, reads as follows:

1   С Муз, геликонских богинь, мы песню свою начинаем.
    На Геликоне они обитают высоком, священном.
    Нежной ногою ступая, обходят они *в хороводе*
    Жертвенник Зевса-царя и фиалково-темный источник . . .

                    .  .  .  .  .  .  .  .  .  .  .  .  .  .  .  .  .

5   Нежное тело свое искупавши в теченьях Пермесса,
    Иль в роднике Иппокрене, иль в водах священных Ольмея,
    На геликонской вершине они *хоровод заводили*,
    Дивный для глаза, прелестный, и ноги их в пляске мелькали.

                    .  .  .  .  .  .  .  .  .  .  .  .  .  .  .  .  .

51  Радуют разум великий отцу своему на Олимпе
    Дщери великого Зевса-царя, олимпийские Музы.
    Семя во чрево приняв от Кронида-отца, *в Пиерии*
    Их родила Мнемосина, царица высот Елевфера,
55  Чтоб улетали заботы и беды душа забывала.

Hesiod's *Works and Days* also begins with an address to the Muses:

    Вас, *пиерийские Музы*, дающие песнями славу,
    Я призываю, — воспойте родителя вашего Зевса![7]

Nevertheless, it should be noted that in the lyric of Sappho, which
underlies the imagery of the whole poem, poetry is symbolized by the
roses of Pieria (fragment No. XLV in Ivanov's translation, No. 44 in
Veresaev's).

The images of poet-bees and poetry-honey in Mandel'štam's poem
are not new; they, too, have literary sources. Nils Nilsson refers to these
sources in his article "Osip Mandel'štam and His Poetry" (*Scando-
Slavica IX*, 1963, 48): "In Greek and Roman poetry poets are often
compared to or compare themselves to bees (cf. the well known ode of
Horace, Carm. IV:2: ego apis Matinae . . .). The metaphor is then
taken up by the Renaissance poets (Ronsard: je ressemble à l'Abeille
. . .)." However, the main source of this image is Plato's dialogue "Ion":
" . . . [poets] tell us that they bring songs from honeyed fountains,
calling them out of the gardens and dells of the Muses; they, like the
bees, winging their way from flower to flower" (English translation by
B. Jowett, 1892).[8] In Old Russian literature, Daniil Zatočnik also

compares himself to a bee: "Az bo ne vo Afinex rostox, ni ot filosof
naučixsja, no byx padaja aki pčela po različnym cvetom i ottudu
izbiraja sladost' slovesnuju i sovokupljaja mudrost', jako v mex vodu
morskuju." Plato's metaphor of poet-bees which gather honey in the
gardens of the Muses was used also by Vjačeslav Ivanov. In Ivanov this
image is complicated still further by the orphic symbol of the black suns
(*Cor ardens* I, 86):

> Когда взмывает дух в надмирные высоты
> Сбирать полночный мед в садах Невест-богинь, –
> Мы, пчелы черных солнц, несли в скупые соты
> Желчь луга — óмег и полынь.

The word *lirnik* (a translation of the Greek εὐλύρας appears both in
Ivanov (No. LXXXa, entitled "Svad'ba Gektora i Andromaxi") and in
Veresaev (No. 118 in the cycle "Svadebnye pesni"). The εὐλύρας in
Sappho is a name for Apollo. In the fragment No. XXXVI (Bergk, 92;
Veresaev, 101) which refers to Terpander, Ivanov translates the Greek
ἀοιδὸς ὁ Λέσβιος as *lirnik lesbijskij* (in Veresaev: *pevec lesbosskij*). G. A.
Levinton, in his article mentioned in note 5 to this chapter indicates as
the main source of Mandel'štam's *slepye lirniki* Vjačeslav Ivanov's
"Èpos Gomera" (a preface to Homer's songs, published in Moscow,
1912); in this article, Ivanov calls the ancient epic poets *lirniki* and
their songs *byliny*. There is no doubt that Mandel'štam had in mind the
Hellenic rhapsodists, in the first place the old blind Homer. It should
also be mentioned that the Russian ethnographical term *lirniki* primarily refers to Ukrainian singers who played the Ukrainian *lira*, an
instrument different from the Greek lyre.

The theme of Hellenic poetry continues in the second stanza of
Mandel'štam's poem, although no longer as the theme of high epic, but
of intimate lyric: Sappho takes the place of the blind rhapsodists, and
the setting is transferred to Lesbos. The entire second stanza is a skillful
montage of Sappho's poetry, in particular of those fragments which are
often grouped by editors under the general heading of "Epithalamia."[9]
The second stanza is a genre picture of preparations for a wedding seen
not by the mind's eye of the poet, but assembled by him from fragments
of poetry by the oldest Hellenic poetess.

The image of spring which appears in the first line — "Bežit vesna
toptat' luga Èllady" — foretokens the joyous, prenuptial atmosphere
of the whole stanza. This image is not an allegory at all, as Przybylski
thinks, but a simple personification, similar to the one in the well-known
lines by Tjutčev:

Весна идет, весна идет!
И тихих, теплых, майских дней
Румяный, светлый хоровод
Толпится весело за ней.

"Bežit vesna toptat' luga Êllady": such a personification of spring is
not out of keeping with the spirit of Sappho's poetry. True, in her poetry,
spring is not personified, but in one very well-known fragment the
goddess of dawn is depicted: Eos in golden sandals. The modern reader
naturally perceives this image as a personification, as Vjačeslav Ivanov
did in his translation (No. LXXIX: "Blizitsja zarja na zolotyx sandal'-
jax"). Veresaev, as usual, was more exact in his rendering (No. 70: "V
zolotyx sandalijax mne nedavno Êos . . ."). Perhaps Mandel'štam also
recalled the words from the preface to *Alkej i Safo*: "Safo, po suždeniju
drevnix, sladostna; s čarujuščej graciej poet ona o krasote i ljubvi, *vesne* i
gal'cionax" (p. 17). In Ivanov's translations, the noun *vesna* and the
adjectives *vesennij* and *vešnij* are found more often than in the poetry of
Sappho herself, namely, in the six fragments (Nos. V, XIII, XXXVII,
LXV, LXVI, LXVIII). The first of them (very freely translated) could
have inspired Mandel'štam:

. . . вьем
Из фиалок и роз венки,
Вязи вяжем из пестрых первин лугов, –
Нежной шеи живой убор,
Ожерелья душистые –
Всю тебя, *как Весну*, уберу в цветы.

Finally, in the first line of Mandel'štam's montage an echo from still
another Ivanov translation (fr. No. XXVII) can be heard:

Критянки, под гимн
Окрест огней алтарных,
Взвивали, кружась,
Нежные ноги стройно,
На мягком *лугу*
Цвет полевой *топтали*.

When he wrote the line "Bežit vesna *toptat' luga Êllady*," it is hardly
likely that Mandel'štam was thinking about a "polemic with the
Parnassians." I strongly believe that precisely the reading of Sappho
in Ivanov's translation inspired Mandel'štam to begin his montage
with a personified image of spring.

As Przybylski has indicated, a fragment from Sappho is enciphered in the second line of the second stanza ("Obula Safo pestryj sapožok"); it reads as follows in the translations of Vjačeslav Ivanov and Veresaev:

(1) V.Iv.XLVIII:

> ... Пестроцветный ногу
> *Сапожок* обул, выписной, любезный
> Неге лидийской;

(2) Ver. 96:

> ... а ноги
> Пестрый ей *ремень* покрывал, лидийской
> Чудной работы.

It should be mentioned that the word μάσλης in the fragment of Sappho's has received various interpretations. One American translator even translated it as "girdle" (P. Maurice Hill, *The Poems of Sappho*, 1954, p. 53): "She wore an embroidered leather / girdle, the ends of which reached / down to her feet, a beautiful / piece of Lydian workmanship." Another American translator went still further and translated it as "gown": "Her gay embroidered gown / draped down to her toes: / fine needlework from Lydia" (Willis Barnstone, *Sappho*, 1965, p. 89). The Polish translator translated μάσλης as *sandały*. Thus, proceeding from her translation, Przybylski supposed that there was a choice before Mandel'štam, *sandalija* or *sapožok*, and draws the conclusion that "the choice of the second version was significant ('znaczący') for Mandel'-štam." As a matter of fact, there was no choice: Mandel'štam simply took what was at hand. The "frivolous," motley little boot of Sappho's actually belongs to Vjačeslav Ivanov.

The next two lines, "I *molotočkami kujut* cikady, / Kak v pesenke poetsja, *perstenek*," again have as a subtext a fragment of Sappho's, which we shall cite in the translations of both Russian translators: (1) V.Iv.LXII: "Čto ž *perstenkom* ty svoim poxvaljaeš'sja?"; (2) Ver. 27: "Čto *kolečkom* svoim tak gordiš'sja ty, duročka?" Again, Mandel'-štam's source is Vjačeslav Ivanov.

In Sappho's time rings began to come into fashion, but only as an adornment, not as an accessory of the wedding rite. Mandel'štam, though, is not an historian, but a poet, and the forging of a ring in this poem becomes part of the preparations for the wedding, just as does the building of a tall house by the stalwart carpenter. The *pesenka* to which Mandel'štam refers ("kak v pesenke poetsja") is most likely the song from Žukovskij's "Svetlana," as G. A. Levinton indicates in the article mentioned above:

Пой, красавица: «Кузнец,
Скуй мне злат и нов венец,
*Скуй кольцо златое,*
Мне венчаться тем венцом,
Обручаться тем кольцом» . . .

The image of the hammering cicadas also interested Przybylski: "After
the Pseudo-Anacreon wrote his ode in honor of cicadas these songstresses
sang in poetry for a whole century." To this one may add that the
cicada sings in Hesiod's works as well (*Works and Days*, lines 582–584,
in Veresaev's translation); from here it migrated to Sappho's contemporary, Alcaeus (No. XVI, "Leto," in Ivanov's translation; in Veresaev's,
*Èllinskie poèty*, p. 291). The image of the singing cicada is found in one
fragment which is attributed by some authors to Alcaeus, and by others
to Sappho herself (J. M. Edmonds, *Sappho revocata*, 1928, p. 94).
Speaking of Russian poetry, Przybylski compares Mandel'štam's cicadas
with Bunin's "typically Parnassian description of a concert of songstresses" ("Nočnye cikady," 1910), and comes to the following conclusion: "So as not to be Parnassian, Mandel'štam's cicadas do not
sing, but hammer out a ring." The image of the cicadas forging with
their little hammers is apparently suggested by Vjačeslav Ivanov's
poetry. One finds cicadas in Ivanov's poems time and again, and in
the poem "Cikady" (*Prozračnost'*, p. 61) they are simply called *kovači*:

Цикады, цикады!
Луга палящего,
Кузницы жаркой
Вы ковачи!
Молотобойные,
Скрежетопильные,
Звонкогремучие
Вы ковачи!

These lines obviously made an impression on Ivanov's readers: in his
brief review of *Prozračnost'*, Blok notes them as an example of good
sound texture (*Sobranie sočinenij* V, 1962, 539). In *Nežnaja tajna*
Ivanov has the poem "Cikada," in which the poet starts a conversation
with the "garden guest" that has flown into his hand and does not
answer his questions:

Ты безмолствуешь в ответ,
Звонкогласная певунья,
Вдохновенная вещунья!

Только пальцы мне живей
*Молоточками* щекочешь . . .

It thus turns out that all of these "anti-Parnassian" diminutives (*sapožok, perstenek, molotočki*) can be traced back to Vjačeslav Ivanov's vocabulary.[10]

The fifth line in the second stanza is also evoked by Sappho's poetry. Here is the corresponding fragment with which Bergk begins the cycle of "Epithalamia":

(1) In the translation of Vjačeslav Ivanov, No. LXXXV:

Стройте кровельку выше –
Свадьбе слава!
Стройте, *плотники*, выше –
Свадьбе слава!
Входит жених, ровно бог-воевода:
Мужа рослого ростом он выше.

(2) In the translation of Veresaev, No. 100:

Эй, потолок, поднимайте, –
О Гименей!
Выше, *плотники*, выше!
О Гименей!
Входит жених, подобный Арею,
Выше самых высоких мужей!

The Polish translator does not have "carpenters" (*cieśle*); she has simple "men" (*mężczyźni*, Safona, *Pieśni*, 1961, p. 34), and that is why Przybylski did not take notice of this fragment of Sappho's.[11]

Finally, the last two lines of the second stanza are a paraphrase of yet another epithalamium which ridicules the doorkeeper, who undoubtedly is a comic figure. Here is that fragment in the versions of both Russian translators:

(1) V.Iv., XCI:

У придверника ноги в семь са́жен;
Сапоги — *из пяти шкур бычачьих*;
Их сапожников шили десяток.

(2) Ver., 107:

В семь сажён у привратника ноги,
На ступнях пятерные подошвы,
В двадцать рук их башмачники шили.

A collation of both these texts again leaves no doubt that the Ivanov translation served as Mandel'štam's source. Thus, there is only one line in the second stanza for which a literary source has not been found: "Na svad'bu vsex peredušili kur."

Proceeding from the assertion that in Arcadia "no one kills anybody," Przybylski comes to the conclusion that here "we are already in the Greece of Homer and Hesiod." However, Mandel'štam is speaking not of "happy Arcadia," but of Sappho's Lesbos. The line about the "throttled hens" in no way sins against her poetry, at any rate not in the form with which Mandel'štam became acquainted in Ivanov's *Alkej i Safo*. Ivanov's translation of fragment XV mentions a blood sacrifice, as well as libations: "Beluju kozu prinesu ja v žertvu, / I na tvoj altar' vozlijat' ja stanu . . ."[12] The line about the throttled hens may have been prompted by the deep rhyme: *škur* — peredušili *kur*.

A person not knowing the literary subtext of the stanza just analyzed will have a great deal of difficulty understanding it. For such a reader, as Przybylski has noted, the simplest answer naturally suggests itself: "The stanza arose as a result of the irrational association of fortuitous elements begotten by fancy." Similarly, one cannot but agree with Przybylski's further assertion: "There is nothing surprising in the fact that these and like fragments have caused Mandel'štam to be called a precursor of the surrealists." As we have seen, a detailed analysis of the stanza clearly reveals its extraordinary structural integrity. But even after this analysis, Mandel'štam's montage remains a modernist poem characteristic of twentieth-century European poetry.

Each age leaves an imprint of its own on literary translations and on literary pastiches. Each age demands its own Shakespeare, its own Sappho. For curiosity's sake we venture to compare Mandel'štam's montage with a pseudo-classical montage of Sappho's "Epithalamia" (*Stixotvorenija Safy*, perevedennye Pavlom Goleniščevym-Kutuzovym, Moscow, 1805, p. 30):

Ода XIV

О вы, которые десницей и умом
Воздвигли славные палаты со столбами!
Украсьте пышными вратами,
Возвысьте сей прекрасный дом.

Уже супруг в чертог вступает,
В нем Марсов бодрый стан, в нем огнь его горит.
Какие в нем черты! — и самый гордый вид
Пред ним чело свое смиряет.

Певец Лесбийский помрачает
Прелестным голосом других Парнасских чад;
Так ты, младый супруг, прелестней всех стократ;
Все пред тобою изчезает.

Под щастливой звездой свершается твой брак,
На всех твоих гостях зришь радости ты знак;
Соединяются теперь желанья многи,
Чтобы тебе во всем способствовали боги.

One cannot but agree that in this "translation" Sappho sounds like Sumarokov.[13]

The third stanza of the poem under consideration places us historically about one century further back in antiquity, in the times of the Lesbian poet Terpander, the forefather of classical Hellenic music. According to one legend, Terpander attached three additional strings to the four-stringed cithara (Vjačeslav Ivanov mentions this in the preface *Alkej i Safo*, p. 11). The image of the tortoise-lyre is associated with the Homeric hymn "To Hermes," which tells how Hermes disemboweled a tortoise, stretched around its rim a cover of oxhide, and fitted on seven strings of sheep-gut, after which he presented this first lyre to Apollo. Nonetheless, the source of this image in Mandel'štam's poem is again found in a fragment of Sappho's. Vjačeslav Ivanov began the cycle "Gimničeskie otryvki" (fr. VII) with it:

Оживись, о священная,
Спой мне песнь, черепаха!

Veresaev gives two versions of this fragment:

46.

Лира, лира священная,
Ты подай мне свой голос.
Точнее:
Черепаха священная,
Стань звучащею ныне.

In Brzostowska's Polish translation (Safona, *Pieśni*, p.40: "Prowadź mnie, boska liro, / uczynię cię wymowną") the image of the tortoise is absent, and therefore Przybylski did not catch the connection between the third stanza and Sappho's poetry. Finally, it should be noted that "Mytilene coins with Sappho's image have on the reverse side the image of her lyre in the shape of a tortoise" (Veresaev's note to fragment No. 46).

"*Solnyško* Ėpira" in the third line of the third stanza aptly echoes the diminutive-hypocoristic terms in the second stanza: *sapožok, pesenka, perstenek,* and *molotočki*; "*nerastoropnaja* čerepaxa" recalls "*neukljužyj* sapožnik." This lexical interplay binds the two central stanzas, which are already connected by a common theme, still closer together. A reader with a rationalistic bent might be struck by the fact that the tortoise lying in the sun of Epirus waits for the poet of Lesbos. To this, one might respond that Mandel'štam did not strive for geographical accuracy: Pieria, Ionia, the Archipelago, Hellas, Epirus are all simply resonant "signal-words" which place the reader in the world of ancient Greece. It is quite probable that the image of the Epirian sunshine simply arose from the sonorous rhyme: *lira–Ėpira*.

We have already indicated the historical chronology in the first three stanzas of the poem "Na kamennyx otrogax Pièrii": the first stanza refers to deepest antiquity, the second, to the sixth century B.C., and the third, to the seventh century. However, the "poetic chronology" of these three stanzas is somewhat different. Here it is a question of "the poetry of grammar," the principles of which have been elaborated by Roman Jakobson in a number of articles which are to be collected in the third volume of his *Selected Writings*. The use of verbal tenses in the poem under consideration forms a well-balanced structure.

In the first stanza, only the past tense is found, four forms in all, two in each quatrain. They are arranged in pairs; the first member of the pair is in the main clause and the second is in the subordinate clause, joined to the main clause with the conjunction *čtoby* signifying purpose: "muzy *vodili* . . . čtoby lirniki *podarili*; xolodkom *povejalo* . . . čtoby *raskrylis'*." Both subordinate clauses have an indirect object in the dative case, *nam* and *pravnukam dalekim*. In this stanza we have the distant past projected into the future — in fact, into the present time. This is indicated by the object given in the form of the personal pronoun *nam*, which identifies *us* with the remote great-grandsons. Thus, the present moment is also fixed in the first stanza.

In the second stanza, three forms of the present tense alternate with four forms of the past: *bežit–obula–kujut–poetsja–postroil–peredušili–rastjanul*. We are dealing here with the so-called historical present, that is, with the present tense in a narrative function. The moment immediately preceding the historical present is designated by four forms of the past tense (from perfective verbs only): "Bežit vesna . . . [a] Safo [uže] obula sapožok, kujut cikady, [a] plotnik [uže] postroil . . . dom," etc.

If we do not consider the zero copula in the first line of the third stanza, then this stanza, just like the second one, has seven verbal forms: three forms of the present tense (historical present), two present gerunds, and two forms of the so-called simple future: *polzet–ležit–greja–prilaskaet–perevernet–ožidaet–predčuvstvuja*. The future tense is found only in the interrogative sentence and therefore designates potential, not real, action. From the point of view of "poetic grammar," all the remaining personal forms in this stanza denote simultaneity with the present-tense forms in the second stanza: spring runs and the cicadas forge at the same time that the tortoise lies in the sun. Thus, Sappho and Terpander become contemporaries. As we see, Mandel'štam the poet does not fully consider either the exact geography of Hellas or its history. However, only a pedantic classicist could demand this of him.

Not counting the two zero copulas in lines four and six, the fourth stanza contains six verbal forms; they are all present-tense forms. But the fourth stanza sharply breaks into two unequal parts [3 + 5]; moreover, the function of the present-tense forms in the second part is different from that in the first. The narrative present in the two central stanzas obviously continues in the first three lines of the last: the spring waters the oaks, the grass rustles, and the melilot smells at the same time that the tortoise-lyre awaits Terpander in sleep and spring runs to tread the meadows of Hellas. There is absolutely no reason for artificially tearing these three lines from the two central stanzas, as Przybylski does. When Mandel'štam wrote these lines he was not in the least thinking about "the ideal landscape of the Vale of Tempe": the imagery of these lines also can be traced to Vjačeslav Ivanov's poetry.

In the fourth line of the last stanza the poet returns us to the present: "O gde že [teper' naxodites'] vy, svjatye ostrova?"; this present time has been hinted in the first stanza, in the indirect object *nam*. In the last four lines all forms of the present tense are used in a nontemporal function: "O gde že vy, svjatye ostrova, / Gde [nikogda] ne edjat nadlomlennogo xleba, / Gde [vsegda] tol'ko med, vino i moloko," and so on. The timelessness of the "holy islands" makes them unreal, illusory. It is as if Mandel'štam's rhetorical question implied the answer: they are nowhere to be found.

As regards the first three lines of the last stanza, it should be noted that the oaks (in the first of these lines) are found in one of Sappho's fragments (No. XXXIV of Ivanov); similarly, the plant "melilot" (*medunica*, μελίλωτος) in No. VI:

> Весь в росе,
> Благовонный дымится луг;
> Розы пышно раскрылись; льют
> Сладкий запах анис и *медуница*.[14]

*Krinica*[15] is also a word from Vjačeslav Ivanov's vocabulary: in *Cor ardens* (I, 76) there is a poem with this word as the title:

> Чисты воды ключевые,
> Родники — струи живые;
> В темном лесе — студенец.
> . . . . . . . . . . . .
> Наклонися у *криницы* . . .

The image of the wasps for whose joy the melilot gives off its aroma belongs to Mandel'štam: there are no wasps in Sappho. In conventional symbolism bees are industrious and bustling, wasps cunning and rapacious. A frightening image of wasps is found, for example, in Annenskij's tragedies: a wasp chasing and harassing the Nymph in *Famira-Kifarèd* and the hungry wasps in the chorus of widows in *Laodamija* (act one):

> Не политы,
> Вянут цветы,
> Страшны голодные осы.
> И завились
> И развились
> Даром тяжелые косы.

Bees are contrasted to wasps in Bal'mont's sonnet "Oxota" (*Sonety solnca, meda i luny*, 1917):

> Шмели — бизоны в клеверных лугах.
> Как бычий рев глухой — их гуд тяжелый.
> Медлительные ламы, ноют пчелы.
> Пантеры — осы, сеющие страх.

In Mandel'štam's poem the rapacious wasps are a pendant to the image of the industrious bees of the first stanza. But here the wasps / bees opposition is only hinted at; the image of the wasps will receive its development and complete motivation in Mandel'štam's later lyrical poems.

As we have said, the theme of the Hellas of the times of Terpander and Sappho ends in the third line of the last stanza. The fourth line is a kind of intonational italics: instead of the anticipated cadence, this line is marked by a strong anticadence (*intonation incitante* in Karcevskij's terms) which particularly draws our attention to the content of the line. Moreover, the line begins with an exclamatory interjection which interrupts the tranquil narrative tone of the preceding text. One must admit that the emotionally charged motif of the "holy islands" (*svjatye ostrova*) is launched in a spectacular manner. The holy islands recall, of course, the Archipelago of the first stanza, but we are immediately given to understand that they are somewhat different, still more idyllic islands than the Lesbos of Sappho and Terpander. On the holy islands not only does no one throttle hens or shell tortoises, but people do not even eat broken loaves ("ne edjat nadlomlennogo xleba"). The image of the "holy islands" goes back to the "dalekie svjatye ostrova" (ἱεραὶ νῆσοι) of Hesiod's *Theogony* (line 1015 in Veresaev's translation),[16] and recalls the "isles of the blessed" (νῆσοι μακάρων) from *Works and Days* (Veresaev, lines 170-174):

Сердцем ни дум, ни заботы не зная, они безмятежно
Близ океанских пучин острова населяют блаженных.
Трижды в году хлебодарная почва героям счастливым
Сладостью равные меду плоды в изобилье приносит.

"Honey, wine and milk" are not only foodstuffs, but are also typically used as libations, that is, bloodless sacrifices. Mandel'štam must have known about them since his schooldays, and therefore Przybylski's reference to the Old Testament does not seem well founded. Perhaps Mandel'štam's creative memory also retained the lines from Majkov's poem "U xrama" (1851):

Это идут они с жертвами к Вакху!
Роз, *молока и вина* молодого,
*Меду* несут и козленка молочного тащут . . .

However, the triad "honey, wine and milk" is also connected with poetic creation as described in Plato's "Ion": "And as the Corybantian revellers when they dance are not in their right mind, so the lyric poets are not in their right mind when they are composing their beautiful strains: but when falling under the power of music and metre they are inspired and possessed; like Bacchic maidens who draw milk and honey from the rivers when they are under the influence of Dionysus but not when they are in their right mind" (English translation by Jowett). Thus, an additional close relation between the imagery of the first and the fourth stanza can be established: the honey which is used for libations becomes closely connected with the Ionian honey of the blind rhapsodists.

The last two lines, "Skripučij trud ne omračaet neba / I koleso vraščaetsja legko," effectively complete the entire poem. Jurij Terepiano, in his memoirs, ascribes the last two lines to Vladimir Makkavejskij.

Mrs. Mandel'štam confirms Terapiano's story, but she attributes to Makkavejskij only the last line (*Vtoraja kniga*, p. 129). The image of the turning wheel fitted very well in the finely balanced structure of the poem. As G. A. Levinton noticed, it recalls the circular dance of the Muses in the first stanza. Since the last line was a kind of impromptu by Makkavejskij, I do not think that one should attempt to identify the "wheel" with a concrete object. Moreover, I believe that within the general theme of the "holy islands" it does not require concrete definition. A reader inclined to symbolic interpretations may recall the Wheel of Fortune.[17]

We remind the reader that the poem "Na kamennyx otrogax Pièrii" was written in 1919, at a time which was characterized as a period of general devastation. The poet's exclamation, "O gde že vy, svjatye ostrova," expresses genuine longing and sadness. The poet will recall these islands again during the hard days in Voronezh, with the former longing in his voice:

> Ты отдай мне мое, остров синий,
> Крит летучий, отдай мне мой труд,
> И сосцами текучей богини
> Напои обожженный сосуд.
>
> Это было и пелось, синея,
> Много задолго до Одиссея,
> До того, как еду и питье
> Называли «моя» и «мое».

One cannot but agree with Przybylski's last lines: "Despair, not wisdom, created the myth of Arcadia. We therefore love poets who leave this myth with regret. And further, in defiance of reason, we like to hear fairy tales about paradise lost, even though historicism and history teach us that it never existed."

The image of the bees and wasps is repeated in Mandel'štam's poem "Sestry — tjažest' i nežnost'," written in March 1920.[18] The themes of time, dying, the transitoriness of life and unrequited love are interwoven in this poem; the theme of bees and wasps is only secondary: "Medunicy i osy tjaželuju rozu sosut" — the industrious bees and the rapacious wasps enjoy with equal rights the beautiful gifts of the earth (since "the rose had been earth"). In this line the word *medunica* is used for the first time instead of *pčela*; it is a word characteristic of Vjačeslav Ivanov's vocabulary. Compare in *Alkej i Safo* (No. LXX): "Net ni medu mne, ni medunicy" (μέλισσα in the original); and also in *Cor ardens*:

... медуница Гимета
К моим миртам льнула с жужжанием звонким,

(I, 63)

Я розу пел на сто ладов,
Из розы пили сто медов,
Мои златые медуницы.

(II, 149)

The visual image of bees and roses occurs so frequently in *Cor ardens*
that there is no need to excerpt all the quotations. We will cite some
examples taken at random:

И медлит весть: тебе ли цвесть, лилея
            Иных полей?
Ах, розы мед, что пчел зовет, алея, –
            Земле милей!

(I, 144)

Золотые реют пчелы
Над кострами рдяных роз.

(I, 188)

... Пчела
Из розы мед полуденный пила
И реяла над сладостной влюбленно.

(II, 56)

... А роза пчелке
Льет нектар, не жалея,
И грезит жала солнца,
Желанием алея ...

(II, 107)

In Vjačeslav Ivanov, to be sure, on the figurative level the symbolism
of roses and bees is more complex and polysemantic than in Mandel'-
štam's line but on the basic, material level they coincide.[19]

   The image of the bees occupies a central place in the poem, "Voz'mi
na radost'," written in November 1920. Here, this image provides, as
it were, the basic frame for the plot of the whole poem:

Возьми на радость из моих ладоней
Немного солнца и немного меда,
Как нам велели пчелы Персефоны.

Не отвязать неприкрепленной лодки,
Не услыхать в меха обутой тени,
Не превозмочь в дремучей жизни страха.

Нам остаются только поцелуи,
Мохнатые, как маленькие пчелы,
Что умирают, вылетев из улья.

Они шуршат в прозрачных дебрях ночи,
Их родина — дремучий лес Тайгета,
Их пища — время, медуница, мята.

Возьми ж на радость дикий мой подарок,
Невзрачное сухое ожерелье
Из мертвых пчел, мед превративших в солнце.

This poem is written in blank verse (unrhymed iambic pentameter),
which in Russian lyric poetry is associated with the genre of monologues,
of poetic meditations, going back to Puškin's masterpieces, "On meždu
nami žil..." and "Vnov' ja posetil..." Mandel'štam used this meter
as early as 1915 in the poem "Ja ne uvižu znamenitoj 'Fedry'." Unlike
Puškin's monologues, which represent an open form with free intonational phrasing, Mandel'štam's monologues are stanzaic, with no
enjambements between stanzas or between lines; in other words, they
represent a closed form.

"Voz'mi na radost'" consists of five tercets in each of which the
poetic images and grammatical forms are distributed according to a
certain system. The image of bees is repeated in all odd tercets, the
images of honey and sun in the first and fifth, and the image of the
beehive appears only in the third (central) tercet. Thus, the odd tercets
provide the basic frame for the plot of the whole poem. The even tercets
are a kind of thematic digression, but they, too, are connected by the
images "*dremučaja žizn'*" and "*dremučij* les." The forms of the first and
second person singular (verbal and pronominal) appear only in the first
and fifth tercets. These are the imperative *voz'mi* and the pronoun *moj*,
which establish the subjective relation: addresser-addressee. In the
third (central) tercet the first and the second person singular are united
in the form of the first person plural personal pronoun *nam*. In the even
tercets the personal forms are either completely absent (in the second),
or else are forms of the objective third person (in the fourth tercet).
Finally, the first and fifth tercets are connected by the repetition of the
adverbial modifier of purpose *na radost'*. All of these words and forms
seemingly shape the "basic signal system" of the entire poem:

I     Возьми на радость . . . из моих . . . солнце . . . мед . . . пчелы . . .
II    Дремучая жизнь . . .
III   Нам . . . пчелы . . . улей . . .
IV   Дремучий лес . . .
V    Возьми на радость . . . мой . . . пчелы . . . мед . . . солнце . . .

The anaphoric repetitions in the first and fifth tercets, which give the whole poem a circular (ring) structure, as well as the symmetrical distribution of all other "fundamental signals" in the tercets, evoke in the reader an impression of completeness, wholeness, and fullness of poetic message. This impression is reinforced by the strict regularity of intonational phrasing and the familiar tranquil tonality of the blank verse, a tonality characteristic of the genre of poetic meditations.

The literary subtext of "Voz'mi na radost' " is the following part of "Poslanie na Kavkaz" by Vjačeslav Ivanov (*Nežnaja tajna*, p. 105):

> Так, милый! так! Нам Касталийский ключ
> Звучит, поет всечасно смутным звоном,
> Но, чу! над ним, за ним поет Печаль . . .
> И диво ли, что ныне ты печален?
> Ведь миндалем Весна одела долы
> Страны твоей загорной, завершинной;
> Ведь юная выходит *Персефона*
> Из недр земных, с улыбкой несказанной,
> Неся цветы лугам и грусть певцу.
> Грусти ж, певец! Но лиру оживи
> Отзвучием *загробного завета*,
> Что нам живым велит одно: *любить*.

"Poslanie na Kavkaz" is also written in the blank verse of poetic meditations. The part cited breaks up into tercets, although these are not as distinct as Mandel'štam's. But Mandel'štam did not merely reproduce Ivanov's "verse-music." The lines quoted also contain the basic theme of Mandel'štam's poem: the commandment of the goddess of fertility and death, who bids us, the living, do one thing: to love.

Perhaps Mandel'štam also remembered lines from Ivanov's poem "Persefona" (*Prozračnost'*, pp. 20–21):

> Весна                 И светлых дней
> Я встаю             Веду хоровод,
> На пажить твою,     И мною твердь
> О смертный род, –     Сияет ясней, –
> Из темного лона!      Царица теней,

Богиня Сна　　　　　И смерть
Весна –　　　　　　Персефона.[20]

There is another subtext from Vjačeslav Ivanov, reflected in Mandel'-
štam's "Voz'mi na radost'." I have in mind his triptych "Rozy" (*Cor
ardens* II, 65–66). Needless to say, the symbolism of Ivanov's images
is somewhat different, even more complex; but in Mandel'štam's poem
it definitely acquires a new quality.

I will not cite the complete text of Ivanov's sonnets, but only those
lines which contain images repeated in Mandel'štam's poem:

|     |     |     |
| --- | --- | --- |
| I | 7 | Моих гостей . . . |
|   | 8 | Невидим лик и *поступь неслышна.* |
|   | 12 | Я буду петь, из темного огня |
|   | 13 | И звездных слез свивая *ожерелье* – |
|   | 14 | *Мой дар тебе* для свадебного дня. |
| II | 1 | Не ты ль поведала подругам *пчелам,* |
|   | 2 | Где цвет цветет и что таит любимый? |
|   | 5 | *Мед,* гостьи божьи, . . . |
|   | 6 | Вы в *улей* собираете родимый . . . |
| III | 11 | И *поцелуй* уж обменен с подругой . . . |

The "word-signals" common to both texts are as follows: *neslyšnaja
postup'* (*ne uslyxat'* . . . *teni*), *ožerel'e, moj dar* (*moj podarok*), *pčely, med,
ulej* and *poceluj.*

In the above-cited article on Mandel'štam's poetry (47–49), Nils
Nilsson gives his own interpretation of Mandel'štam's poem "Voz'mi na
radost'." From the very beginning, he identifies the Ionian honey of the
blind rhapsodists from the poem "Na kamennyx otrogax Pièrii" with the
honey of Persephone's bees, and interprets the entire poem "Voz'mi na
radost' '" as a kind of allegory. For Nilsson, bees are words, honey is
"the secret beauty of the words," and sunshine is poetry. "As bees, so
words in a way die, vanish when they are spoken . . . So what the poet is
able to offer his reader is . . . a necklace of dead bees, a string of simple,
common words." I do not believe that the addressee of Mandel'štam's
poem is an impersonal reader, and I doubt that the honey from "Voz'mi
na radost' '" should be identified with the Ionian honey from "Na
kamennyx otrogax." It is true that in Mandel'štam one comes across
recurrent images having the same meaning; though, very often, we are
simply faced with repeated "word-signals," which acquire different

meanings in new contexts. We may recall what Mandel'štam himself wrote about the "word" in his essay "Slovo i kul'tura": "Slovo Psixeja. Živoe slovo ne oboznačaet predmeta, a svobodno vybiraet, kak by dlja žil'ja, tu ili inuju predmetnuju značimost', veščnost', miloe telo. I vokrug vešči slovo bluždaet svobodno, kak duša vokrug brošennogo, no ne zabytogo tela." I will attempt to prove that in the poem "Voz'mi na radost' " the word "bee" chose three different "bodies."

"Voz'mi na radost' iz moix ladonej" is a love poem; the second person singular form of address in the first line is unmistakably understood by the Russian reader as the poet speaking to the woman he loves.[21] The bees of the first stanza are the "industrious bees" of Hellenic poetry. Moreover, here they are concretized: they are the servants of the goddess of fertility who transmit to mortals her commandment: to enjoy life. Mandel'štam is not a symbolist; he does not create new symbols, but he never avoids the old, accepted ones. Honey is a usual, frequently occurring symbol of the sweetness of life; the sun has always been a symbol of light and warmth. These common figurative meanings of sun and honey are the basic key to the interpretation of Mandel'-štam's poem. The same simple meanings are the basis of sun and honey symbolism in Bal'mont's book of poetry *Sonety solnca, meda i luny* (published in Moscow, 1917):

(1)    Оно прекрасно ласкою привета,
Всегда слепые смотрят на него.
И чувствуют. И любят. *Оттого,*
*Что в нем огонь есть нежный, кроме света.*

Оно в сознаньи расцвечает лето.
*Кто счастлив здесь, он счастлив чрез него,*
*Лишь им живое в мире не мертво.*
Лишь с ним мечта рубинами одета.

(«Оно прекрасно»)

(2)    В пылании томительных июлей,
Бросали пчелы рано утром улей,
Заслыша дух цветущей крутизны.

Тот мед, что пчелы собрали с цветка, –
Я взял. *И вся пчелиная затея*
*Сказала мне, чтоб жил я не робея,*
*Что жизнь смела, безбрежна и сладка.*

(«Сонеты солнца»)[22]

As we will see later, honey also has erotic connotations in poetic tradition, as does the image of the sun representing a cosmic fertilizing power. Erotic overtones are present, for example, in Vjačeslav Ivanov's lines: "A roza . . . *grezit žala solnca,* / *Želaniem aleja*" (*Cor ardens* II, 107).

It is not accidental, I believe, that sun and honey merge, as it were, into one image in both Bal'mont's and Vjačeslav Ivanov's poetry (as they do in Mandel'štam's):

(1) Bal'mont (sonnet "Orar' " in *Sonety solnca, meda i luny*):

> Когда на сотне верст чуть слышно хрустнет лед
> В одной проталине, тот звук и дуновенье
> Тепла весеннего вещают льду крушенье,
> И в *Солнце* в этот миг есть явно зримый *мед*.

(2) In Vjačeslav Ivanov (*Cor ardens*, I, 13):

> Млеет длительно, все *мед и нега*, – Солнце.

and much later in "Rimskie sonety" (*Svet večernij*, 1962, p. 110):

> Пью медленно *медвяный солнца свет*,
> Густеющий, как долу звон прощальный;
> И светел дух печалью беспечальной,
> Весь полнота, какой названья нет.
>
> *Не медом ли воскресших полных лет*
> Он напоен сей кубок Дня венчальный?

It is not difficult to imagine the real, material level of the symbolism in Mandel'štam's first tercet: extended palms holding a piece of honeycomb, and a ray of sunlight playing on them.[23]

The second tercet is a kind of thematic digression. It develops the theme of "somnolent life," of the impossibility of any kind of action (three infinitives with negation: *ne otvjazat', ne uslyxat', ne prevozmoč* ). While in the first tercet we are given the theme of summer Persephone, we spontaneously associate several images of the second tercet with winter Persephone, the goddess of death. Thus, the "unfastened boat" evokes, perhaps unjustifiably, the image of Charon's boat. But it recalls also the empty boat in a dry river ("V suxoj reke pustoj čelnok plyvet") in the second poem of Mandel'štam's "twin-poems," written in 1920, probably a few months before "Voz'mi na radost' ": "Kogda Psixeja-žizn' spuskaetsja k tenjam" and "Ja slovo pozabyl, čto ja xotel skazat'." The "poetic space" of these poems is the underground kingdom of Persephone. Moreover, the "unfastened boat" reminds us of the image of a sinking bark in "Čto pojut časy-kuznečik," which was discussed in Chapter Four. "The shadow shod in furs" most probably signifies an inaudibly approaching danger, and again one spontaneously associates it with the next world ("Kogda Psixeja-žizn' spuskaetsja *k tenjam*"). The only subtext found so far for this line is Ivanov's "guests whose faces are invisible and whose footfalls are soundless."[24] The last line of the second tercet, "Ne prevozmoč' v dremučej žizni *straxa*," requires commentary both on the biographical and historical levels. Before this line was written, Mandel'štam had already been in a Wrangel jail in Theodosia and in a Menshevik jail in Tiflis. Here is how Anna Axmatova describes Petrograd at the end of 1920 (*Sočinenija* II, 172):

Как воспоминание о пребывании Осипа в Петербурге в 1920 г., кроме изумительных стихов О. Арбениной, остались еще живые, выцветшие как наполеоновские знамена афиши того времени — о вечерах поэзии, где имя Мандельштама стоит рядом с Гумилевым и Блоком. Все старые петербургские вывески были еще на своих местах, но за ними, кроме пыли, мрака и зияющей пустоты, ничего не было. Сыпняк, голод, расстрелы, темнота в квартирах, сырые дрова, опухшие до неузнаваемости люди. В Гостином дворе можно было собрать большой букет полевых цветов. Догнивали знаменитые петербургские торцы. Из подвальных окон «Крафта» еще пахло шоколадом. Все кладбища были разгромлены. Город не просто изменился, а решительно превратился в свою противоположность.

In this oppressive atmosphere, the only salvation, the only refuge, was love: "Nam ostajutsja tol'ko pocelui." These are not allegorical kisses, but quite real ones, as in Vjačeslav Ivanov: "I poceluj už obmenen s podrugoj." These are not prickly masculine kisses, but fluffy feminine ones ("moxnatye"): it does not take much imagination to picture to oneself the light down on the upper lip of the woman to whom the poem is written. Thus, bees in the third tercet are not symbolic at all; they serve as second member in the simple simile which is based on tactile sensation: "Moxnatye, kak malen'kie pčely." Mandel'štam used bees, as the second member of the simile based on a visual perception, in the poem, "Dombi i syn" (1913):

> В конторе сломанные стулья,
> На шиллинги и пенсы счет;
> Как *пчелы, вылетев из улья,*
> Роятся цифры круглый год.

Mandel'štam's comparison of kisses to dying bees apparently comes from Maeterlinck's *La Vie des abeilles* (see my "Tri zametki," *IJSLP* XII, 167). Maeterlinck's description of the nuptial flight of the queen-bee during which the lucky prince-consort pays with his life for a moment of ecstasy is followed by this reflection of the author's "Le Vol nuptial," IV):

La plupart des êtres ont le sentiment confus qu'un hasard très précaire, une sorte de membrane transparente, sépare la mort de l'amour, et que l'idée profonde de la nature veut que l'on meure dans le moment où l'on transmet la vie. C'est probablement cette crainte héréditaire qui donne tant d'importance à l'amour. Ici du moins se réalise dans sa simplicité primitive cette idée dont le souvenir plane encore sur *le baiser* des hommes.

Kisses are compared to bees in a somewhat different way in Longus's novel *Daphnis and Chloe*: "Whatever is Chloe's kiss doing to me? Her lips are softer than roses, but her kiss hurts more than the sting of a bee." (Compare also Verlaine's: "J'ai peur d'un baiser / Comme d'une abeille"). However, the motif of death is also present in Daphnis's monologue: "My breath's coming in gasps, my heart's jumping up and down, my soul's melting away — but all the same I want to kiss her again. Oh, what an unlucky victory! Oh, what a strange disease — I don't even know what to call it. Had Chloe drunk poison just before she kissed me? If so, how did she manage not to be killed?" Longus also compares a kiss to honey: "But what revived him most of all was the kiss she gave him with her soft lips — a kiss that was like honey." Mandel'-štam knew Longus's novel; he wrote about it in his essay "Konec romana":

Жития святых, при всей разработанности фабулы, не были романами, потому что в них отсутствовал светский интерес к судьбе персонажей, а иллюстрировалась общая идея; но греческая повесть «Дафнис и Хлоя» считается первым европейским романом, так как эта заинтересованность впервые в ней появляется самостоятельной, движущей силой.

Deržavin's poem "Mščenie" (1805) is a translation of a German poem by Johann Nikolaus Goetz, an elaboration of Longus's imagery at two removes:[25]

> Бог любви и восхищенья
> У пчелы похитил сот,

И пчелой зато в отмещенье
Был ужален тут Эрот.
Встрепенувшися, несчастный
Крадены, сердясь, соты
В розовы уста прекрасны
Спрятал юной красоты.
«На, — сказал, — мои хищеньи
Ты для памяти возьми,
И отныне наслажденьи
Ты в устах своих храни.
С тех пор Хлою дорогую
Поцелую лишь когда,
Сласть и боль я в сердце злую
Ощущаю завсегда.
Хлоя, жаля, услаждает,
Как пчелиная стрела:
Мед и яд в меня вливает,
И, томя меня, мила.

Possibly Deržavin's "Pčelka" (1796) also attracted Mandel'štam's attention:

Пчелка златая!
Что ты жужжишь?
Все вкруг летая
Прочь не летишь?
Или ты любишь
Лизу мою?

Соты ль душисты
В желтых власах,
Розы ль огнисты
В алых устах,
Сахар ли белый
Грудь у нее?

Пчелка златая!
Что ты жужжишь?
Слышу, вздыхая,
Мне говоришь:
К меду прилипнув
С ним и умру.

Mandel'štam's poetry contains many reminiscences from Deržavin (for example, Deržavin's "Penočka" and "Seročka" are enciphered in the ninth line of "Grifel'naja oda").

Finally, we may also mention Lermontov's kisses melting (that is, dying) on the lips:

Она поет — и звуки тают,
Как поцелуи на устах.

It is not surprising that Mandel'štam's bee-kisses die as they leave
the hive: from time immemorial, lovers have been dying in each other's
embraces, and from time immemorial love's ecstasy has been identified
with death, a "sweet death." Let us only recall a stanza from Blok
written in 1915 ("Pered sudom"):

> Ты всегда мечтала, что, сгорая,
> Догорим мы вместе — ты и я,
> Что дано, *в объятьях умирая,*
> *Увидать блаженные края.*

The poem "Voz'mi na radost' " is part of a small cycle of love poems
written in Petrograd (November-December 1920) during Mandel'štam's
brief romance with Ol'ga Arbenina, an actress in the Alexandrine
Theater. Mrs. Mandel'štam attributes to this cycle the following poems
(*Vtoraja kniga*, pp. 67–70): "Mne žalko, čto teper' zima," "Voz'mi na
radost' iz moix ladonej," "Za to, čto ja ruki tvoi ne sumel uderžat',"
"Ja naravne s drugimi xoču tebe služit'," and, possibly, "Ja v xorovod
tenej . . . " Despite her denial, I believe that the poem "V Peterburge
my sojdemsja snova" (November 25, 1920) should also be included in
that cycle.[26] G. Dal'nij (Gabrièl' Superfin) asserts that the autograph of
"Voz'mi na radost' " contains a dedication to Arbenina (*Vestnik russkogo
studenčeskogo xristianskogo dviženija* 97, 1970, 143). It is very characteristic that throughout this cycle Mandel'štam depicts the lips and
mouth of his beloved:

> В тебе все дразнит, все поет,
> Как итальянская рулада.
> *И маленький вишневый рот*
> Сухого просит винограда.
>                     («Мне жалко, что теперь зима»)

> За то, что я руки твои не сумел удержать,
> За то, что я предал *соленые, нежные губы,*
> Я должен рассвета в *дремучем* акрополе ждать.
> Как я ненавижу плакучие древние срубы.
>                     («За то, что я руки твои не сумел удержать»)

> Не утоляет слово
> Мне пересохших уст,
> И без тебя мне снова
> *Дремучий* воздух пуст.
>             . . . . . . . . . . .

И, словно преступленье,
Меня к тебе влечет
Искусанный, в смятенье,
*Вишневый нежный рот.*

(«Я наравне с другими»)

In these quotations the motif of "somnolent life" appears as well, drawing all of these poems together with "Voz'mi na radost'."

The fourth tercet of "Voz'mi na radost' " is a thematic digression: it develops the motif of love. The tercet begins with a realized metaphor of bee-kisses which, before dying, "rustle in the transparent wild woods of the night." This line echoes the beginning of the first of the twin-poems mentioned above:

Когда Психея-жизнь спускается к теням
*В полупрозрачный лес,* вослед за Персефоной,
Слепая ласточка бросается к ногам
С стигийской нежностью и веткою зеленой.

The image of the semitransparent forest in ancient Hades is further developed in the third and fourth stanzas of the poem:

Кто держит зеркало, кто баночку духов –
Душа ведь женщина, — ей нравятся безделки,
*И лес безлиственный прозрачных голосов*
Сухие жалобы кропят, как дождик мелкий.

И в нежной сутолке не зная, что начать,
Душа не узнает *прозрачные дубравы;*
Дохнет на зеркало, и медлит передать
Лепешку медную с туманной переправы.

As we see, both even tercets in "Voz'mi" contain reminiscences from the twin-poems. However, there is a substantial difference between the "prozračnye debri" from "Voz'mi" and the "prozračnye dubravy" from "Kogda Psixeja-žizn' ": the former belongs to this world, the latter to the nether world. Thus the image of the "transparent wild woods" in "Voz'mi" does not indicate death, but rather serves as a reminder of dying. The image of "transparent spring" in the 1916 poem: "Mne xolodno. Prozračnaja vesna / V zelenyj pux Petropol' odevaet" has a similar function.[27] It is an old truism that themes of love and death are inseparable in poetry. And in the love poem "Voz'mi" images which can be associated with death are interwoven in all five tercets: Persephone in the first, the boat and the shadow in the second, dying bees in the third, transparent woods in the fourth, and dead bees in the fifth.

As Nils Nilsson noted, the homeland of the bees in the fourth tercet is not fertile Hymettos, famed for its bees, but the wild impenetrable forest of Taygetos, a massif in the south of the Peloponnesus. The theme of the "happy islands" is given here only obliquely. Nilsson assumes that the honey produced by these bees has a darker, wilder taste, different from that of the sweet honey of Hymettos. The food of these bee-kisses is "time, melilot and mint." The first element is, I believe, an allusion to the special way in which time is experienced during the love ecstasy (when time either stops or flies). Herbs with a spicy smell and taste, melilot and mint, might suggest heightened erotic sensations. They are reminiscent of the "anise and melilot" in a poem of Sappho's (No. LI in Ivanov's translation). Thus, the night from the first line of this tercet could also be associated with love.[28] The erotic symbolism of bees is often found in Vjačeslav Ivanov, too, and even in the triptych "Rozy" it is present as an allusion: "I bliže l'net žužžaščix *lask* ugroza."

The last tercet is a variation of the first: instead of honey and sun, the poet offers his beloved a wild (absurd) gift: "an uncomely, dry necklace of dead bees, which have transformed honey into sunshine." Here, we shall quote once again the apparent subtext from Vjačeslav Ivanov:

> Я буду петь, из темного огня
> И звездных слез свивая ожерелье –
> Мой дар тебе для свадебного дня.

A necklace is a work of great craftsmanship; for both poets it symbolizes not poetry in general, but specific poems: in Vjačeslav Ivanov's sonnet, lines about love and tears; in Mandel'štam's poem, lines about the bee-kisses which turned the sweetness of life into light and warmth.[29]

The last tercet of Mandel'štam's "Vozmi na radost'" echoes the *pointe* of his earlier poem "Ne verja voskresen'ja čudu" (1916):[30]

> Нам остается только имя –
> Чудесный звук, на долгий срок.
> *Прими ж ладонями моими*
> *Пересыпаемый песок.*

Here the poet offers his addressee another "absurd gift" from his palms. However, the serious tonality of the last two lines indicates that this is not innocent play on the seashore or on the river bank. This gift obviously has a symbolic meaning. And again the explanation of this symbolism is found in Vjačeslav Ivanov's book, of which Mandel'štam was so fond in 1909 (*Po zvezdam*, p. 273):

Пересыпание золотого песку есть образ нечуждый символике религиозной: он имеет отношение к высшим состояниям мистического созерцания. Как же пользуется им Vielé-Griffin? Для прославления химеры, для апофеоза иллюзии. Горсть песку достаточна для поэта, чтобы вообразить себя владельцем груд золота. Самые тусклые дни самого ничтожного существования он волен превратить мечтой в «духовную вечность» (éternité spirituelle).

It is noteworthy that Mandel'štam compared eternity to sea sand as early as 1913 ("V taverne vorovskaja šajka"). In his 1917 poem "Ešče daleko asfodelej" there is another enigmatic image connected with sand:

И раскрывается с шуршаньем
Печальный веер прошлых лет,
Туда, где с темным содроганьем
*В песок зарылся амулет;*
Туда душа моя стремится,
За мыс туманный Меганом,
И черный парус возвратится
Оттуда после похорон!

I believe that the image of the "amulet buried in the sand" should be deciphered as "poetry addressed to the reader in posterity."[31] To my understanding, Mandel'štam refers here to the image of the "bottle found in the sand" in the following passage from his essay "O sobesednike" (1913):

У каждого человека есть друзья. Почему бы поэту не обращаться к друзьям, к естественно близким ему людям? Мореплаватель в критическую минуту бросает в воды океана запечатанную бутылку с именем своим и описанием своей судьбы. Спустя долгие годы, скитаясь по дюнам, я нахожу ее в песке, прочитываю письмо, узнаю дату события, последнюю волю погибшего. Я имел право сделать это. Я не распечатал чужого письма. Письмо, запечатанное в бутылке, адресовано тому, кто найдет ее. Нашел я. Значит, я и есть таинственный адресат.

Мой дар убог, и голос мой не громок,
Но я живу — и на земли мое
Кому-нибудь любезно бытие:
Его найдет далекий мой потомок

В моих стихах; как знать? душа моя
С его душой окажется в сношеньи,
И как нашел я друга в поколеньи,
Читателя найду в потомстве я.

Читая стихотворение Боратынского, я испытываю то же самое
чувство, как если бы в мои руки попала такая бутылка. Океан
всей своей огромной стихией пришел ей на помощь — помог испол-
нить ее предназначение, и чувство провиденциального охватывает
нашедшего. В бросании мореходом бутылки в волны и в посылке
стихотворения Боратынским есть два одинаково отчетливо вы-
раженных момента. Письмо, равно и стихотворение, ни к кому в
частности определенно не адресованы. Тем не менее оба имеют
адресата: письмо — того, кто случайно заметит бутылку в песке,
стихотворение — «читателя в потомстве». Хотел бы я знать, кто
из тех, кому попадутся в глаза названные строки Боратынского,
не вздрогнет радостной и жуткой дрожью, какая бывает, когда
неожиданно окликнут по имени.

In the 1923 poem "A nebo buduščim beremenno," longing for an
irretrievably lost golden age of humanity gives place to a dim hope for
a future golden age:

Давайте все покроем заново
Камчатной скатертью пространства,
Переговариваясь, радуясь,
Друг другу подавая брашна.
На круговом, на мирном судьбище
Зарею кровь оледенится.
В беременном глубоком будущем
*Жужжит большая медуница.*

There is no doubt that the buzzing honeybee (a metaphor for an airplane)
is one of the servants of the goddess of fertility.[32]

In the 1930s, bees are mentioned in the humorous verses to Anna
Axmatova, "Privykajut k pčelovodu pčely" (1930), and in a variant of
the poem "Ariost" (1933–1936): "Nad rozoj muskusnoj žužžanie pčely."
In the latter poem, the buzzing bee, together with the grasshopper and
the cicadas, enlivens the southern landscape. In October 1930, the
rapacious wasp appears in Mandel'štam's reminiscences of childhood:

Вспомнишь на даче осу,
Детский чернильный пенал,

Или чернику в лесу,
Что никогда не сбирал.[33]

Mandel'štam's principal poem about wasps was written in Voronezh
on February 8, 1937. There wasps acquired a metaphoric meaning:

Вооруженный зреньем узких ос,
Сосущих ось земную, ось земную,
Я чую все, с чем свидеться пришлось,
И вспоминаю наизусть и всуе.

И не рисую я, и не пою,
И не вожу смычком черноголосым:
Я только в жизнь впиваюсь и люблю
Завидовать могучим хитрым осам.

О, если б и меня когда-нибудь могло
Заставить, сон и смерть минуя,
Стрекало воздуха и летнее тепло
Услышать ось земную, ось земную . . .

Mandel'štam composed this poem while he was working on his notorious
"Stixi o Staline" (see in Mrs. Mandel'štam's *Vospominanija*, the chapter
"Oda," pp. 216–220). Despite Mrs. Mandel'štam's assertion that this
"Ode" was destroyed, at least one copy of it (made in Moscow, 1937),
fortunately, has been preserved. In the first stanza of the "Ode" the
metaphoric meaning of the world's axis has plausible historical-political
connotations:

Когда б я уголь взял для высшей похвалы –
Для радости рисунка непреложной, –
Я б воздух расчертил на хитрые углы
И осторожно и тревожно,
Чтоб настоящее в чертах отозвалось,
В искусстве с дерзостью гранича,
Я б рассказал о том, *кто сдвинул мира ось*,
Ста сорока народов чтя обычай.

One should not, however, simplify the message of "Vooruzennyj zren'em
uzkix os" interpreting it exclusively as the reflection of a specific epoch.
The meaning of the image of wasps is far broader: the mighty, rapacious wasps are the strong of this world in general. These wasps do not
suck the heavy rose, but the very axis of the Earth, on which is supported
and around which revolves our world. The poet does not identify

himself with the rapacious wasps: he merely envies them, although he has learned to see with their eyes. The poem reveals the poet's great experience of life, his perception of all the phenomena to which he was a witness. Yet, nevertheless, the poet only dreams that he might understand and comprehend the essence of things: "to hear the Earth's axis, the Earth's axis."[34]

The second quatrain of Il'ja Sel'vinskij's 1958 poem "Tvorčestvo" seems to be a direct response to Mandel'štam's "Vooružennyj zren'em uzkix os," published in 1955 (*Prostor* 4):

> Говорят, что композитор слышит
> На три сотни звуков больше нас,
> Но они безмолвствуют иль свищут,
> Кляксами на ноты устремясь.
>
> Может быть, трагедия поэта
> В том, что основное не далось:
> Он поет, как птица, но при этом
> *Слышит*, как скрипит *земная ось*.

Mandel'štam is a difficult poet, a poet of cryptic messages. In order to understand him one must indeed assimilate his culture. To reveal all his literary subtexts is the fundamental problem which stands before investigators of his poetry. "Postepenno rasširjaja oblast' bezuslovnogo i obščeobjazatel'nogo znanija o poète, my rasčiščaem dorogu ego posmertnoj sud'be" — so wrote Mandel'štam in "Barsuč'ja nora."[35]

# VI

## THE SOIL AND DESTINY

О, знал бы я, что так бывает,
Когда пускался на дебют,
Что строчки с кровью — убивают,
Нахлынут горлом и убьют!

От шуток с этой подоплекой
Я б отказался наотрез.
Начало было так далеко,
Так робок первый интерес.

Но старость — это Рим, который
Взамен турусов и колес
Не читки требует с актера,
А полной гибели всерьез.

Когда строку диктует чувство,
Оно на сцену шлет раба,
И тут кончается искусство,
И дышат почва и судьба.

Пастернак

### The Third Rome

The poem "Na rozval'njax, uložennyx solomoj" was written at the
end of March during Mandel'štam's visit to Moscow in February-June,
1916. It seems to have been his first encounter with the "senior" capital
of Russia. Certainly the theme of Moscow begins in his poetry at this
time.

I    1.  *На розвальнях, уложенных соломой,*
     2.  Едва прикрытые рогожей роковой,
     3.  От Воробьевых гор до церковки знакомой
     4.  *Мы ехали* огромною Москвой.

<table>
<tr><td>II</td><td>5.</td><td>А в Угличе играют дети в бабки,</td></tr>
<tr><td></td><td>6.</td><td>И пахнет хлеб, оставленный в печи.</td></tr>
<tr><td></td><td>7.</td><td>*По улицам меня везут* без шапки,</td></tr>
<tr><td></td><td>8.</td><td>И теплятся в часовне три свечи.</td></tr>
<tr><td>III</td><td>9.</td><td>Не три свечи горели, а три встречи –</td></tr>
<tr><td></td><td>10.</td><td>Одну из них сам Бог благословил,</td></tr>
<tr><td></td><td>11.</td><td>Четвертой не бывать, а Рим далече, –</td></tr>
<tr><td></td><td>12.</td><td>И никогда он Рима не любил.</td></tr>
<tr><td>IV</td><td>13.</td><td>*Ныряли сани* в черные ухабы,</td></tr>
<tr><td></td><td>14.</td><td>И возвращался с гульбища народ.</td></tr>
<tr><td></td><td>15.</td><td>Худые мужики и злые бабы</td></tr>
<tr><td></td><td>16.</td><td>Переминались у ворот.</td></tr>
<tr><td>V</td><td>17.</td><td>Сырая даль от птичьих стай чернела,</td></tr>
<tr><td></td><td>18.</td><td>И связанные руки затекли;</td></tr>
<tr><td></td><td>19.</td><td>*Царевича везут*, немеет страшно тело, –</td></tr>
<tr><td></td><td>20.</td><td>И рыжую *солому* подожгли.</td></tr>
</table>

As often happens in poems with an odd number of stanzas, the central stanza (III) is the most prominent. It conveys the philosophical message of the poem: the idea of "Moscow, the Third Rome." All the other stanzas are descriptive. Stanzas I and IV, on the one hand, and stanzas II and V, on the other, parallel each other. The former two are characterized by the image of the sledge and by the past tense of the verbs of motion (*Na rozval'njax . . . my exali: Nyrjali sani*). In the latter two, the verb of motion is in the present tense (*vezut*). The third line of the fifth stanza, varies, as it were, the same line of the second (*Po ulicam menja vezut: Careviča vezut*). Finally, the straw (*soloma*) from the first stanza is repeated in the last. Thus, the poem acquires a ring-like composition.

In the poem, a clear reference is made to Russia at the turn of the seventeenth century. Uglič mentioned in the second stanza, definitely points to the Time of Troubles, as does the image of the Tsarevich brought to Moscow a prisoner, his hands bound. However, Marina Cvetaeva indicates in her memoirs ("Istorija odnogo posvjaščenija," *Oxford Slavonic Papers* XI, 1964, 134) that this poem was written to her, when she "was giving Moscow as a present to Mandel'štam" ("Kogda ja Mandel'štamu darila Moskvu").[1] In that case, we may assume that there is a double time guage in this poem, a device which Mandel'štam used, for example, in "Peterburgskie strofy" (1913), where Evgenij from Puškin's *Mednyj vsadnik* inhales gasoline and, ashamed of his poverty, curses his fate ("Čudak Evgenij — bednosti styditsja, / Benzin vdyxaet i sud'bu kljanet").

People from St. Petersburg used to call Moscow a "big village" (*bol'šaja derevnja*). Mandel'štam might have been surprised to see yard-keepers dressed like peasants (lines 15 and 16: "Xudye mužiki i zlye baby / Pereminalis' u vorot"). The "znakomaja cerkovka" from the first stanza might be the famous *Iverskaja časovnja* at the *Voznesenskie vorota* of the *Kitaj-gorod*, a chapel which was built after 1648. But, in any case, the entire scenario can be applied to seventeenth-century Moscow as well.

Cvetaeva compared herself to Maryna Mniszek on several occasions; for example in the 1916 poem "Dimitrij! Marina!" (*Versty*, 1922), in the cycle "Marina" (April 1921; *Remeslo*, 1923), or in the "Poèma konca" (1924): "Takova u nas, Marinok, / Spes', u nas poljaček to . . ." Is this the reason that Mandel'štam identified himself with Dimitrij, since he was infatuated with Cvetaeva? The poem "Dimitrij! Marina!" was written on March 29-30, during Mandel'štam's stay in Moscow. I shall quote its beginning:

> Димитрий! Марина! В мире
> Согласнее нету ваших
> Единой волною вскинутых,
> Единой волною смытых
> Судеб! Имен!

Later in the poem Cvetaeva speaks of herself:

> Марина! Царица — Царю,
> Звезда — самозванцу!
> Тебя пою,
> Злую красу твою,
> Лик без румянца.
> Во славу твою грешу
> Царским грехом гордым.
> Славное твое имя
> Славно ношу.

"Predstavim sebe," Lidija Ginzburg writes in her article "Poètika Osipa Mandel'štama" (*Izvestija AN SSSR, Serija literatury i jazyka*, 1972, no. 4, 322), "čto stixotvorenie 'Na rozval'njax' soprovoždaetsja posvjaščeniem — Marine Cvetaevoj. Imja Marina daet associaciju s puškinskim 'Borisom Godunovym' i ključ k skrytoj ljubovnoj teme stixotvorenija. Ona — Marina, poètomu on — Dimitrij, i v to že vremja

on tot, kto pišet o Dimitrii i Marine." Be it as it may, these associations
are entirely outside of the text; most likely they only explain the first
impulse for writing the poem. "Na rozval'njax" is by no means a love
poem. Mandel'štam's infatuation with Cvetaeva has no bearing what-
soever on the main message of the poem, that is, on the problem broached
in the third stanza. A vacillation between Catholicism and Orthodoxy
was characteristic of the first Pretender. It was Mandel'štam's own
problem as well. As is known, he formally converted to Lutheranism in
order to be able to enter the University of St. Petersburg (that means,
before the fall semester, 1911).[2] In 1913 and 1914 he gravitated toward
Catholicism, under the influence of Čaadaev's Catholic universalism
(see his essay "Petr Čaadaev," published in *Apollon*, in 1915). Obviously,
in 1916 he was already emotionally attracted by Orthodoxy, probably
influenced by Pavel Florenskij's writings.[3] As for Marina Cvetaeva,
she had always been a devout Orthodox believer.

Now let us approach the poem from another chronological perspective, recalling the events of the Time of Troubles. From this point of
view, we may consider the entire poem to be an internal monologue of
the Tsarevich, a first person narration, as it were. In the last stanza,
however, the Tsarevich speaks of himself in the third person in order to
emphasize his royal title: "Careviča vezut, nemeet strašno telo," varying
the line from the second stanza: "Po ulicam vezut menja bez šapki."

Mandel'štam's Tsarevich is not a historical personality, but rather
a generalized type of those pretenders that appeared during the Time of
Troubles (several Dimitrijs, Ivan and Petr). The only Tsarevich who
was brought to Moscow as a prisoner under the guard of *strelcy* (in 1614)
was Ivan, the son of Maryna Mniszek by *Tušinskij Vor*. However,
Mandel'štam's Tsarevich is obviously not a three-year-old child, and,
moreover, Tsarevich Ivan was hanged, while Mandel'štam's Tsarevich
is to be burned (since the straw covering the sledge in the first stanza is
apparently the same "yellow straw" that is being set to fire in the last
stanza). As is known, the corpse of the first Pretender was exhumed and
burned in the winter of 1606. It is possible that from all these historical
facts Mandel'štam composed a generalized type of Tsarevich, a victim
of inhuman cruelty. There is no doubt that Mandel'štam had known of
the various pretenders since his school years.

It is already implied in the first stanza that the ride in the sledge is
not a simple pleasure trip. The "fatal bast mat" (*rokovaja rogoža*)
from the second line introduces a disturbing note. The Tsarevich's
thoughts have turned to Uglič, where many years before Tsar Ivan's son
Dimitrij was killed while playing a Russian popular game, *svajka*, with
other children. In Uglič a normal life is going on. New children are

playing another popular game in which animal knucklebones are used. However, the *igra v babki* serves as a reminder of death in Mandel'štam's poems written in 1923, "Našedšij podkovu" ("Deti igrajut v babki pozvonkami umeršyx životnyx. / Xrupkoe letoisčislenie našej èry prixodit k koncu") and "Grifel'naja oda" ("I v babki nežnaja igra"). The *igra v babki* intersects with other images from "Vek" (*pozvonki, xrebet, xrjašč rebenka, temja žizni, razbityj pozvonočnik*) and from "Jazyk bulyžnika" (*nežnye l'vjata* and *igra kljatvoj kak jablokom;* compare also in "Našedšij podkovu": "Tak *rebenok* otvečaet: 'Ja dam tebe *jabloko*,' ili: 'Ja ne dam tebe *jabloka*' "), etc. This complex imagery is analyzed in D. M. Segal's article "Grifel'naja oda" (*Russian Literature* 2, 1972) and in Steven Broyde's book mentioned above, *Osip Mandel'štam and His Age: A Commentary on the Themes of War and Revolution in the Poetry, 1913–1923* (1975). I cannot but agree with D. M. Segal's conclusion: " . . . i v 'Grifel'noj ode' nesomnenno soxranjaetsja svjaz' igry v babki s *vremenem:* igrajut deti, predstavljajuščie mladenčestvo, *molodoe* vremja, a sami babki — èto simvol smerti, *starejuščego, umirajuščego* vremeni, no odnovremenno i *pamjati, sleda,* ibo oni xranjatsja v zemle 's odinakovoj počest'ju' narjadu s 'raznoobraznymi mednymi, zolotymi i bronzovymi lepeškami' ('Našedšij podkovu')." I have only one small reservation: I would prefer to speak of "analogue" rather than "symbol."

The image of the three candles in the chapel is not quite clear: people light candles in churches both for the living and the dead. From these three candles the Tsarevich's thoughts leap to the three crucial meetings of humanity in the next stanza. These three meetings are Rome, Byzantium, and Moscow, that is, the three meetings of mankind and Providence. Our Lord, says Mandel'štam, never liked Rome. Which of the other two meetings did He then bless: Byzantium, the cradle of the true Faith, or Moscow, its heir? It is more likely that Byzantium was the blessed one.

Mandel'štam must have known the legends about the foundation of Constantinople, the miraculous dream of Constantine, and the tracing by the emperor, walking spear in hand, of the boundary of the destined capital: "The growing circumference was observed with astonishment by the assistants, who, at length, ventured to observe that he had already exceeded the most ample measure of a great city. 'I shall still advance,' replied Constantine, 'till He, the invisible guide who marches before me, thinks proper to stop'."[4] These words are to be compared with the beginning of the poem "Ajja-Sofija" (1912):

Айя-София — здесь остановиться
Судил Господь народам и царям!

The church of St. Sophia, too, was founded by Constantine and re-placed, after its destruction during the Nika Riot, by a magnificent temple during the reign of Justinian.[5]

However, Byzantium had perished and the Grace of God had passed over to Russia.

The doctrine of "Moscow, the Third Rome" was elaborated during the reign of Ivan III (1462–1505) and Vasilij III (1505–1533). It was aphoristically formulated by a monk of the Eleazar monastery in Pskov, the *starec* Filofej, in a letter to the *d'jak* Mixail Munexin of Pskov: "I da vesi, xristoljubče i bogoljubče, jako vsja xristianskaja carstva preidoša v konec i snidošasja vo edino carstvo našego gosudarja, po proročeskim knigam, to est' rossijskoe carstvo; *dva ubo Rima padoša, a tretij stoit, a četvertomu ne byti.*" In his essay "Petr Čaadaev," Mandel'-štam spoke about this doctrine rather skeptically: ".... Čaadaev i slovom ne obmolvilsja o 'Moskve — Tret'jem Rime'. V ètoj idee on mog uvidet' tol'ko čaxluju vydumku kievskix [sic] monaxov. Malo odnoj gotovnosti, malo dobrogo želanija, čtoby 'načat'' istoriju. Ee voobšče ne myslimo *načat'*. Ne xvataet preemstvennosti, edinstva." When he wrote that, he still believed that continuity and unity were found in Catholic universalism. By 1916, his attitude had changed: he used the doctrine of "Moscow, the Third Rome" quite seriously as a poetic myth.

Not much remains to be said about the last two stanzas. The fourth stanza is descriptive. As was mentioned, line 13 continues the motif of the ride in the sledges from the first stanza. In the last stanza the Tsarevich reveals his royal identity. The straw set afire echoes the frightening image of the "fatal bast mat" from the first stanza.

In *Vtoraja kniga* (p. 279) Mrs. Mandel'štam also identifies the poet with the Tsarevich: "Bednyj moj carevič — on pomnil, čto ego krov' otjagoščena 'nasledstvom ovcevodov, patriarxov i carej'." She points out that in "Na rozval'njax" we see reflected the premonition of deportation and a terrible death ("predčuvstvie nasil'nogo uvoza i strašnoj smerti"). This motif appeared for the first time in Mandel'štam's poetry in precisely this poem. Did it result from a naïve Marina–Dimitrij game with Cvetaeva? Or was it not a prophetic premonition?

### The Silence

The theme of silence appears in the young Mandel'štam's work in a 1909 poem:

Ни о чем не нужно говорить,
Ничему не следует учить . . .

and in a 1910 poem which has the Tjutčevian title "Silentium." As E. A. Toddes has shown (*IJSLP* XVII, 1974), Mandel'štam's "conversation" with Tjutčev started in his earliest poems (1908–1909) and continued through his entire life.

The thematic "frame-work" of Mandel'štam's "Silence" is the myth of Aphrodite. Its poetic space and time is the world before the embodiment of the goddess of beauty:

> Она еще не родилась,
> Она и музыка и слово,
> И потому всего живого
> Ненарушаемая связь.
>
> Спокойно дышат моря груди,
> Но, как безумный, светел день,
> И пены бледная сирень
> В мутно-лазоревом сосуде.
>
> Да обретут мои уста
> Первоначальную немоту,
> Как кристаллическую ноту,
> Что от рождения чиста!
>
> Останься пеной, Афродита,
> И слово в музыку вернись,
> И сердце сердца устыдись,
> С первоосновой жизни слито!

Stylistically and syntactically, the poem breaks into two equal parts [2 + 2]. The first two stanzas are narrative-descriptive. The description is objective (the present tense zero copula and the form *dyšat* refer to the third person, singular or plural, respectively). The verb which appears in the perfective past is modified by the negative particle *ne*; this negation actually abolishes the reference to the past time: "Ona [Afrodita] ešče ne rodilas' " = *ee ešče net*. The third and fourth stanzas are rhetorical; they contain four verbs in the imperative. High-style Slavonicisms in the ninth line signal a transition from a "calm" narrative to an "elated" rhetoric ("*Da obretut* moi *usta*"). There are no "elevated" words in the first two stanzas.

The thematic division of the poem does not coincide with the syntactic; the first, second, and fourth stanzas develop the theme of Aphrodite. The third stanza is a solemn rhetorical digression, the poet's address to himself. Strictly speaking, the poem would have even greater compactness without this stanza. However, the fact that this stanza is thus set off is artistically significant: it contains the basic message of the entire poem.

Victor Terras pointed out the theme of the "reversed flow of time" in Mandel'štam's "Silentium," a theme which in general is characteristic of Mandel'štam (it is most vividly expressed in "Lamark," 1932). Terras characterized the entire poem as "the poet's nostalgia for primordial unity with the cosmos."[6] As early as 1916, Gumilev called "Silentium" an incantatory summoning of the state of pre-being.[7]

Mandel'štam's "Silentium" is not a restatement of Tjutčev's poem; it is, rather, a poetic polemic with Tjutčev. To Tjutčev's subjective world of "mysterious and enchanting thoughts" Mandel'štam opposes an objective world, material (bright day, the calmly breathing bosom of the sea, the shell [*mutno-lazorevyj sosud*], the pale lilac of the foam from which Aphrodite has not yet been born) and spiritual ("the undisturbed bond between all that is alive" — beauty). Whereas Tjutčev emphasizes the *impossibility* of poetic creation:

> Как сердцу высказать себя?
> Другому как понять тебя?
> Поймет ли он, чем ты живешь?
> Мысль изреченная есть ложь . . .

Mandel'štam speaks of its *uselessness*:

> Да обретут мои уста
> Первоначальную немоту,
> Как кристаллическую ноту,
> Что от рождения чиста.

One should not disturb the primordial "bond between all that is alive." We do not need Aphrodite, and the poet adjures her not to be born. The word is also not necessary; the poet bids it revert to music. Of course, the subject here is not our human music, but rather metaphysical music: the spontaneous language of being. In this poem Mandel'štam is still a symbolist.[8] The appeal for human hearts to shy away from each other is a direct reply to Tjutčev's rhetorical questions. Mandel'štam answers that there is no need to express oneself; we do not need to seek understanding from others. Man's most sublime spiritual experience lies in merging with the original essence of life, the primeval harmony of the universe. Let this be only a comforting myth; yet it speaks to us of the full value of being that man finds in the mute contemplation of the world and its beauty.

Thus, the theme of both poems is *voluntary creative silence* which is differently motivated by the two poets. This theme, of course, is only the "lyrical subject." Naturally the poets did not heed the inner voice which summoned them to silence. Both wrote their poems at the beginning of their poetic careers and thereafter enriched Russian poetry with their unique poetic worlds.

The theme of *compulsory creative silence* was to appear in Mandel'-štam's later work. This was something of which Tjutčev could not have even dreamed. The theme is already outlined in the elegy "1 janvarja 1924":

> Я знаю, с каждым днем слабеет жизни выдох,
> Еще немного, — оборвут
> Простую песенку о глиняных обидах
> И губы оловом зальют.

This theme is most sharply expressed in the poem "Ne govori nikomu," written in October 1930, in Tiflis, after a five-year silence. Thus, the theme in this poem is not only creative silence, but actual silence as well, silence in its most usual, earthly sense:

> Не говори никому,
> Все, что ты видел, забудь –
> Птицу, старуху, тюрьму,
> Или еще что-нибудь . . .
>
> Или охватит тебя,
> Только уста разомкнешь,
> При наступлении дня
> Мелкая хвойная дрожь.
>
> Вспомнишь на даче осу,
> Детский чернильный пенал,
> Или чернику в лесу,
> Что никогда не сбирал.

In contrast with the first "silence," this poem forms one syntactical period with a very clear-cut structure. The conjunction *ili*, which begins the second stanza, is used with an adversative meaning: "a ne to, inače, v protivnom slučae." The connective conjunction *i* inevitably suggests itself between the second and third stanzas. Thus, the syntactic structure of the entire period acquires the following appearance: "[Ni o čem] ne govori nikomu, vse . . . zabud' . . . [a ne to] oxvatit tebja . . . drož' [i ty] vspomniš' . . . osu . . . penal . . . ili černiku."

All of the verbs in this poem are used in the second person only; in the main clauses, which comprise the "core" of the syntactic period, they are encountered only in the imperative (in stanza 1) and simple future (stanzas 2 and 3). The past tense is found only in object clauses (with the relative pronoun *čto*). The poem is directed to a specific addressee. The second and third stanza narration pertains to the potential (conditional) future. Judging by the autobiographical hints in the second and third stanzas (which will be discussed later) the addressee of the poem is the poet himself. In this respect, Mandel'štam's second "silence" is closer to Tjutčev's "Silentium!" than to his own "Silentium" of 1910. Mandel'štam's *ne govori* clearly echoes Tjutčev's *molči*.

The theme of the first stanza is a summons to silence and oblivion. The first line is elliptical, but the implied member of the clause is easily supplied: "[Ni o čem] ne govori nikomu" — do not say anything to anybody, that is, speak with nobody. This line should be compared with a fragment of a poem from 1931 which Mandel'štam destroyed. Here, the predicate, not the object, is omitted:

> Замолчи! *Ни о чем, никогда, никому –*
> Там в пожарище время поет . . .

Both lines have the same meaning.

The triad "ptica, staruxa, tjur'ma" is autobiographical. It is a reminiscence of Mandel'štam's incarceration in a Wrangel jail in Theodosia at the end of 1919 or the beginning of 1920, under a charge which normally resulted in death by firing squad.[9] Mandel'štam's autobiographical prose piece "Feodosija" (1925) is devoted to that time. In the second sketch, titled "Staruxina ptica," the theme of life's troubles is clearly heard. We will cite a subtext from this section for two of the three images in the aforementioned triad:

В одной из мазанок у *старушки* я снял комнату в цену куриного яйца. Как и все карантинные хозяйки, старушка жила *в предсмертной праздничной чистоте*. Домишко свой она не просто прибрала, а *обрядила* . . . Пахло хлебом, керосиновым перегаром матовой детской лампы и чистым старческим дыханием . . . Я был рад, что в комнатах надышано, что кто-то возится за стенкой, приготовляя обед из картошки, луковицы и горсточки риса. Старушка жильца держала как *птицу*, считая, что ему нужно переменить воду, почистить клетку, насыпать зерна. *В то время лучше было быть птицей, чем человеком*, и соблазн стать старухиной птицей был велик.

Nevertheless, the poetic imagery of this triad is not completely disclosed by the subtext. The triad is not a simple auto-reminiscence. The contrasting juxtaposition of bird and jail continues the tradition of the prison theme in Russian poetry; it evokes for the reader Puškin's and Lermontov's lines:

Сижу за решеткой в темнице сырой.
Вскормленный в неволе орел молодой,
Мой грустный товарищ, махая крылом,
Кровавую пищу клюет под окном . . .
. . . . . . . . . . . . . . . . . .
Зачем я не птица, не ворон степной,
Пролетевший сейчас надо мной?
Зачем не могу в небесах я парить
И одну лишь свободу любить?

In the compressed poetic line, the three members of the triad fuse into one complex "jail" image; and the good-natured Crimean landlady is transformed into a frightful old woman.[10] The last line of the first stanza, "Ili ešče čto-nibud'," points to the open-ended flow of the reminiscences, which will continue in the third stanza.

The second stanza begins with the adversative conjunction *ili* (*a neto*) which sounds like a threat. The theme of this stanza is fear of execution. The key to this interpretation is given in the metonymy of the execution (in the adverbial modifier of time): *pri nastuplenii dnja.* As is known, executions in general, and execution by firing squad in particular, are usually carried out at dawn. Thus, "melkaja, xvojnaja [koljuščaja] drož' " is not simply trembling caused by the morning cold; it is death trembling.

There is a great deal of testimony offered by people who have looked death in the eye (people drowning, led to execution) concerning the vivid stream of chance recollections which occur at the fatal moments. In Mandel'štam's poem these are the three touching reminiscences of childhood; they are in sharp contrast with the ominous jail triad of the first stanza.[11] These reminiscences are also autobiographical. In "Pute-šestvie v Armeniju," written in 1931, Mandel'štam shared the following confession with his readers: "V detstve iz glupogo samoljubija, iz ložnoj gordyni ja nikogda ne xodil po jagody i ne nagibalsja za gribami." The author seemingly regrets his childhood whim, is sorry about his refusal to take part in the simple joys of children. Viewed against this background, the "never" of the last line can be interpreted as projecting itself into the future as well, meaning "nevermore": "i nikogda ne budeš' sbirat'."

Mandel'štam's second "silence" is not a myth, not a "lyrical subject";

it is a staggering truth of art and life. But even here the poet did not pay heed to his inner voice — he did not fall silent. On the 6th of July 1931, he began to speak "at the top of his voice":

> Я больше не ребенок.
>
>                                Ты, могила,
> Не смей учить горбатого — молчи!
> Я говорю за всех с такою силой,
> Чтоб нёбо стало небом, чтобы губы
> Потрескались, как розовая глина.[12]

At this time, the "wolf cycle" had already been written. Afterwards, two years later, in November 1933, the poet wrote his notorious invective "My živem, pod soboju ne čuja strany"; thereupon he began his road to Calvary . . .

### The Poet in His Grave

In August 1836, Aleksandr Puškin, brought to bay by malicious harassment, wrote the lines which entered all schoolbooks:

> Я памятник себе воздвиг нерукотворный,
> К нему не зарастет народная тропа . . .
> . . . . . . . . . . . . . . . . . . . . . .
> Слух обо мне пройдет по всей Руси великой,
> *И назовет меня всяк сущий в ней язык . . .*

A century later, in May 1935, another persecuted Russian poet, Osip Mandel'štam, wrote the tragic lines that echo those of Puškin:

> Да, я лежу в земле, губами шевеля,
> *Но то, что я скажу, заучит каждый школьник . . .*

The most recent investigator of Puškin's "Monument" writes:[13]

Едва ли мы погрешим против истины, если предположим, что стихотворение «Я памятник себе воздвиг» мыслилось поэтом как предсмертное, как своего рода прощание с жизнью и творчеством в предчувствии близкой кончины, потому что и самое слово «памятник» вызывало прежде всего представление о надгробии. «Кладбищенская» тема в лирике Пушкина последнего года его жизни была темой навязчивой, постоянно возвращавшейся в его сознание. . . .

The "graveyard theme" is even more directly expressed in Mandel'štam: in his Voronezh exile, the poet sees himself as already buried.

1. Да, я лежу в земле, губами шевеля,
2. Но то, что я скажу, заучит каждый школьник:
3. На Красной площади всего круглей земля,
4. И скат ее твердеет добровольный,
5. На Красной площади земля всего круглей,
6. И скат ее нечаянно раздольный,
7. Откидываясь вниз до рисовых полей,
8. Покуда на земле последний жив невольник.

The last line clearly echoes Puškin's "Pamjatnik," too: "...dokol' v podlunnom mire / Živ budet xot' odin piit." Thus, while reading Mandel'štam's poem, we hear Puškin's voice, in the same way as Mandel'štam heard Puškin's ballad about the poor knight when he read Nekrasov's "Vlas" (see Chapter One, p. 18).

The noun *zemlja* is probably the most suggestive of this poem. It is repeated four times: twice in the nominative, in the function of subject (lines 3 and 5) and twice in the prepositional (locative) case, in the function of adverbial modifier of place (lines 1 and 8). Lines 5 and 6 actually are a variation of the previous two (3 and 4). Only the epithets of the slope (*skat*) are different (*dobrovol'nyj* and *nečajanno razdol'nyj*). As we will see later, the interplay of these two epithets is very significant. The two locatives are opposed to each other (*v zemle: na zemle*); the sharp contrast between them is achieved by juxtaposition of the two prepositions: "*in* the earth" and "*on* the earth."[14]

The interplay of rhymes in the poem is meaningful, as well. Its rhyme pattern can be represented by the following scheme: a $B_1$ a $B_2$ c $B_2$ c $B_1$, in which the small letters indicate masculine rhymes and the capital letters feminine ones. The subscript figures point out pairs of exact rhymes: $B_1$–$B_1$; $B_2$–$B_2$. The pairs $B_1$–$B_2$ and $B_2$–$B_1$ are inexact rhymes. On the one hand, all even lines are linked together by one continuous rhyme. On the other, lines two:eight and four:six are tied together even more closely. Thus, the rhyme *nevol'nik* recalls its exact counterpart from line two: *škol'nik*. When we notice this, we may recollect the entire text of the first two lines; then the contrast of prepositions in the adverbial modifiers *v zemle* and *na zemle* becomes even more conspicuous.

There are other parallelisms in the poem; they are readily apparent. The repeated phrases "*na Krasnoj ploščadi*" (lines 3 and 5) and "*i skat ee*" (lines 4 and 6) are connected (semantically and syntactically) with the subject *zemlja.* Thus, the "Earth" becomes the central image of the entire poem.

The image of "moving lips" is Mandel'štam's favorite metaphor for the process of poetic creation. It recurs in the quatrain which directly follows the poem under investigation in the Voronezh Notebook:

> Лишив меня морей, разбега и разлета,
> И дав стопе упор насильственной земли,
> Чего добились вы? Блестящего расчета:
> Губ шевелящихся отнять вы не могли.

In the "coercive land," in Voronezh exile, the poet goes on composing his inspired songs. It will be noted that the image of the sea in this quatrain is the same Puškinian image of the free element (*svobodnaja stixija*).[15]

The "poetic lips" are an image which Mandel'štam frequently associates with the theme of death. Such a leitmotif appeared in his poetry as early as November 1920, in the poem "Ja slovo pozabyl, čto ja xotel skazat' "

> Но я забыл, что я хочу сказать,
> И мысль бесплотная в чертог теней вернется.
>
> Все не о том прозрачная твердит,
> Все ласточка, подружка, Антигона . . .
> *А на губах как черный лед горит*
> *Стигийского воспоминанье звона.*

In the poem "Xolodok ščekočet temja" (1922), this leitmotif undergoes a modification. Here it clearly expresses the theme of death as the price that the poet has to pay for his poetry:

> Видно даром не проходит
> *Шевеленье этих губ,*
> И вершина колобродит,
> Обреченная на сруб.

This stanza has much in common with the lines from "1 janvarja 1924," which anticipate the mood of the Voronezh poems:

> Я знаю, с каждым днем слабеет жизни выдох,
> Еще немного, — оборвут
> Простую песенку о глиняных обидах
> *И губы оловом зальют.*

Almost a decade later, in May 1933, the poet ends his monologue on the art of poetry, "Ne iskušaj čužyx narečij," with the image of the sponge soaked in vinegar and meant for his lips:

> И в наказанье за гордыню, неисправимый звуколюб,
> *Получишь уксусную губку ты для изменнических губ.*

Thus the autobiographic image of crucifixion, common to a number of twentieth-century Russian poets (Belyj, Blok, Majakovskij, Xlebnikov, Pasternak, and others) finds its way also into the poetry of Mandel'štam.[16]

In the central lines of the poem (3–6) there appears the image of the Red Square, which is actually a convex surface, its convexity being particularly conspicuous if one looks from the Historical Museum in the direction of the cathedral of Vasilij Blažennyj. The hyperbolic superlative degree *vsego kruglej* clearly indicates that the image is metaphoric; actually, it is but a paraphrase of another stock metaphor, *pup zemli*.[17]

Since the phrase *zemlja vsego kruglej* deciphers as the "hub of the universe," the modifier "vsego kruglej" acquires positive semantic value. The positive image of the earth is sharply opposed to the negative one, the "coersive land" (*nasil'stvennaja zemlja*) from the poem which follows in the Voronezh Notebook "Da, ja ležu v zemle." The noun *zemlja* itself is rather neutral, and in both cases the modifiers assign the whole phrase either to the positive or negative semantic field. Thus, the second poem reveals the other side of the coin.

The verb *tverdet'* is apparently used with metaphoric meaning: "stanovit'sja vse bolee rešitel'nym, stojkim, nepokolebimym," which is a positive concept. Thus, the hardening of Red Square's slope might be explained as a mataphor for its growing determination to fulfil its historic mission, to achieve the goal stated in the last line of the poem.

The first adjective modifying the noun *skat*, *dobrovol'nyj*, undoubtedly belongs to the positive semantic field. The second adjective, *razdol'nyj* (wide, free, thus: untrammeled), normally has a more or less positive value. However, it is modified by the adverb *nečajanno* (*neožidanno, nepredvidenno*) which might have a negative shade of meaning. Does the epithet *nečajanno razdol'nyj* indicate that the hardening of the slope might go out of control?

Mandel'štam has a negative image of the earth's slope, in his poem "Stixi o russkoj poezii, II" (1932):

> Гром живет своим накатом –
> Что ему до наших бед?
> .  .  .  .  .  .  .  .  .  .  .  .  .

Зашумела, задрожала,
Как смоковницы листва,
До корней затрепетала
С подмосковными Москва.
Катит гром свою тележку
По торцовой мостовой
И расхаживает ливень
С длинной плеткой ручьевой.

И *угодливо-поката*
Кажется *земля* пока,
И в сапожках мягких *ката*
Выступают *облака*.

In the last stanza the clouds are characterized as the executioner; the earth is a submissive victim. Here again the adjective *pokatyj* is modified by the adverb *ugodlivo*, which transfers its negative shade of meaning to the entire image. Mandel'štam, naturally, always had before his eyes the dark side of the picture, as well.

In April 1935, Mandel'štam used the image of the Red Square in the following poem:

Наушники, наушнички мои,
Попомню я воронежские ночки:
Недопитого голоса́ Аи
И в полночь с Красной площади гудочки . . .

Ну, как метро? Молчи, в себе таи,
Не спрашивай, как набухают почки . . .
А вы, часов кремлевские бои –
Язык пространства, сжатого до точки.

I often had the opportunity to observe that young people who have never seen radio sets with earphones do not understand these lines. Actually there is nothing obscure in them: at midnight, the poet listens to a news broadcast from Moscow, followed by the Kremlin chimes. Anyone who has heard this broadcast knows that the din of the city, including automobile honks, comes from the Red Square for a few seconds before the clock begins to chime. But the poet also hears other voices, the voices of his past life with its pleasures cut short. While the question that opens the second stanza testifies to the poet's interest in current events, such as the construction of the Moscow Underground, the following sentence, on the contrary, suggests withdrawal from life and turning inward. The swelling buds, a metonymy of spring, appeared in a much earlier poem of Mandel'štam, "Vek" (1923), in which the image is more developed:

И еще набухнут почки,
Брызнет зелени побег . . .

I do not think that one should seek any metaphoric meaning in the "swelling buds" of "Naušniki, naušnički moi."

The last two lines provide the poem with a pointed conclusion: if the striking of the Kremlin clock is the language of the space condensed to a dot, then the Kremlin itself turns out to be the center of the world. Thus we are once again confronted with the poetic myth of "Moscow, the third Rome," discussed in the first part of this chapter. One should bear in mind that all myths predicting the bright future of humanity have, among others, this distinctive function: to console the people, to raise their hopes.[18]

The image of rice fields in the penultimate line is a plausible metonymy of China. It will be recalled that in the thirties the semifeudal, semi-colonial China was frequently used in the Soviet phraseology as a typical example of the "enslavement of man by man."

The last line, "Pokuda na zemle poslednij živ nevol'nik," clearly foreshadows the end of the poem "Oboronjaet son svoju donskuju son' " (written on February 13, 1937), which is, in its turn, connected with the poem "Naušniki, naušnički moi" by the image of the Kremlin chimes:

И слушает земля — другие страны — бой
Из хорового падающий короба:
— *Рабу не быть рабом, рабе не быть рабой!*
И хор поет с часами рука об руку.

The third line, which contains an onomatopoeia of the Kremlin chimes ($bu — by — bom \,||b'e — by — bo\underset{.}{i}$), may be interpreted as "the language of the space condensed to a dot." It should also not be forgotten that in the thirties the midnight striking of the Kremlin chimes was followed by the *Internationale*.

Mandel'štam's attitude to his own time, the so-called "period of the personality cult," was sharply negative, and found a frank expression in his poetry and prose. "Da, ja ležu v zemle" tells of the historic mission of the poet's country and expresses his hope in the bright future of all humanity. This is his testament from the grave. And as has been shown, we hear Puškin's voice, too, when we read Mandel'štam's poem. Mandel'štam, I believe, would never misuse Puškin's voice to convey a false message. "K Puškinu u Mandel'štama bylo kakoe-to nebyvaloe, počti groznoe otnošenie — v nem mne čuditsja kakoj-to venec *sverx-čelovečeskogo celomudrija*" (Axmatova, "Listki iz dnevnika").

There is much in common between the messages of the poems "Na rozval'njax, uložennyx solomoj" and "Da, ja ležu v zemle." Both poems deal with the historical mission of Russia, on the one hand, and the cruelty and the victims of history, on the other. In the first poem, the bound Tsarevich is such a victim; in the second poem, the victim is the poet himself, buried alive.

During his lifetime, Mandel'štam could not even dream of having his poem appear in print. Apparently, he addressed it to that "reader in the future generation" of whom he wrote at the very beginning of his literary path (the essay "O sobesednike," 1913). Nor could Puškin think of publishing his "Monument."[19] Nevertheless, both poets were convinced that their poetry would outlive them and reach the generations to come:

> *Нет*, весь я не умру — душа в заветной лире
> Мой прах *переживет* и тленья *убежит* . . .
>
> *Да*, я лежу в земле, губами шевеля,
> Но то, что я скажу, *заучит* каждый школьник . . .

# NOTES
# AUTHOR'S NOTE
# INDEXES

# NOTES

## Chapter I: Concert at the Railroad Station

1.  This is a good example of a later text explaining an earlier metaphor.
2.  In the first four lines of the poem, music is joined with poetry, as it were, and thus the aim of art in a more general sense is clearly stated: it must follow the mood and aspirations of the people. Such artists as Schubert, Mozart, and Goethe followed this principle in their creative work. In regard to Mandel'štam's own poetry, this idea is expressed with the greatest power in a fragment written in 1931:

> Я больше не ребенок.
> 
> Ты, могила,
> Не смей учить горбатого — молчи!
> *Я говорю за всех* с такою силой,
> Чтоб нёбо стало небом, чтобы губы
> Потрескались, как розовая глина.

See also "Narodu nužen stix tainstvenno-rodnoj,/Čtob ot nego on večno prosypalsja" ("Ja nynče v pautine svetovoj," 1937).

One might ponder Mandel'štam's mentioning Hamlet among great artists. By the image of "frightened steps" he describes Hamlet's behavior as man; he presumably considers him also a poet. Not the poem which he (Hamlet) attempted to write, but all his monologues are thus to be considered high poetry. The fact, however, that they were written by Shakespeare, leaves Hamlet in the company of Schubert, Mozart, and Goethe — as a metonym for Shakespeare.

3.  "V citadeli revoljucionnogo slova," *Puti tvorčestva*, Kharkov, 1919, no. 5. Fragments of this article were reprinted in B. Livšic, *U nočnogo okna* (Moscow, 1970), p. 185.

4.  "Pis'mo o russkoj poèzii" (1922), *Sobranie sočinenij* III, 1969, 34.

5.  The poet's widow also asserts that Mandel'štam had Xlebnikov's poems in Samatixa, where he was arrested on May 2, 1938. See Nadežda Mandel'štam, *Vtoraja kniga* (Paris, 1972), p. 107.

6.  "On Reading Mandel'štam," Osip Mandel'štam, *Sobranie sočinenij* I, 2nd ed.; 1967, xiv.

7.  "Kstati, zametila: lučšie poèty (osobenno nemcy: voobšče — lučšie iz poètov) často, berja èpigraf, ne prostavljajut otkuda, živopisuja — ne prostav-

ljajut — kogo, čtoby pomimo iskonnoj sokrovennosti ljubvi i govorenija vešči samoj za sebja dat' lučšemu čitatelju ètu — po sebe znaju! — nesravnennuju radost': v sokrytii otkrytija" ("Istorija odnogo posvjaščenija," *Oxford Slavonic Papers* XI, 1964, 123).

8. The idiom from *Slovo* was used by Mandel'štam also in his translation (dated January 4–8, 1934; Belyj died on January 8) of the 319th sonnet of Petrarch ("Promčalis' dni moi . . ." — "I dí miei piú leggier che nesun cervo"):

О, семицветный мир лживых явлений –
*Печаль жирна* и умиранье наго!
(*Sobranie sočinenij* I, 2nd ed.; 1967, No. 491)

9. Steven Broyde, my former student, called my attention to this *tanka*.

10. In another poem dedicated to the memory of Belyj ("Golubye glaza i gorjaščaja lobnaja kost'") the image of the dragonflies is repeated once more:

Как *стрекозы садятся, не чуя воды, в камыши*,
Налетели на мертвого жирные карандаши.

This image, likewise, recalls a similar one in *Kubok metelej*:

Озеро, зажженное искрами, казалось застывшим зеркалом . . . испод ветром колеблемых *камышей* взлетали *стрекозы* (99) . . . Вот она скрылась в зеленых *камышах:* там слетела с нее одежда; там *пляшущие стрекозы садились* к ней на плечи и грудь (100) . . .

I am also tempted to compare the image of dragonflies in one of Mandel'štam's earliest poems, "Medlitel'nee snežnyj ulej" (1910), with Belyj's "Zima" (1907):

И, если *в ледяных алмазах*
Струится вечности *мороз*,
Здесь — трепетание *стрекоз*
Быстроживущих, синеглазых.
(Мандельштам)

Пусть за стеною, в дымке блеклой,
Сухой, сухой, сухой *мороз*, –
Слетит веселый рой на стекла
*Алмазных*, блещущих *стрекоз*.
(Белый)

In both poems dragonflies appear in a cheerful description of winter. In Mandel'-štam, the dragonflies are a metaphor for a turquoise-blue veil (*birjuzovaja vual'*); in Belyj, they serve as a metaphor for snowflakes. However, Mandel'štam used a frightening image of dragonflies (a metaphor for military airplanes) as early as 1922 ("Veter nam utešen'e prines"):

. . . в лазури почуяли мы
Ассирийские крылья стрекоз . . .

И военной грозой потемнел
Нижний слой помраченных небес . . .

11. "Slovo i kul'tura" was published in the almanac *Drakon* (1921). When
Mandel'štam reprinted the essay in his book *O poèzii* (1928), the sentence quoted
above was changed: "Kto skazal, čto pričina revoljucii — golod v mežduplanet-
nyx prostranstvax?" This is obviously a rhetorical question: Mandel'štam
knew the answer.

12. This poem was published for the first time in the almanac *Lët* (1923) as
a part of the cycle which included two other poems dealing with the theme of
aviation: "Veter nam utešen'e prines" (1922) and "Kak tel'ce malen'koe krylyškom" (1923). See a discussion of these poems in Steven Broyde's *Osip Mandel'-
štam and His Age; A Commentary on the Themes of War and Revolution in the
Poetry, 1913–1923*, Harvard Slavic Monographs I (Cambridge, Mass., 1975).

13. Gurdžiev used to promulgate his teaching in circles of his followers in
Moscow and Petrograd (1915–1917), and in the Caucasus (Essentuki, Sochi,
Tiflis, 1917–1919). In 1919, he even opened the Institute for Harmonious
Development of Man in Tiflis. In June 1920, he left Georgia for Constantinople
"with a fairly large company." Mandel'štam could have heard about Gurdžiev's
teaching either in Moscow or in Petrograd, but most probably in Tiflis, where
he spent the summer and fall of 1920.

Gurdžiev's cosmology was described by P. D. Uspenskij (Ouspensky) in his
book *In Search of the Miraculous* (New York: Harcourt, Brace, and Company,
1949). Uspenskij quotes the following statement made by Guržiev at the beginning of World War I (p. 24): "What is war? *It is the result of planetary influences.*
Somewhere up there two or three planets have approached too near to each
other; tension results ... For them it lasts, perhaps, a second or two. But here,
on the earth, people begin to slaughter one another, and they go on slaughtering
maybe for several years ... They fail to realize to what an extent they are mere
pawns in the game. They think they signify something; they think they can move
about as they like; they think they can decide to do this or that. But in reality
all their movements, all their actions, are the result of planetary influences.
And they themselves signify literally nothing. Then the moon plays a big
part in this. But we will speak about the moon separately." The role of the
Moon is explained on p. 57: "The evolution of large masses of humanity is
opposed to nature's purposes. The evolution of a certain small percentage may
be in accord with nature's purposes ... There exist, therefore, special forces
(of a planetary character) which oppose the evolution of large masses of humanity and keep it at the level it ought to be. For instance, the evolution of humanity
beyond a certain point, or, to speak more correctly, above a certain percentage,
would be fatal for the *moon*. The moon at present *feeds* on organic life, on humanity. Humanity is a part of organic life; this means that humanity is *food* for the
moon. If all men were to become too intelligent they would not want to be
eaten by the moon" (see also p. 139). This "cosmic conflict," according to
Gurdžiev, can be solved by the evolution of organic life (p. 305): "Organic life
... has to evolve, to adapt itself to the needs of the planets and the earth.
Likewise also the moon can be satisfied at one period with the food which is
given her by organic life of a certain quality, but afterward the time comes
when she ceases to be satisfied with the food, cannot grow on it, and begins to
get hungry. Organic life must be able to satisfy this hunger, otherwise it does

not fulfill its function, does not answer its purpose. This means that in order to answer its purpose organic life must evolve and stand on the level of the needs of the planets, the earth and the moon."

Mandel'štam's *pšenica sytogo èfira* might be compared also to Esenin's *lunnyj xleb* and to his image of cosmic satiation and happiness:

> Закинь его [мир, шар] в небо,
> Поставь на столпы!
> Там лунного хлеба
> Златятся снопы.
>
> Там голод и жажда
> В корнях не поют,
> Но зреет однаждный
> Свет ангельских юрт.
>
> («Отчарь», 1917)

14. See Chapter Five, pp. 96–98.

15. See my paper "O vzaimootnošenii stixotvornogo ritma i tematiki," *American Contributions to the Fifth International Congress of Slavists* I (The Hague: Mouton and Co., 1963).

16. The standard Russian idiom for the "horse in a lather" is "lošad' *v myle*." See Ušakov's *Tolkovyj slovar' russkogo jazyka,* the second meaning of *mylo:* "Belaja pena pota na sil'no razgorjačennoj lošadi. *Lošad' vsja v myle,*" and the third meaning of *pena:* "Gustaja, belovataja, s puzyrjami sljuna, tekuščaja iz pasti nekotoryx životnyx, preimuščestvenno v sostojanii ustalosti. *Udila, pokrytye penoj.*" Puškin used these two words exactly in the meaning given by Ušakov: (1) "A poutru otopreš konjušnju, / Kon' ne tix, *ves' v myle,* žarom pyšet"; (2) "Počuja mertvogo xrapjat / I b'jutsja koni, *penoj* beloj / Stal'nye močat udila." Likewise in Mandel'štam: (1) "S rozovoj *penoj* ustalosti u mjagkix gub / Jarostno volny zelenye roet byk" (1922); (2) "Kon' ležit v pyli i xrapit *v myle*" ("Našedšij podkovu," 1923). True, one may say also: "Kon' ves' pokryt penoj," but in this case *pena* would be a less usual metaphor.

17. The bows in this line can be understood as a metonym for the violinists. However, there is no need to insist on such a rationalistic explanation.

18. In *Sobranie sočinenij* (vol. I, 2nd ed.) these three lines are published as the second part of a six-line poem (No. 287, dated December 1933). However, this is not an original poem by Mandel'štam, but a variant of lines 9–14 of his translation of the 164th sonnet by Petrarch, published in the same edition as No. 489 (dated December 1933–January 1934). In the full text of the sonnet the end is different:

> Тысячу раз на дню, себе на диво,
> Я должен умереть на самом деле –
> И воскресаю так же сверхобычно.

The later version is closer to the original.

19. There is no doubt in my mind that the word *tverd'* in "Koncert na vokzale" means "sky," "firmament." The entire image of the first stanza is

ascensional, as it were: first the suffocating atmosphere ("nel'zja dyšat' "),
then — the blackness of the sky swarming with worms, then the stars, and
finally — the music which is *above us*.

In Russian poetic usage, the word *tverd'* primarily refers to the sky. When it
means "earth," "terra firma," it is usually used in combination with sky ("nebo
i tverd' "") or it is modified by the adjective *zemnaja*. Mandel'štam used this
noun seven times in his poetry, but never in the sense of "earth."

In five instances it means the actual sky:

(1)   *Твердь умолкла, умерла.*
    С колокольни отуманенной
    Кто-то снял колокола.
                                    («Скудный луч холодной мерою», 1911)

(2)   Только там, где *твердь светла,*
    Черно-желтый лоскут злится.
                                      («Дворцовая площадь», 1915)

(3)   Нельзя дышать и *твердь кишит червями* . . .
                                        («Концерт на вокзале», 1921)

(4)   Умывался ночью на дворе –
    *Твердь сияла грубыми звездами* . . .
                                            (1921)

(5)   Под высокую руку берет
    *Побежденную твердь Азраил.*
                                 («Ветер нам утешенье принес», 1922)

There is a striking similarity between examples (3) and (4). Both were written
in the same year, and in both an unfriendly sky is depicted. To the best of my
understanding, in the remaining two instances *tverd'* also means "sky": the
sky painted on a porcelain plate (*stekljannaja tverd'* in "Na blednogoluboj
èmali," 1909), or on the wall (*stenobitnaja tverd'* in "Tajnaja večerja," 1937).

20. There is a difference, however, between Mandel'štam's and Burljuk's
sky. In Mandel'štam, the black visible firmament is full of worms; in Burljuk
the worms are the stars themselves.

An inquisitive reader may ask whether Burljuk's poem does not already
contain a hidden polemic with Lermontov's "Vyxožu odin ja na dorogu."
Is it not the Lermontovian mist in the second line of "Mertvoe nebo" (which,
incidentally, is a trochaic pentameter)? Even if Burljuk did not have Lermontov
in mind, could not Mandel'štam understand his poem as a polemic with Lermontov and drive the point home? See my "Tri zametki o poèzii Mandel'štama,"
*IJSLP* XII, 1969, 165–166.

21. See the commentary to "Koncert na vokzale" in *Sobranie sočinenij* I,
2nd ed.; 1967, 462–463, where the reminiscences from Lermontov and Tjutčev
are mentioned.

22. S. Bobrov, "Zaimstvovanija i vlijanija," *Pečat' i revoljucija* VIII,
1922, 72–92.

23.  Mandel'štam's conclusion of "Koncert na vokzale" repeats even the rhythmic-syntactic pattern of these lines (and *zvučit* rhymes with *predstoit*).

24.  One may further compare Tjutčev's "golye steny" and "pustaja xramina" with Mandel'štam's "vokzala šar stekljannyj," "železnyj mir," and "stekljannyj les vokzala": the concert, like the Lutheran service, is held in austere surroundings.

25.  "... dlja Skrjabina xarakterno to, čto Iskupitelem, kotoryj prineset s soboj novoe nebo i novuju zemlju, budet muzykant, artist, a ne moral'nyj propovednik, pričem imenno xudožnik prineset miru vseobščuju garmoniju — ljubov' i spravedlivost' " (I. I. Lapšin, *Zavetnye dumy Skrjabina*, Petrograd, 1922, p. 23).

26.  There may be a third subtext by Tjutčev in "Koncert na vokzale," the image of the dear shadow (*milaja ten'*) possibly coming from the last stanza of Tjutčev's poem "Ona sidela na polu":

> Стоял я молча в стороне
> И пасть готов был на колени, –
> И страшно грустно стало мне,
> *Как от присущей милой тени.*

27.  That is, lastočka-dočka.

28.  In Russian minds, the unpretentious, fragrant bloom of *čeremuxa* is associated with the beauty and poetry of everyday life. See Chapter Four, p. 79–80.

29.  See Vjačeslav Vs. Ivanov, "Dva primera anagrammatičeskix postroenij v stixax Mandel'štama," *Russian Literature* 3, 1972, 86. I do not agree that the *"blažennoe, bessmyslennoe slovo"* in Mandel'štam's early poems and in his poems of the twenties was self-contained ("bylo samodovlejuščim") and that he became a *smyslovik* (as he called himself) only in the thirties. To my understanding "Solominka" (1916), "Čto pojut časy-kuznečik" (1917), "Grifel'naja oda" (1923), "Armenija" (1931), "Stixi o neizvestnom soldate" (1937), and some other Voronezh poems are based on the same poetic method. The *"blažennoe, bessmyslennoe slovo"* from "V Peterburge my sojdemsja snova" (1920) should be interpreted as the "mladenčeskij lepet," the "detskaja zaum'," expressing joy (see Chapter Three, note 23).

30.  According to the editor of Mandel'štam's poems in the "Biblioteka poèta" (1974), N. I. Xardžiev, the man who read the "Ulalume" was Mandel'štam's friend, Vladimir Pjast, poet and translator, "an apologist of Edgar Allan Poe's 'Titanic creativity'." There is no doubt that Pjast had a very good command of English.

## Chapter II: The Hayloft

1.  An actual event, a night spent in a hayloft, provided the impetus for the writing of these two poems. Mandel'štam had a companion at this time (nowhere mentioned in the text), his wife Nadežda Jakovlevna. In both poems the motif of difficult breathing is present. At this time, "u Mandel'štama ešče ne bylo i sledov astmy, no u Nadeždy Jakovlevny bylo čto-to v ètom rode (ili čto-to allergičeskoe, tipa sennoj lixoradki); ne otsjuda li — čerez 'simpatiju' — ...

podčerkivanie *dušnosti* i *dyxanija?*" (quoted from a personal letter to me from Jurij Levin).

2.   The noun *senoval* is unique in the poem (semantic field: building, sheltered lodging). But if we divide the field *Nature* into *Landscape* and *Cosmos*, then "hayloft" can, in the final analysis, be grouped in *Landscape*.

3.   Good examples of similar semantic analysis can be found in the articles of Jurij Levin ("Semantičeskij analiz stixotvorenija," *Teorija poètičeskoj reči i poètičeskaja leksikologija*, Šadrinsk, 1971, and "Razbor dvux stixotvorenij Mandel'štama," *Russian Literature* 2, 1972), and D. M. Segal ("O nekotoryx aspektax smyslovoj struktury 'Grifel'noj ody' O. È. Mandel'štama," *Russian Literature* 2, 1972). Segal, not limiting himself only to the text, at times draws upon a larger context as well as several "subtexts" (Lermontov, Deržavin, Tjutčev).

4.   The example from Tynjanov might, to a skeptically inclined reader, appear doubtful. A more convincing example can be found in Levin's commentary to Pasternak's line, "Kak v ad, cejxgauz i arsenal": "*ad* priobretaet nečto 'voennoe', *cejxgauz i arsenal* — nečto 'infernal'noe'; akcentiruetsja nabor sem *mračnoe pomeščenie:* mnogie semy zatuševyvajutsja i nejtralizujutsja" ("O nekotoryx čertax plana soderžanija v poètičeskix tekstax," *Strukturnaja tipologija jazykov*, 1968, p. 214).

5.   The omission of line 12 still remains very strange: the noun *tmin* can be included in the semantic field *Šuršaščee*, as well as the verb *zašit'* (the latter at least phonetically).

6.   *Krovi suxaja voznja* recalls *šelest krovi* from "Xolodok ščekočet temja":

А ведь *раньше лучше было,*
И пожалуй не сравнишь,
Как ты *прежде шелестила,*
Кровь, как нынче шелестишь.

Both phrases are easily included in the semantic field *Dry, Rustling*. Whereas, in Lidija Ginzburg's opinion, the *suxaja voznja* acquires a negative meaning in the 1920 poem (and I agree with her), the former *šelest krovi* can in no way be said to have negative implications (since "formerly it was better"). For "rustle" (of fever and blood) see Chapter Four, p. 74 and note 11.

7.   In her article quoted above (pp. 323–324), Lidija Ginzburg points out only one such particular image of Mandel'štam's, the image of the "living swallow which fell on the hot snow" (in "Čut' mercaet prizračnaja scena"), an image which Mandel'štam himself deciphered in *Egipetskaja marka* as the death of the Italian singer Angiolina Bosio (in St. Petersburg in 1859). See also A. Dymšic's article, " 'Ja v mir vxožu . . . ' (Zametki o tvorčestve O. Mandel'-štama)," *Voprosy literatury*, 1972, no. 3, 89.

8.   The autobiographical elements in *Egipetskaja marka* have been pointed out on many occasions. Nadežda Mandel'štam writes in her memoirs that at one time Osip Èmil'evič "almost confused himself with Parnok" ("on počti sputal sebja s Parnokom, čut' ne prevratil ego v svoego dvojnika," *Vospominanija*, 1971, p. 181).

9. From the poem "Kak tel'ce malen'koe krylyškom." The "splinter in the azure" (*zanoza v lazuri*) is deciphered as an airplane by Mandel'štam himself, in the sketch "Xolodnoe leto," published in July 1923:

Тот не любит города, кто не ценит его рубища, его скромных и жалких адресов, кто не задыхался на черных лестницах, путаясь в жестянках, под мяуканье кошек, кто не заглядывался в каторжном дворе Вхутемаса *на занозу в лазури, на живую, животную прелесть аэроплана* . . .

10. The comparison of the poet to a seashell is found in an early Mandel'štam poem (1909):

Дыханье вещее в стихах моих
Животворящего их духа,
Ты прикасаешься сердец каких –
Какого достигаешь слуха?

Или пустыннее напева ты
Тех раковин, в песке поющих,
Что круг очерченной им красоты
Не разомкнули для живущих?

However, the image of a "seashell without pearls" (*rakovina bez žemčužin*, rhyming with *nenužen*) probably goes back to Gumilev ("Otkrytie Ameriki," 1910):

Раковина я, но без жемчужин,
Я поток, который был запружен, –
Спущенный, теперь уже *ненужен*.

There are many subtle observations on the semantics of "Rakovina" in E. Toddes's article, "Mandel'štam i Tjutčev," *IJSLP* XVII, 1974, 73.

11. In "Silentium!" it is precisely the opposition of night to day, so significant for Tjutčev, which is emphasized with "rhythmic italics": amphibrachic lines in an iambic context (lines 4 and 5 in the first stanza and line 5 in the third). The common rhythmic index for these amphibrachs and mixed iambic lines is three beats (the last four lines in both the first and third stanza have three stresses). In fact, one might call this a shift of the second ictus from the fourth syllable to the fifth in the fourth variation of the iambic tetrameter. This is how it takes place in the first stanza:

4. $x / x / x x x /$     (iamb, var. IV)
5. $x / x x / x x /$     (amphibrach)

Whether we read the text in a normal or slightly muffled tone of voice, there remains a sharp rhythmic shift. And when this shift is repeated in the third stanza, it evokes in our memory the rhythmical pattern of the fourth and fifth lines of the first stanza along with their contents. "Silentium!" has yet one more instance of "rhythmic italics," in the fourth line of the second stanza: "*Mýsl'* izrečénnaja *est'* lóž'" (variation VI with nonmetrical stresses on the first and seventh syllables). For a commentary on the recent polemics about the rhythmical structure and tonality of Tjutčev's "Silentium!" see B. Ja. Buxštab,

*Russkie poèty*, 1970, pp. 62–63. Mandel'štam's polemics with Tjutčev's poem will be discussed in Chapter Six.

12. For a discussion of Tjutčev's and Mandel'štam's night, see Segal, *Russian Literature* 2, pp. 82–87, 91–93, as well as the Tjutčev poems quoted by him ("Kak ptička ranneju zarej," written before 1836, and "O veščaja duša moja," 1855). Segal notes that in *Kamen'*, immediately after "Rakovina" a 1911 quatrain on the theme of the day is printed (pp. 82–83):

Учитывая, что поэт придавал огромное значение порядку следования стихов в сборнике, соседство рядом стихов о *ночи* и *дне* неслучайно. Неслучаен и характер взаимоотношения между *ночью* и *днем*. В стихотворении «Раковина» «ночь» — это некоторая *старшая, учительская стихия* ... По сравнению с этим *день* выглядит как нечто бесплотное, преходящее:

> О небо, небо, ты мне будешь сниться!
> Не может быть, что ты совсем ослепло,
> И день *сгорел*, как белая страница:
> Немного дыма и немного пепла.

13. Concerning Mandel'štam's *Kamen'* and his stones, see Omry Ronen, "Mandel'štam's *Kaščej*," *Studies Presented to Professor Roman Jakobson by His Students* (Cambridge, Mass., 1968); also his "Leksičeskij povtor, podtekst i smysl v poètike Osipa Mandel'štama," in *Slavic Poetics: Essays in Honor of Kiril Taranovsky* (1973).

14. The quotation is from Annenskij's "Košmary."

15. In these selections we have not quoted from the poem "Za to, čto ja ruki tvoi ne sumel uderžat' " (stanzas two and four), since the image of blood in it does not have a straightforward meaning. If the "dry rustle of blood" probably is the blood of the poet "who betrayed the salty tender lips," then the blood which "gushed towards the ladders and went to the attack" relates in the first place to the "Achaean men who equipped the horse in the darkness." But even this simplified interpretation cannot be accepted without reservation. As Lidija Ginzburg writes in the article mentioned above (p. 313): " 'Za to, čto ja ruki tvoi ne sumel uderžat'' odno iz lučšix stixotvorenij o ljubvi v russkoj poèzii XX v. V nem poèt okazyvaetsja učastnikom antičnogo dejstva, a osaž-dennaja Troja, axejskie muži, nenazvannaja Elena — èto obraznye oboločki proryvajuščegosja skvoz' nix naprjažennogo lirizma." See also Victor Terras, "Classical Motives in the Poetry of Osip Mandel'štam," *SEEJ*, 1966, no. 3, 261–262.

16. A poem from 1909 supports the idea that in these lines breathing is connected with poetic creation: "Dyxan'e veščee v stixax moix / Žyvotvorjaščego ix duxa." Mandel'štam was still a symbolist in 1909.

17. In the line "Protiv šersti mira poem" Mandel'štam is playing on the Russian colloquial idiom *gladit' protiv šersti*, that is, to talk or act in defiance of someone. Compare the English "to rub the wrong way."

18. See Ryszard Przybylski, "Osip Mandel'štam i muzyka," *Russian Literature* 2, 1972, 123.

19. Contrary to what many think, the attribute "tonic" is not a slip on the

poet's part. Mandel'štam obviously heard or read somewhere that the use of the word "tonic" in relation to Russian accentual verse which is based on the *relative loudness of the vowels* was a clear misunderstanding. The term "tonic," by that time, was being used in comparative metrics in relation to verse based on the relative *pitch of the vowel tones* (for example, Chinese). Mandel'štam knew that the prosodic base of ancient Greek verse was the *relative length of the vowel tones.* In his poem the *dolgota glasnyx — toničeskie stixi — cezura — dlinnoty — celaja nota* create one central image, the *image of the lengthened phonation of Homeric verse.* The *"toničeskie stixi"* in the second line of the poem and the *"bogatstvo celoj noty"* in the last line are semantically tied together (*ton: nota*). Changing the adjective *toničeskij* to *metričeskij* would be impossible: it would destroy the image.

20.  Note that the "darkness" in the third stanza not only *rings* (like the "mosquito prince" in the first "Hayloft"), but *swells* and *grows* (*nabuxaet, rastet*). The last two verbs mean "increase from within." This is how Segal (*Russian Literature* 2, p. 88) defined the general meaning of the verbs *naryvat'* and *zret'* in the following line from "Grifel'naja oda": "Plod naryval. Zrel vinograd." I believe that these two images are also connected with the process of creation. See a commentary on these lines in Chapter One, p. 2.

21.  *Voz* is a Russian dialectic name for the constellation Ursa major. *Voz* (with this meaning) enters the semantic field *Cosmos,* but also becomes a part of the semantic field *Hay-mowing* (*Senokos*): *kosari* (haymowers) — *voz* (cart) — *senoval* (hayloft).

22.  Compare, too, Fet's old translation ("Ja vyxožu, ili to pogreben'e bylo bez trupa./Neoprjatnyj spustiv kosmy na sumračnyj lik") and Ja. Golosovker's new translation ("Vyvralsja. Trup ne živoj? Pogrebennyj, no bez pogreben'ja . . . /Šerst'ju obrosšij idu, dikij, s kosmatym licom"). Perhaps Mandel'štam also remembered lines 19–20 from the tenth elegy of book three: "Pellibus et sutis arcent mala figora bracis,/ Oraque de toto corpore sola patent" (in Fet's translation: "V škurax da sšityx portax ot zloj zaščiščajutsja stuži / Tol'ko otkryto odno v tele to celom lico"). Obvious reminiscences from this elegy can be heard in the third stanza of Mandel'štam's 1914 poem "O vremenax prostyx i grubyx":

> Привратник, царственно ленив,
> Встал, и звериная зевота
> Напомнила твой образ, скиф!
>
> [Скиф тех (простых и грубых) времен],
> III  Когда с дряхлеющей любовью
> Мешая в песнях *Рим и снег,*
> Овидий пел *арбу воловью*
> *В походе* царственных *телег.*

The "ox cart" and the "march of the wagons" derive from lines 33–34 and 59–60 of elegy III, X; Rome (*urbs*) is mentioned in the second line of Ovid, and snow (*nix*) in the thirteenth.

23.  In the sketch "Vozvraščenie" (1923?), Mandel'štam calls Villon his "friend and favorite." In his 1937 poem, "Čtob prijatel' i vetra i kapel'," Mandel'-štam returns to Villon:

Рядом с готикой жил озоруючи
И плевал на паучьи права
Наглый школьник и ангел ворующий,
Несравненный Виллон Франсуа.

The image of the *belka v kolese* is repeated in "Stixi o russkoj poèzii, III" (1932): "I belok krovavoj belki / Krutjat v strašnom kolese."

24. "The ringing of the arm-like dry grasses" is not a poetic translation, but rather an analytic explanation of Mandel'štam's image "travy suxorukij zvon." This puzzling image, as I understand it, is based both on similarity (metaphor) and on contiguity (metonymy). It originated, I believe, in a metaphor: "suxie stebli travy, poxožye na ruki > *suxie ruki travy.*" The final image is a result of metonymical thinking: "zvon suxix ruk travy > *travy suxorukij zvon.*" It is surprising how both literary critics and scholars working in structural poetics neglect metonymy in their analyses, despite stimulating articles by R. Jakobson ("Randbemerkungen zur Prosa des Dichters Pasternak," *Slavische Rundshau* VII, 1935), Nils Nilsson ("Life as Ecstasy and Sacrifice: Two Poems by Pasternak," *Scando-Slavica* V, 1959), and Michel Aucouturier ("The Metonymous Hero or the Beginnings of Pasternak the Novelist," *Books Abroad*, Spring 1970). Critics and scholars often do not realize that in Russian post-symbolist poetry metonymy is a very important device (both as a trope and as a compositional principle). There is no essential difference between a plausible Puškin metonymy: "*Mladoj i svežij poceluj* < poceluj mladyx i svežyx ust" (*Evgenij Onegin*) and more unusual metonimies in Pasternak: "*krasnoščekaja i kurnosaja samouveren-nost'* < somouverennoe vyraženie krasnoščekogo i kurnosogo lica" ("Detstvo Ljuvers"), or in Mandel'štam: "*prostovolosye žaloby nočnye* < nočnye žaloby prostovolosyx ženščin" ("Tristia") and: "Aptečnye telefony delajutsja iz samogo lučšego *skarlatinovogo dereva* < iz dereva zaražennogo (i zaražajuščego) skarlatinoj" (*Egipetskaja marka*). My explanation of the last example is supported by the further development of scarlet fever imagery: "Ne govorite po telefonu iz peterburgskix aptek: trubka šelušitsja i golos obescvečivaestsja." It is well known that skin peeling occurs in the last, most contagious stage of scarlet fever and that during the illness the throat is affected and the voice becomes hoarse. Quite naturally, the scarlet fever tree grows in an "enema grove" (*klistirnaja rošča*). Many children would enjoy such a "materialization" of poetic tropes. One wonders how adult and learned literary professionals refuse to understand such images, labeling them simply as surrealistic.

25. See another statement of Mandel'štam's about Xlebnikov ("O prirode slova," 1922): "Xlebnikov vozitsja so slovami kak krot, meždu tem on proryl v zemle xody dlja buduščego na celoe stoletie."

### Chapter III: The Black-Yellow Light

1. The poem "V xrustal'nom omute kakaja krutizna" (1919) contains references to both the Old and New Testaments. The Judaic themes are rein-terpreted here in the light of Christianity: Jacob's ladder serves the Holy Spirit, the Credo is joined with King David's Psalms, and so on: "S visjačej lestnicy

prorokov i carej / Spuskaetsja organ Svjatogo Duxa krepost'"; "Krutoe Veruju i psalmopevca rozdyx." The first image echoes Mandel'štam's words from his essay "Petr Čaadaev" (1915): "Istorija — èto lestnica Iakova, po kotoroj angely sxodjat s neba na zemlju. Svjaščennoj dolžna ona nazyvat'sja na osnovanii *preemstvennosti duxa blagodati*, kotoryj v nej živet." The poem "V xrustal'nom omute" elaborates the idea of the historical succession of the spirit of grace by means of poetic imagery. But there is no mention of Palestine in the last line. This line should read: "Kak *Palestriny* pesn' nisxodit blagodat'."

2. See Mandel'štam's black and yellow tallith in "Xaos iudejskij": "Vdrug deduška vytaščil iz jaščika komoda *černo-želtyj platok*, nakinul ego na pleči i zastavil povtorjat' za soboj slova, sostavlennye iz neznakomyx šumov, no, nedovol'nyj moim lepetom, rasserdilsja, zakačal neodobritel'no golovoj. *Mne stalo dušno i strašno.*"

3. This is a quotation from Puškin's *Cygany*. The "holy man" is Ovid.

4. The main sources of Mandel'štam's "Hellenism" are writings of F. F. Zelinskij (Tadeusz Zieliński), primarily his two books: *Drevne-grečeskaja religija* and *Religija èllenizma*, published in Petrograd, 1918 and 1922 respectively. In the first of these books Mandel'štam might have found the strong opposition of Hellenism and Judaism (pp. 27, 86, and 152–160), as well as the image of the *hearth*: "V centre *sem'ji*, t.e. ob"edinennoj obščnost'ju doma i krova jačejki graždanskogo obščežitija, stojalo božestvennoe suščestvo, *očag* — i glubokaja religioznaja vdumčivost' èllinov skazalas' v tom, čto u nix — (i, kažetsja, u nix odnix) èto suščestvo predstavljaetsja ženskogo pola, kak boginja *Gestija*. Buduči odnim iz drevnejšix božestv, ona, možno skazat', na našix glazax vyrostaet iz immanentnogo, kakim ee tol'ko i znaet Gomer, v transcendentnoe: uže dlja Gesioda ona boginja-ličnost', sestra Zevsa naravne s Geroj i Demetroj, no v otličie ot nix — devstvennica; èto potomu, čto ee stixija — očažnoe plamja. Ee pozdnjaja transcendentalizacija imela posledstviem i to, čto ee redko izobražali: daže v obščestvennye xramy ne stavili ee kumirov, ee počitali v ee simvole, pylajuščem na altare vnutri xrama neugasimom ogne. V dome i podavno" (p. 66); "Tak kak gosudarstvo bylo liš' razvitiem sem'i, gorod — razvitiem doma, to my ne udivimsja, najdja i v gosudarstve-gorode očag-sredotočie i ego boginju Gestiju" (p. 79); "... Del'fy polučili svoe preobladajuščee položenie sredi grečeskix gorodov, kak 'obščij očag vsej Èllady'..." (p. 82). In Chapter Five we will see that Mandel'štam learned something about ancient Greek mythology and the Hellenic tradition from the writings of Vjačeslav Ivanov, as well. However, Ivanov's Dionysian obsession (particularly in *Cor ardens*) was entirely alien to him; he obviously preferred Zelinskij's appreciation of the "Apollonian religion of joy" (p. 92). Compare also Mandel'štam's "tončajšee teleologičeskoe teplo" in the second quotation above and Zelinskij's "ujutnoe teplo pod lučami Gestii" (p. 72).

5. Concerning the inner, spiritual freedom which is the lot of the chosen people, Mandel'štam wrote his 1914 poem "K ènciklike papy Benedikta XV." It contains an overt polemic with Tjutčev's "Encyclica." In his poem, Tjutčev predicts the destruction of Pius IX because of his encyclica *Quanta cura* which denied the freedom of conscience (December 8, 1864): "Ne ot meča pogibnet

on zemnogo, / Mečom zemnym vladevšij stol'ko let, — / Ego pogubit rokovoe slovo: / 'Svoboda sovesti est' bred'." The first stanza of Mandel'štam's "K èncyklike" sounds like a direct reply to Tjutčev: "Est' obitaemaja duxom / Svoboda — izbrannyx udel. / Orlinym zren'em, divnym sluxom / Svjaščennik rimskij ucelel." In 1914, Mandel'štam was attracted by Catholicism. The same year he wrote his poem "Abbat" about an abbot who predicted to the poet that he would die a Catholic.

6. It is noteworthy that the pool in the second poem has a *window* which evokes the visual image of a room full of water. This image leads to such later poems of Mandel'štam's as his masterpieces: (1) "Bessonnica. Gomer. Tugie parusa" (1915), (2) "Solominka, I–II" (1916), and (3) "Masterica vinovatyx vzorov" (1934).

"Bessonnica" is linked with the second of the 1910 "twin-poems" by its water imagery, by the word signal *izgolov'e*, and the motif of falling asleep (found in the last quatrain of both poems). In "V orgomnom omute" the poet must stay at the head of his bed and lull himself to sleep. In "Bessonnica" the black sea is penetrating into his room, and the poet falls asleep to its "heavy roaring." Dropping off to sleep is often associated with sinking into the water. Despite Cvetaeva's recollections, Mandel'štam's *more černoe* is by no means a geographical reference. "Black" (*černyj*) is a Homeric epithet (*černyj pont* in Gnedič's translation, *Iliada* II). Mandel'štam's line "I more černoe, vitistvuja, šumit" is a reminiscence from Puškin ("Otryvki iz putešestvija Onegina": "Liš' more Černoe šumit"), and Lermontov ("Pamjati A. I. Odoevskogo"): "A more Černoe šumit, ne umolkaja" (note the interplay of the two gerunds: Lermontov's *ne umolkaja* and Mandel'štam's *vitijstvuja*). The sea is an old symbol of life (cf. *pučiny mirovye* in Mandel'štam's 1909 poem "Ni o čem ne nužno govorit' "). The Homer in the last stanza is a symbolic metonym for poetry: both life and poetry are governed by love. The poet has stopped reading Homer ("Gomer molčit"); he is listening to the voice of life and is falling asleep, lulled by its roar. The expression "the Achean men" is also Homeric and is found in Gnedič (*Iliada* II). Mandel'štam's *poezd žuravlinyj* and *žuravlinyj klin* were suggested by Gnedič's lines found approximately in the middle of the "ship catalogue" of Agamemnon's expedition (*Iliada* II, lines 484–785): "Ix plemena kak ptic pereletnyx neščetnye stai, / Dikix gusej, žuravlej, il' stada lebedej dolgovyjnyx ..." Compare in "Bessonnica": "Ja spisok korablej pročel do serediny." There is no doubt that Mandel'štam read the *Iliad* in Gnedič's translation. See also Nils Nillson's article "Osip Mandel'štam's 'Insomnia' Poem," *IJSLP* X, 1966, 148–154.

The famous "Solominka" is connected with "Bessonnica" by the motif of insomnia and with the 1910 "twin-poems" by the motif of existence on the border of reality and dream, of being and non-being; and it is, of course, related to the three previous poems by its water imagery. Both in "Solominka" and in "Bessonnica" the water is filling up the room ("V orgomnoj komnate tjaželaja Neva / I golubaja krov' struitsja iz granita"). The following are the word signals in "Solominka" which serve as a link with the preceding poems: *solominka — bessonnica — omut*. True, in "V ogromnom omute" the *solominka* is the poet's heart, and in the 1916 poem *solomka, solominka* is a woman, while *omut* in the latter poem is a metaphor for a mirror. One can find still more lexical correspondences between these poems: *"ogromnyj* omut" — *"orgomnaja* komnata"; *"tomjas'* toskoj" — *"tomitel'nyj* pokoj," and so on. The water is also a symbol of death (the "invitation to death"), but the main theme of "Solominka" is not death as such but rather *dying (umiran'e)* and reminders of death ("Dvenadcat' mesjacev pojut o smertnom čase"). The Solominka is by no means dead. She has only had some knowledge and experience of death. A line from an earlier version of "Solominka," quoted by Axmatova in "Listki iz dnevnika" and taken by her as an epigraph to her poem "Ten'" (1940) — "Čto znaet ženščina odna o smertnom čase" — may serve as a comment to the line "Vsju smert' ty vypila i sdelalas' nežnej." Axmatova's "Ten'" is addressed to Salomeja Andronikova, Mandel'štam's Solominka ("Solomenkoj tebja nazval poèt"). Incidentally, it contains a clear reminiscence from Mandel'štam's "Bessonnica": "Flober, bessonnica i pozdnjaja siren'." The mention of Flaubert in this line, I believe, is not accidental. Axmatova's reading of his "Hérodias" might have evoked an association of the biblical Salome with Salomeja — Solominka. Another argument for the fact that *Solominka* is alive is the idiom *ubita žalost'ju* (the pattern: *ubit gorem*). She is tender, lacking vitality, heart-broken, stricken with pity, but not dead (see the lexical figurative meaning of *neživoj: "lišennyj žiznennoj ènergii"*).

But the problem arises, perhaps she has a different identity, perhaps she is a potential Salome? In the first poem, the poet rejects such a possibility: no, she is not Salome; she is rather a fragile straw ("Ne Salomeja, net, solominka skorej"). But in the last two lines of the second poem he is still in doubt: "A ta, solominka, *byt' možet* Salomeja, / Ubita žalost'ju i ne vernetsja vnov'." The name Salome appears with three other names, Lenore, Ligeia and Séraphita, the three unearthly, incorporeal women, mentioned by Théophile Gautier in his essay on Charles Baudelaire (Teofil' Got'e, *Šarl' Bodler*, Petrograd, 1915, p. 34), as N.I. Xardžiev has pointed out in his commentary to Mandel'štam's poems in "Biblioteka poèta": " ... Večno želannyj i nikogda ne dostižymyj ideal, verxovnaja božestvennaja krasota, voploščennaja v obraze èfirnoj, besplotnoj ženščiny ... kak ... Ligeja ... i Èleonora Èdgara Po i Serafita-Serafit Bal'zaka ..." (quoted after Xardžiev). In the light of the subtext from Gautier the *pointe* of the second poem indicates, I believe, that Mandel'štam's Solominka might be different from the other three ideal women, she might turn out to be an earthly woman of flesh and blood. Moreover, in this context the name *Salomeja* must have a literary source, which is, I strongly believe, Oscar Wilde's *Salomé*. At the beginning of this century, performances in Europe both of Oscar Wilde's play and Richard Strauss's opera enjoyed a kind of *succès de scandale*. In November 1908, Wilde's *Salomé* was staged in Komissarževskaja's Dramatic Theater in St. Petersburg, but was banned after the dress rehearsal by the church censorship. Its staging was very expensive; the theater could not surmount the financial crisis and was closed very soon afterward. Mandel'štam knew Wilde's play very well and must have been aware that any contemporary reader would unambiguously identify his *Salomeja* with Wilde's heroine.

The poem "Masterica vinovatyx vzorov" reflects Mandel'štam's brief infatuation with a young poetess, Marija Petrovyx, in 1934. A fine semantic analysis of this poem is found in Jurij Levin's article "Semantičeskij analiz stixotvorenija," mentioned above (Chapter Two, note 3). In contrast to "Solominka," the water in "Masterica" has erotic connotations (for example, *poluxleb ploti*). This aspect of water symbolism is frequently found both in Western European poetry (for example, Novalis) and in Russian (for example, Baratynskij, Tjutčev, Bal'mont, Majakovskij, Cvetaeva). The most puzzling problem of "Masterica" is the fish imagery. Levin is not interested in *realia*; for his analysis he has no need to know whether there was an aquarium with the goldfish in the room. Having some, but very limited knowledge of how *realia* are reflected in certain of Mandel'štam's poems, I would prefer to believe that there was an aquarium and that fish became, in the poet's imagery, an analogue of his human wishes: he asks his addressee to feed them with *poluxleb ploti*. In this poem, too, the water imagery is connected with the motif of death ("Nužno smert' predupredit', usnut' "). This is not surprising: the themes of water, dream (or sleep), and death are inseparable in poetry (see already in the first quatrain: *utoplennica-reč'*). In the last quatrain, the poet calls his beloved: "Ty, Marija, — gibnuščim podmoga." Thus, he compares his beloved to the Holy Virgin Hodigitria. There are several famous icons of *Bogorodica-Odigitrija* (*Putevoditel'nica*) in Russia. Mandel'štam might have known them; in any case, he knew the church of Santa Maria della Salute in Venice. Finally, he might have recalled Kuzmin's lines: "Ty že iz buri, pučiny, pogibeli reva, / Vyvedi k pristani nas, Odigitrija-Deva" ("Voditel'nica-Odigitrija" in *Osennie ozera*).

There are two other water-filled rooms in Russian poetry from the 1920s. In Majakovskij's *Pro èto* (1923) the water is present as the realization of the standard hyperbole "slezy [tekut] ruč'em" ("Otkuda voda? / Počemu mnogo? / Sam naplakal"). However, later in *Pro èto*, the water acquires a complex, symbolic meaning. In Cvetaeva's "Popytka komnaty" (1926), water has a definite erotic connotation: "A potom? / Son est': v ton. / Byl pod"em. / Byl naklon // Lba — i lba. / Tvoj vpered / Lob. Gruba / Rifma: rot. / / Ottogo l', čtob ne stalo sten — / Potolok dostoverno kren / Dal. Liš' zvatel'nyj, cvel padež / V rtax. A pol — dostoverno breš'! / / *A skvoz' breš' zelena kak Nil.* / Potolok dostoverno plyl." ... "Nad ničem dvux tel / Potolok dostoverno pel — / Vsemi angelami."

On water symbolism, see Gaston Bachelard's book, *L'Eau et les rêves*. It offers many fine examples of water imagery in European literature.

7. As Omry Ronen has pointed out, this poem contains reminiscences from Xomjakov ("K I. V. Kireevskomu" and "Široka, neobozrima"). "Gde tebe, naš putnik smelyj / *Solnce novoe vzošlo*"; "*Iz vorot Erusalima* / Šla narodnaja tolpa." The end of the second poem vaguely recalls the black sun: "A nejdet kak burja zlaja, / Ves' odejan *černoj mgloj*, / *Plameneja i sverkaja* / Nad trepeščuščej zemlej." Later, in 1932, Mandel'štam used the same reminiscence in a humorous poem ("Dajte Tjutčevu strekozu"): "A ešče, bogoxranima, / Na gvozdjax torčit vsegda / *U vorot Erusalima* / Xomjakova boroda." Here, Xo

mjakov's beard appears as the equivalent of Prince Oleg's shield on the gates of Constantinople. See O. Ronen, "Leksičeskij povtor, podtekst i smysl v poètike Osipa Mandel'štama," *Slavic Poetics: Essays in Honor of Kiril Taranovsky* (The Hague, 1973), p. 383.

8.   There is another black sun — this one in the first poem of *Tristia* (written in 1916), the sun of Phaedra. It derives from Racine's play. The lines of the chorus "Černym plamenen Fedra gorit / Sredi belogo dnja" vary Racine's image: "Je voulois en mourant prendre soin de ma gloire, / Et dérober *au jour une flamme si noir*" (I, IV). Compare also *"le feu fatal"* (II, V), *"ma flamme adultère"* (III, III), "La fureur *de mes feux*, l'horreur de mes remords," " . . . et moi *je brûle* encore" (IV, IV), "Le ciel mit dans mon sein *une flamme funeste*," " . . . *un feu* qui lui [Hippolyte] faisait horreur" (V, VII). From this imagery emerged Mandel'štam's image of the black sun:

> И для матери влюбленной
> *Солнце черное* взойдет.
> . . . . . . . . . . . . . . . . . .
> *Любовью черною* я солнце запятнала . . .
> . . . . . . . . . . . . . . . . . .
> Мы же, песнью похоронной
> Провожая мертвых в дом,
> *Страсти дикой и бессонной*
> *Солнце черное* уймем.

There are other reminiscences from Racine in Mandel'štam's poem. Its very beginning: "— Kak ètix pokryval i ètogo ubora / Mne pyšnost' tjažela sred' moego pozora" is an elaborated paraphrase of the following line of Racine (which, in its turn, can be traced to Euripides): "Que ces vains ornements, que ces voiles me pèsent!" Possibly Mandel'štam's "pogrebal'nyj fakel" also was suggested by Racine: "Tandis que de vos jours prêts à se consumer / Le *flambeau* dure encore et peut se rallumer." There are various kinds of black suns in mythological traditions and many metaphors in world poetry using this image with different meanings. One thing is clear: Phaedra's black sun in Mandel'štam bears no relation either to the symbolism of the Dionysian or Orphic cults or to Gérard de Nerval's "El Desdichado" (*"le soleil noir de la mélancholie"*) and Gumilev's "Dagomeja" (*Šater*, 1921): "I blestelo lico u vladyki, / *Točno černoe solnce podzemnoj strany*." The origin of Mandel'štam's image is clear enough, and its meaning is explained by the poet himself: it is the "black sun of *wild and sleepless passion*." If one wants to look for similar images in Russian poetry of the twentieth century, one may cite Brjusov's lines from "Svidanie" (*Urbi et orbi*):

> Как Сириус палит цветы
> Холодным взором с высоты,
> Так надо мной восходишь ты,
> *Ночное солнце — страсть!*

Mandel'štam's two black suns, which are strongly negative, should not be confused with his images of the "night sun," "yesterday sun," and the "burial of the sun" which are always positive in his poetry. The only ambiguous "night sun" is found in his prose (*Šum vremeni*, in the sketch "Sem'ja Sinani"): "Nočnoe solnce v oslepšej ot doždja Finljandii, konspirativnoe solnce novogo Austerlica!" The "sun of the new Austerlitz" for Finland is a symbol of the awaited freedom; for Russia, it signifies the new defeat. All other "Russian" night and yesterday suns symbolize cultural and spiritual light which has gone out:

(1)  Когда в темной ночи замирает
      Лихорадочный форум Москвы,
      И театров широкие зевы
      Возвращают толпу площадям,

      Протекает по улицам пышным
      Оживленье *ночных похорон* . . .
      . . . . . . . . . . . . . .
      Зто *солнце ночное хоронит*
      Возбужденная играми чернь,
      Возвращаясь с полночного пира.

                                              (1918)

(2)  В Петербурге мы сойдемся снова
      Словно солнце мы похоронили в нем . . .
      . . . . . . . . . . . . . . .
      Что ж, гаси, пожалуй, наши свечи
      В черном бархате всемирной пустоты,
      Все поют блаженных жен крутые плечи,
      *А ночного солнца не заметишь ты.*

                                              (1920)

Thus, Mandel'štam's "night sun" is not black; it is only invisible.

(3)  Человек умирает, песок остывает согретый,
      *А вчерашнее солнце на черных носилках несут.*
                   («Сестры — тяжесть и нежность», 1920)

In "Listki iz dnevnika," Axmatova asserts that the "yesterday sun" is Puškin, having in mind Mandel'štam's lines addressed to her in "Kassandre" (1917):

      Касатка, милая Касандра,
      Ты стонешь, ты горишь — зачем
      Сияло солнце Александра
      Сто лет назад, сияло всем?

and a sentence from the first fragment of Mandel'štam's essay "Puškin i Skrjabin": "Noč'ju položili solnce v grob, i v janvarskuju stužu proskripeli poloz'ja sanej, uvozivšix dlja otpevanija prax poèta." Mandel'štam's image from "Sestry — tjažest' i nežnost'," I believe, has a broader meaning: every "yester-day sun" should be borne on a black stretcher. True, there is an enigmatic "night sun" in the same fragment of "Puškin i Skrjabin" which is not necessarily positive, and whose meaning remains unclear, since the last sentence of the following quotation is incomplete:

Я вспоминаю картину пушкинских похорон, чтобы вызвать в вашей памяти образ ночного солнца, образ последней греческой трагедии, созданной Еврипидом — видение несчастной Федры.

В роковые часы очищения и бури мы вознесли над собой Скрябина, чье солнце-сердце горит над нами, но — увы! — это не солнце искупления, а солнце вины. Утверждая Скрябина своим символом в час мировой войны, Федра-Россия . . .

We do not know how Mandel'štam motivated his image of Phaedra-Russia. There is no night sun in Euripides' *Hippolitus*, as there are no "classical military phalanges of swallows" in the *Divina Commedia*, swallows which Mandel'štam attributes to its author in his *Razgovor o Dante*. Obviously, he gave a new, more complex meaning to his own image of Phaedra's black sun, since it is juxtaposed with Skrjabin's sun-heart, the sun of guilt. But we will never know the real explanation unless the complete text of the essay is found. (See editors' note, "Černoe solnce," in *Sočinenija* III, 1969, 404–408; N. Mandel'štam, *Vtoraja kniga*, in the chapter "Molodoj levit," and Chapter Four of Steven Broyde's book *Osip Mandel'štam and His Age*).

9.  Mrs. Mandel'štam makes reference to the New Testament (John 19.31): "No kak togda byla pjatnica, daby ne ostavit' tel na kreste v subbotu (*ibo ta subbota byla den' velikij*), prosili Pilata, čtoby perebit' u nix goleni i snjat' ix." The Russian text of John's Gospel was obviously the source of Mandel'štam's imagery, since *peleny* are mentioned only in this text (19.40: ". . . oni vzjali telo Iisusa i obvili ego *pelenami* s blagovonijami); the Church Slavonic text has *rizy*; the other three evangelists have *plaščanica* both in the Russian and in the Church Slavonic texts. Mrs. Mandel'štam also refers to "our Passover Christ," having in mind probably "Pasxa Xristos Iskupitel' " from the Easter hymns or from the first epistle of St. Paul to the Corinthians (5.7: "Pasxa naša, Xristos, zaklan za nas").

10.  Mandel'štam's black and yellow coloration, as well as his image of the black sun, were discussed in detail in my Harvard seminar of spring 1968. Jurij Levin gives a very fine interpretation of "Leningrad" in *Russian Literature* 2, 1972, 37–44.

11.  It often happens in Mandel'štam's poetry that a poem is inspired by the image of a woman, but that the main theme of the poem is his own philosophical problem. So it is with "Čto pojut časy-kuznečik," inspired by Axmatova, and with "Na rozval'njax uložennyx solomoj," connected with Cvetaeva. The latter poem reflects the poet's early vacillation between Catholicism and Orthodoxy and deals with the theme "Russia, the Third Rome." The presence of Cvetaeva in this poem is suggested only in the first stanza: "Ot Vorob'evyx gor do cerkovki znakomoj / *My* exali ogromnoju Moskvoj" (see Chapter Six, pp. 116–118). The poem "V Peterburge my sojdemsja snova" belongs to the "Arbenina cycle" but is only vaguely connected with Mandel'štam's brief romance with her (see Chapter Five, note 26.)

Thanks to the memoirs of Mandel'štam's widow, we may now establish a "Miss Xazina–Mrs. Mandel'štam cycle" in his poetry, 1919–1925. It seems that five poems are connected with her in one way or another. In chronological order they are as follows: (1) "Na kamennyx otrogax Pièrii" (1919); (2) "Vernis' v smesitel'noe lono" (1920); (3) "S rozovoj penoj ustalosti u mjagkix̦ gub" (1922); (4) "Xolodok ščekočet temja" (1922); (5) "Ja budu metat'sja po taboru ulicy temnoj" (1925). The first poem has only a very tenuous relation to Miss Xazina. Besides the "salient brow" attributed to the Muses (see below), possibly Sappho's "small motley boot" is also suggested by her physical appearance at that time. "Iz perevodov [Vjačeslava Ivanova]," Mrs. Mandel'štam writes in *Vtoraja kniga* (p. 38), "i prišel 'pestryj sapožok'. Prišelsja on ko dvoru, potomu čto za otsutstviem pristojnoj obuvi ja nosila nelepye kazanskie sapožki s kievskoj jarmarki, nazyvavšejsja 'kontrakty'. . . Nakanune my 'obvenčalis',' to est' kupili vozle Mixajlovskogo monastyrja dva sinix kolečka za dva groša, no tak kak 'venčanie' bylo tajnoe, na ruki ix ne nadeli." What kind of "wedding" it was, Mrs. Mandel'štam recounts on p. 129: ". . . nas blagoslovil v grečeskoj kofejne moj smešnoj prijatel' Makkavejskij, i my sčitali èto vpolne dostatočnym, poskol'ku on byl iz sem'i svjaščennika." Their "wedding" may explain the "merry pre-nuptial atmosphere" of the second stanza, which is a montage from Sappho's "Epithalamia" (see the analysis of "Na kamennyx otrogox" in Chapter Five). The poem "S rozovoj penoj ustalosti" was written when the Mandel'štams were already living together. This poem is a poetical description of Serov's painting, "Poxiščenie Evropy." Mrs. Mandel'štam reveals in her memoirs an allegorical meaning for the poem (which, as it happens, is in no way even hinted at in the text iteself): "V stixax . . . o bednjažke Evrope, kotoroj xočetsja udrat' ot bezvesel'nogo grebca xot' na dno morskoe — 'i soskol'znut' by xotelos' s šeršavyx kruč' — est' žalost' k devočke-ženščine, i on ponimaet, naskol'ko ej 'milej uključin skrip, lonom širokaja paluba, gurt ovec,' slovom mirnaja žizn' s obyknovennym mužem-dobytčikom, a ne s bykom-poxititelem, besputnym brodjagoj, kotoryj taščit ee neizvestno kuda. I vnešne, Mandel'štam skazal, ja byla poxoža na Evropu so slaboj kartinki Serova — skoree vsego udlinennym licom i dikim ispugom." Whatever the interpretation is, this poem cannot be considered one of Mandel'štam's high artistic achievements. Poems (4) and (5) will be discussed in Chapter Four, pp. 79–81, and poem (1) in Chapter Five, pp. 83–98. In the thirties, we find many poems addressed to Mrs. Mandel'štam, including such masterpieces as "My s toboj na kuxne posidim" (1931), "Polnoč' v Moskve" (1931; note: "Vyp'em, družok, za naše jačmennoe gore, — / Vyp'em do dna! . . ."), "Tvoj zračok v nebesnoj korke" (1937), and so forth. She is, of course, the "niščenka-podruga" from "Ešče ne umer ty, ešče ty ne odin" (1937).

12. I understand the genitive singular in these two lines as a simple synecdoche (singular instead of plural). I do not believe that the "salient brow" belongs either to Artemis or to Sappho, who appears only in the second stanza (see Victor Terras, "Classical Motives in the Poetry of Osip Mandel'štam," *The Slavic and East European Journal* X, 1966, no. 3, 261). I read the first stanza as follows: "Na otrogax Pièrii vodili muzy pervyj xorovod, i xolodkom povejalo ot [ix] vypuklo-devičeskogo [= vypuklogo, devičeskogo] lba."

13. This Leah and her sister Rachel appear in a poem of Mandel'štam's

written after the death of Andrej Belyj. There they function as two hypostases of Belyj's complicated and controversial Muse. In the traditional biblical exegesis, Leah is a symbol of the active and Rachel of the contemplative life. However, Mandel'štam's image should not be traced directly to the Bible; he borrowed it from Dante's *Purgatorio* (XXVII, lines 94–108). See my "Tri zametki," *IJSLP* XII, 1969, 169–170.

14.　The names *Lija* and *Elena* both contain a glide /j/ and a sharped liquid /l'/. But they are opposed to each other since the two phonemes appear in them in reverse order: /l'/ – /j/: /j/ – /l'/.

15.　The idiom "bog s toboj" (translated: "and so be it") is by no means a well-wishing formula of parting. Its meaning in this context is: "nu, i isčezaj" (see *Slovar' russkogo jazyka Imp. akademii nauk*, 1895: "*Bog s nim*, ja otkazyvajus' ot nego").

16.　The small masterpiece "Kuvšin" is a description of an ancient Greek pitcher. The Voronezh museum had a good collection of Greek pottery. Incidentally, the pitcher is also a piece of *domašnjaja utvar'*.

17.　See Gleb Struve: "Ital'janskie obrazy i motivy v poèzii Osipa Mandel'-štama", *Studi in onore de Ettore Lo Gatto e Giovanni Maver* (Rome, 1962), pp. 601–614; and D. M. Segal, "Fragment semantičeskoj poètiki O. È. Mandel'-štama," *Russian Literature* 10–11, 1975, 59–146.

18.　The last line of the poem paraphrases the traditional ending of a Russian fairy tale. Puškin used similar paraphrases three times: in *Ruslan i Ljudmila* ("I tam ja byl, i med ja pil"), in "Skazka o care Saltane" and "Skazka o mertvoj carevne" ("Ja tam byl, med, pivo pil, / Da usy liš' območil"). Mandel'štam, I believe, is making a reference to Puškin's *Ruslan i Ljudmila* since Puškin's poem continues the tradition of Ariosto and Tasso (through French intermediaries) and since Mandel'štam mentions "Puškinian sadness" in characterizing the language of Ariosto.

19.　In *Sobranie sočinenij* this line reads as follows: "Ja skažu 'seljam' načal'-niku evreev." Mrs. Mandel'štam corrects this error, replacing the Arabic greeting with the biblical exclamation "selah." The meaning of the Hebrew word is unclear. In the Latin and Church Slavonic Bible the *selah* is omitted. In Russian translations of the Psalms it is rendered as *selá*, with the second syllable stressed. Obviously, the Russian text was Mandel'štam's source. For him the *selá* was a "beatific, senseless word" (*blažennoe, bessmyslennoe slovo*).

20.　See Mrs. Mandel'štam's analysis of the epithet *malinovyj* (*Vtoraja kniga*, pp. 619–622). The poet, according to Mrs. Mandel'štam, could have associated it with the coloration of Rembrandt's painting: "Teplyj ton 'Bludnogo syna' stal dlja Mandel'štama voploščeniem vozvrata v otčij dom."

21.　Mandel'štam must have known Valentin Parnax's book *Ispanskie i portugal'skie poèty, žertvy inkvizicii* (1934). However, the source of the biography retold by Mrs. Mandel'štam must be a different one. As I have learned, R. D. Timenčik is studying the mutual relations between Mandel'štam and Parnax.

22.　On the Germanic-Russian theme see Steven Broyde's book, *Osip Mandel'štam and His Age*, and G. A. Levinton's article, "K probleme literaturnoj citacii," *Sbornik studenčeskix naučnyx rabot* (Tartu, 1973).

23. Compare: "Ešče čto menja porazilo — èto *infantiľnosť itaľjanskoj fonetiki, ee prekrasnaja detskosť, blizkosť k mladenčeskomu lepetu,* kakoj-to izvečnyj dadaizm." ". . . Dant vvodit detskuju zaum' v svoj . . . slovar'."

24. In some copies of the poem, the second line reads: "*Arabskix* peskov geometr" (a personal communication from G. A. Levinton, confirmed by N. I. Xardžiev, editor of Mandel'štam's selected poems in *Biblioteka poèta*). This variant (probably an earlier one) confirms the high credibility of my interpretation of the poem.

## Chapter IV: The Clock-Grasshopper

1. See, for example, Gleb Struve, "O. È. Mandel'štam," in *Sobranie sočinenij* (New York, 1955), p. 22.

2. Axmatova's footnote: "Krome togo, ko mne v raznoe vremja obraščeny četyre četverostišija: (1) 'Vy xotite byt' igrušečnoj' (1911); (2) 'Čerty lica iskaženy' (10-ye gody); (3) 'Privykajut v pčelovodu pčely' (30-ye gody); (4) 'Znakomstva našego na sklone' (30-ye gody)."

3. Axmatova's memoirs are quoted here according to a variant which has not appeared in print. In the text of "Listki iz dnevnika" published abroad there is no mention made of the poem "Čto pojut časy-kuznečik." The following poems are part of the "Axmatova cycle": (1) "Kassandre" ("Ja ne iskal v cvetuščie mgnoven'ja"), from which Axmatova cites the "prediction which partly came true"; (2) "V tot večer ne gudel strel'čatyj les organa"; (3) "Tvoe čudesnoe proiznošen'e"; (4) "Čto pojut časy-kuznečik." Perhaps a fifth poem also belongs to the "Axmatova cycle," "Kogda na ploščadjax i v tišine kelejnoj," where a "stubborn friend" ("uprjamaja podruga") is mentioned, who will refuse to try the white wine of Valhalla.

4. It is interesting to draw a parallel between the real facts lying at the basis of the poem "Čto pojut časy-kuznečik" and the twin-poems of 1922 which were discussed in Chapter Two above. In both cases a woman was present at the event which served as the starting point for the "plot." However, in neither of these poems is her presence felt. The poet attributed to himself the physical condition of his companion (see Chapter Two, note 1).

5. Indirect proof of the fact that Blok's lines were in Mandel'štam's creative memory at one time is the latter's poem "Veter nam utešen'e prines" (1922). As Blok's poem does, this concludes with the name *Azrail* rhyming with *kryl.*

6. Perhaps I should also mention another "insect-clock" in twentieth-century Russian poetry, Annenskij's "Stal'naja cikada." I do not consider it an obvious subtext of Mandel'štam's poem. There are no textual correspondences between Annenskij and Mandel'štam, and thematically their poems are rather dissimilar. However, Annenskij's "cicada" is reflected beyond any doubt at the beginning of "V ne po činu barstvennoj šube" (*Šum vremeni*): "Buločnye, ne stesnennye časom torgovli, sdobnym parom dyšali na ulicu, no *časovščiki* davno zakryli lavki, napolnennye gorjačim lopotan'em i zvonom *cicad.*"

7. I do not think that lines 7 and 8 are an example of an anacoluthon. "Swallow" and "daughter" vary one and the same subject and therefore the singular predicate results.

8.  The syntactic pattern *čto–èto* is typical of Russian colloquial language. Recently, I heard the following utterance: "Čto on ploxo zanimaetsja, — èto vsë jubki. Nu, i marixuana." In general, Mandel'štam's syntax is very close to the colloquial.

In the discussion after my lecture on Mandel'štam at Yale University (April 1972) Professor Edward Stankiewicz noticed that the three complex sentences analyzed above are reminiscent of the structure of riddles. Actually, the subordinate clauses (beginning with *čto*) represent the riddle itself, while the main clause (beginning with *èto*) contains its solution. Needless to say, the latter looks like a quasi-solution before a close analysis of the imagery involved is performed. The problem of riddles in reference to Mandel'štam's poetics is discussed in general terms by Omry Ronen in his article "Leksičeskij povtor, podtekst i smysl v poètike Mandel'štama," *Slavic Poetics: Essays in Honor of Kiril Taranovsky* (The Hague, 1973), pp. 376–384. This problem is very interesting, and it should be explored further. As an example, Ronen also quotes the second tercet of Mandel'štam's poem "Voz'mi na radost' '' (which will be analyzed in Chapter Five). This tercet follows the pattern of Russian tripartite riddles containing three infinitives; for example, "Otcova sunduka ne podnjat', / Sestrina točiva ne sobrat', / Bratnina konja ne pojmat'."

9.  The imperative *prosti* undoubtedly preserves both meanings, "proščaj" and "prosti [menja]." In the Russian language, and especially in Russian folklore, these meanings are very closely connected. In *Tristia* and *Vtoraja kniga* lines 11 and 12 read: "No čeremuxa uslyšit / I na dne morskom *prostit*." This variant might be explained as follows: "No čeremuxa uslyšit i prostit [menja, naxodjaščegosja] na dne morskom."

10.  The metaphoric use of substantives is in general characteristic of Mandel'štam's poetics: "K čemu objazatel'no osjazat' perstami? A glavnoe, začem otoždestvljat' slovo s vešč'ju, s travoju, s predmetom, kotoryj ono oboznačaet? Razve vešč' xozjain slova?" ("Slovo i kul'tura," 1921).

11.  The "rustle of blood' (*"šelest krovi,"* placed in quotation marks) is found in Annenskij's poem "Košmary." A. F. Fedorov writes as follows in his notes to Annenskij's *Stixotvorenija i poèmy* (Biblioteka poèta, 1959): " 'Šelest krovi' — citata iz XV gl. povesti Turgeneva 'Posle smerti (Klara Milič)': 'I vot emu (Jakovu Aratovu, geroju povesti, – A. F.) počudilos': kto-to šepčet emu na uxo ... Stuk serdca, šelest krovi, – podumal on.' Èto mesto Annenskij citiruet i v svoej stat'e 'Umirajuščij Turgenev' ('Kniga otraženij', SPb., 1906, str. 64)." In his turn, Mandel'štam cites Annenskij's "Košmary" in his 1922 article "O prirode slova." This poem was vividly impressed on his memory.

12.  The metaphors "red silk," "black silk," probably go back to Belyj's poetry. His poetry and poetic prose have many examples of such "textile imagery." For example, in *Severnaja simfonija* (p. 66): "Pered nim potreskivalo plamja, i kazalos' on byl objat skvoznym, *krasnym* šelkom"; in *Urna*: "Nad kryšeju purgovyj kon' / Pronessja v noč' ... A iz kamina / Streljaet *šelkovyj ogon'* / Strueju žaljaščej *rubina*. / ... A v okna snežnaja volna / *Atlasom* v'etsja nad derevnej ..."; cf. in *Severnaja simfonija: atlasnye/golubye* noči (p. 38); in *Kubok metelej: zlatobarxatnyj* sumrak (p. 10), *sinij barxat* noči (p. 27), *sinij barxat*

večera (p. 47), *belyj barxat* snegov (p. 134), noč' moja — žarka i *barxatna* (p. 161); in *Zoloto v lazuri*: golubejuščij barxat èfira (p. 4), *želtobarxatnyj* cvet zari (p. 17), černyj barxat (=nočnoe nebo, p. 228); in *Pepel: sinij barxat* noči, *belyj barxat* (snega, p. 27), and so forth.

13. The image of mice as a destructive force goes back to ancient myths. Since this poem is connected with Axmatova, we may suppose that Mandel'štam remembered her line: "Tak že *myši* knigi *točat*" ("Skol'ko raz ja proklinala," 1915). Mandel'štam "used" her lines in other instances. For example, the well-known line in "Tristia" (1918): "Kak belič'ja rasplastannaja škurka" is borrowed from Axmatova ("Vysoko v nebe oblačko serelo," 1911).

14. The transluscent gray spring of the asphodels is a metaphor for death. In ancient Greek mythology, asphodels grow in Hades. Cf. *Asfodilonskij lug* in book XI of the *Odyssey*: ". . . duša Axillesova s gordoj osankoj / Šagom širokim, po rovnomu Asfodilonskomu lugu / Tixo pošla . . ." (Žukovskij's translation). Mandel'štam found the image of the "transluscent spring" in Vjačeslav Ivanov's "Èllinskaja religija stradajuščego boga" (*Novyj put'*, January 1904, p. 127):

Так и в весенней радости греки не забывали о смерти. Весна как бы говорила им: «глядите, смертные: я — цвету, я — Кора Персефона! Недолго быть мне с вами, и вы не увидите меня, и снова увидите меня». И то же говорит Дионис. В этом его глубочайший пафос. *Весна была прозрачна для взора древних: она была цветущая Смерть.* Нигде, быть может, не высказываются виднее хтонические корни дионисической веры. Смерть только обратная сторона жизни: это было сознано народной душой прежде, чем провозглашено мудрецами, прежде, чем Гераклит Темный стал учить, что жизнь представляется смертью умершим, как смерть является смертью только живым.

See also Chapter Five, note 27. Persephone is a goddess of the nether world and a goddess of fertility. She spends the winter in Hades and in spring returns to the earth.

15. Valerij Brjusov, in an unkind and unjust review of *Vtoraja kniga* (*Pečat' i revoljucija*, 1923, no. 6, 64–66), reproached Mandel'štam for being inexact in reproducing an ancient Greek myth: "Persefona, esli i srezala lokon na golove umirajuščego, nikogda sama ne vodila duš v carstvo tenej." But Mandel'štam did not think this at all, as is obvious from the 1917 poem. "Vosled za Persefonoj" therefore can mean only "kak Persefona," "sleduja primeru Persefony," "po puti, projdennomu Persefonoj."

16. Let us compare the following lines from the first and second poems:

I     3 Слепая ласточка [душа] бросается к ногам [теней]

       4 С стигийской нежностью и веткою зеленой . . .

II   1 Я слово позабыл, что я хотел сказать.

       2 Слепая ласточка [душа?, слово?] в чертог теней вернется . . .

II  11 . . . [слово] мертвой ласточкой бросается к ногам

    12 С стигийской нежностью и веткою зеленой . . .

II  19 Но я забыл, что я хочу сказать,

    20 И мысль бесплотная в чертог теней вернется . . .

At first reading, line II, 2, is naturally associated with I, 3: swallow-soul. A new meaning of swallow is revealed in lines II, 11–12. The behavior of the soul and of the word turns out to be analogous (I, 3–4, and II, 11–12). Both the soul and the word carry a green branch to Hades (of course, it comes from our earthly world), but they have already been imbued with Stygian tenderness. Note also the parallelism of II, 1–2, and II, 19–20, as well. In these lines "slepaja lastočka" is identified with "besplotnaja mysl'." The new meaning of swallow (word, thought) is affirmed by lines II, 9–10, II, 21–22, which contain the image of Antigone. Finally, *podružka* from II, 23, recalls *tovarka* from I, 6.

17. "Slovo i kul'tura" (1921); the last image in this quotation is an obvious reminiscence of Tjutčev's lines: "Kak duši smotrjat s vysoty / Na imi brošennoe telo" ("Ona sidela na polu").

18. The complicated imagery of the poems "Kogda Psixeja-žizn'" and "Ja slovo pozabyl" (as well as "Ja v xorovod tenej" which is thematically connected with them) deserves detailed investigation. We will limit ourselves here to a few cursory remarks. In these poems Mandel'štam used the following images from ancient myths: (1) Persephone, (2) "mednaja lepeška" — a small coin put into the mouth of a dead person to pay Charon for ferrying to the gates of Hades, (3) "nočnoj tabun" — horses grazing in Hades (*Aeneid* VI, lines 652–655).

The comparison of the soul to a swallow can be found in an early Mandel'štam poem, "Pod grozovymi oblakami":

> В священном страхе тварь живет,
> И каждый совершит душою,
> Как ласточка перед грозою
> Неописуемый полет.

In learned poetry it goes back to Deržavin's "Lastočka." Many legends connect the swallows' winter absence with the underground, and sometimes, even with the underwater world (for example, in A. Cruden's *A Complete Concordance to the Holy Scriptures* [see "Swallow"]). There are also many legends about the winter death and spring resurrection of swallows (for example, in medieval bestiaries). Deržavin knew one of these legends:

> Всю прелесть ты видишь природы,
> Зришь лета роскошного храм,
> Но видишь и бури ты черны
> И осени скучной приход;
> И прячешься в бездны подземны,
> Хладея зимою, как лед.
> Во мраке лежишь бездыханна, –
> Но только лишь придет весна
> И роза вздохнет лишь румяна,
> Встаешь ты от смертного сна;
> . . . . . . . . . . . . . . . . .
> Душа моя! гостья ты мира:
> Не ты ли перната сия? –

Воспой же бессмертие, лира!
Восстану, восстану и я . . .

In "Lastočki" Fet compares their flight with the inspiration of the human spirit:

Не так ли я, сосуд скудельный,
Дерзаю на запретный путь,
Стихии чуждой, запредельной,
Стремясь хоть каплю зачерпнуть.

Incidentally, Fet's poem is reflected in Mandel'štam's "Kazino" (1912):

*Fet:* Люблю, забывши все кругом,
Следитъ за ласточкой стрельчатой . . .

*Mandel'štam:* Люблю следить за чайкою крылатой . . .

There is a mysterious connection between swallows and blindness. We will cite a legend from Pliny's *Natural History* (see "Chelidonia"; Cruden reproduced this legend in his *Concordance*): "by means of it [celandine] swallows cure the eyes of the chicks in the nest and restore the sight, as some hold, even when the eyes have been torn out." Of course, this legend does not explain Mandel'-štam's image "slepaja lastočka." Nonetheless, it shows that future investigation in this direction may prove to be fruitful.

In the triad, "lastočka, podružka, Antigona," the third name of the "besplot-naja mysl' " is very interesting. Without making any definite suggestions, we should recall that Antigone, the loving and devoted daughter, daughter of Oedipus who tore out his eyes, was born of an incestuous marriage. When talking about the connection between poetry and blindness, we should recall the "blind poets" who gave us "Ionian honey" (from "Na kamennyx otrogax Pièrii"). A parallel text from "Slovo i kul'tura" may be cited with reference to the phrases "zrjačie pal'cy" and "vypuklaja radost' uznavan'ja": "Piši bez-óbraznye stixi, esli smožeš', esli sumeeš'. Slepoj uznaet miloe lico, edva priko-snuvšis' k nemu *zrjačimi pal'cami*, i slezy radosti, nastojaščej *radosti uznavan'ja*, bryznut iz glaz ego posle dolgoj razluki. Stixotvorenie živo vnutrennim obrazom, tem zvučaščim slepkom formy, kotoryj predvarjaet napisannoe stixotvorenie. Ni odnogo slova ešče net, a stixotvorenie uže zvučit. Èto zvučit vnutrennij obraz, èto ego osjazaet slux poèta. — I sladok nam liš' uznavan'ja mig!"

Singing grasshoppers are connected with ancient (anacreontic) lyric poetry. Actually, in classical poetry, cicadas and not grasshoppers sang; but in Russian poetry, Lomonosov translated the ancient Greek τέττιξ as *kuznečik*, and this usage was simply accepted. "Ja slovo pozabyl" is connected with "Čto pojut časy-kuznečik" not only by the images of the "swallow" and "daughter," but also by the image of the untied / empty bark (*čelnok*). Both these barks are similar to the "unfastened boat" (*neprikreplennaja lodka*) in "Voz'mi na radost' iz moix ladonej" (1920), which will be discussed in Chapter Five. Moreover, "Ja slovo pozabyl" and "Čto pojut časy-kuznečik" have in common the image of grasshoppers and a similar model of the metaphors "černyj šelk *gorit* [blestit]" — "černyj led *gorit* [žžet]." Without doubt, Mandel'štam remembered his 1917 poem when he was writing about the swallow-soul and swallow-word.

19. Both in this poem and in "Čto pojut časy-kuznečik" *čeremuxa* is connected by sound repetition to the epithet *černyj*. This repetition emphasizes the contrast white:black.

20. Mrs. Mandel'štam confirms that such an event actually took place, but she dismisses all Kataev's "fictional embellishments" (private communication). She asserts, however, that this poem reflects Mandel'štam's infatuation with Ol'ga Vaksel' in 1925. This is undoubtedly true for the third tercet. In that case "Ja budu metat'sja" would belong both to the Mrs. Mandel'štam and to the Mrs. Vaksel' cycles. See Chapter Three above, note 11. There are two other poems addressed to Ol'ga Vaksel': (1) a love poem, "Žizn' upala, kak zarnica" (1925), and "Vozmožna li ženščine mertvoj xvala?" (1935). In the latter poem there is a reminiscence from "Ja budu metat'sja." Compare: "Ja budu metat'sja . . . *za mel'ničnym šumom*" (1925) and "*No mel'nic kolesa zimujut* v snegu" (1935).

21. That the lilac branch (*sirenevaja vetv'*) is metaphoric in this stanza is proved by the third stanza, where the pronoun *ty* is repeated (in the genitive case: *ot tebja*). In this stanza the garden is nurtured by the poet's yearning ("moej toskoju vynjančen") and is covered with "thorns" from the lilac branch (which is not a real one, but obviously figurative). The thorns, too, are of course metaphoric.

22. Mandel'štam himself, in "Zametki o Šen'e" called romantic poetry a "necklace of dead nightingales" (*ožerel'e iz mertvyx solov'ev*). There is reason to think that Pasternak's "Opredelenie poèzii" was written during the summer of 1917. Mandel'štam, though, could not have known it then, as it was first published in 1922.

23. The poem "Čto pojut časy-kuznečik" can be compared as well to the following stanza from the "Axmatova cycle": "Pust' govorjat: ljubov' krylata, / Smert' okrylennee stokrat; / Ešče duša bor'boj ob"jata, / A naši guby k nej [ = k smerti] letjat" ("Tvoe čudesnoe proiznošen'e"). Both poems, perhaps, deal not only with a premonition of death, but with an attraction toward it, too. In the first poem, the image of the "sea" may symbolize "the invitation to death" (see Gaston Bachelard, *L'Eau et les rêves*).

24. While it is obvious that the imagery in these two poems ("Čto pojut časy-kuznečik" and "Xolodok ščekočet temja") is different, I would like to call the reader's attention to the rhymes in both: inexact, very free in the first, and exact, traditional in the second. Let us note, too, that the first poem is saturated with sound repetitions, whereas they are hardly noticed in the second. But this question goes beyond the limits of this essay.

25. Concerning the image of "poetic lips," see Chapter One p. 2 and Chapter Six, pp. 128–129. In Mandel'štam's work, "the movement of lips" is not just a metaphor. It has been reported that Mandel'štam, when composing a poem, actually moved his lips silently. The lips in the penultimate line of "Ja slovo pozabyl" are also, of course, poetic lips.

26. Gumilev, "Duša i telo, II":

> – Но я за все . . .
> За все печали радости и бредни,

Как подобает мужу заплачу
*Непоправимой гибелью последней.*

## Chapter V: Bees and Wasps

1. These poems and letters are published in *Sobranie sočinenij* II, 2nd ed., 1971. In a postcard mailed June 20 (July 3), 1909, Mandel'štam wrote: "Vaši semena gluboko zapali v moju dušu i ja pugajus', gljadja na gromadnye rostki." The letter dated August 13/26, 1909, contains an enthusiastic appraisal of Ivanov's book *Po zvezdam* ("Vaša kniga prekrasna krasotoj velikix arxitekturnyx sozdanij i astronomičeskix sistem"). In the same letter Mandel'štam asks Ivanov a favor: "Esli u Vas est' lišnij, soveršenno lišnij èkzempljar 'Kormičix zvezd' — ne možet li on kakim-nibud' sposobom popast' v moi berežnye ruki?"

2. See N. Mandel'štam, *Vtoraja kniga*, pp. 37 and 129. See also Chapter Three above, p. 61 and note 11.

3. This article was reprinted with certain changes in Przybylski's book *Et in Arcadia ego* (Warsaw, 1966).

4. The term "Arcadia" can be applied to Mandel'štam's "idyl" only in its broadest meaning. Mandel'štam goes back neither to Virgil's Arcadia, nor to the bucolic poetry of Theocritus. His sources are older still: Hesiod and Sappho.

5. True, in the second version of his article, Przybylski quotes the first fragment both in Ivanov's and Veresaev's translations, but the second fragment remains only in Polish. Here again Przybylski did not thoroughly study Mandel'-štam's possible sources. In the second version the harsh expression "aleksandryj-ska fuszerka" is also removed.

Nadežda Mandel'štam confirms in her memoirs (*Vtoraja kniga*, p. 37) that she gave Mandel'štam Ivanov's book of translations from Alcaeus and Sappho before he wrote "Na kamennyx otrogax" (in the beginning of May 1919). However, her statement that Mandel'štam only leafed through ("perelistal") the book may be questioned: I believe that my analysis of the poem will prove that he read the book very carefully. In his yet unpublished article " 'Na ka-mennyx otrogax Pièrii' Mandel'štama: Materialy k analizu," G. A. Levinton assumes that Mandel'štam worked with all the Russian translations, giving deliberate preference to V. Ivanov's.

6. Perhaps Mandel'štam, in mentioning the "tender tombs of the Archi-pelago" also thought of archeology which, without the oldest epic poetry, cannot alone revive the world of ancient Hellas. But one should not insist on this overly rationalistic explanation of the stanza.

7. All of Veresaev's translations from ancient poets are quoted according to the edition *Èllinskie poèty* (Moscow, 1963).

8. Several years ago, during my Harvard seminar on Mandel'štam (1968) O. Ronen called my attention to Plato's dialogue. Unfortunately, my "Tri zametki," *IJSLP* XII (1969) were at that time in press, and I could not in-clude this information in my *"Post scriptum* k stat'je o pčelax i osax." Mrs. Mandel'štam also indicates "Ion" as a source of the bees and honey in "Na kamennyx otrogax" (*Vtoraja kniga*, p. 129).

9. Theodorus Bergk, *Poetae lyrici Graeci* III, 4th ed., 1882, 110–127; Vjačeslav Ivanov *Alkej i Safo*, 183–198; Veresaev, *Ēllinskie poèty*, 256–260.

10. Mrs. Mandel'štam does not believe that the source of Mandel'štam's cicadas should be traced to Ivanov's poetry. She claims that the only source of Mandel'štam's image is Deržavin's lines: "Ščastliv zolotoj kuznečik, / Čto v lesu kuješ odin." These lines came to my mind when I was writing my article, but I did not consider them as a subtext for Mandel'štam's poem: the forging grasshoppers are a commonplace in Russian poetry, because of the etymological connection: *kuznec* (blacksmith) and *kuznečik* (grasshopper). To the best of my knowledge, only Ivanov and Mandel'štam have *forging cicadas;* moreover, both Ivanov's and Mandel'štam's cicadas have *small hammers*. I shall go even further and assume that Mandel'štam did not want to introduce grasshoppers in the merry prenuptial mood of the second stanza: grasshoppers in his *Tristia* are connected with the motif of death. In his poem "Čto pojut časy-kuznečik" the singing of the clock-grasshopper is "the music of death" (see the discussion of this poem in Chapter Three above), and in the poem "Ja slovo pozabyl, čto ja xotel skazat' " grasshoppers are inhabitants of the underground kingdom of Persephone.

11. Brzostowska did not put the "Epithalamia" into a separate cycle. In her translation the corresponding fragments are scattered throughout the whole book. For this reason Przybylski did not sense the "prenuptial atmosphere" of Mandel'štam's montage.

12. In the extant Greek text this line is very corrupt and only admits of a conjectural translation. Veresaev translates it more cautiously (No. 59): "Na altar' tebe ot kozy ja beloj . . . / I sveršu tebe vozlijan'e . . ."

13. Unfortunately, we have not been able to determine which text Goleniščev-Kutuzov used for his translation. Most likely, it was a French source. Even in this montage, it is not difficult to recognize the fragments published by Bergk as Nos. 91 (73) and 92 (69). We have already quoted the first of them in the translations of Vjačeslav Ivanov and Veresaev. Veresaev translated the second fragment in the following way: "Vyše, naskol'ko pevec lesbosskij [Terpandr] drugix prevyšaet" (No. 101).

14. In Veresaev's translation: *kervel'* and *donnik* (No. 24).

15. *Krinica* is a Ukrainism in Russian poetic language, and it recalls, naturally, the Ukrainian *lirniki* of the first stanza.

16. *Svjaščennye ostrova* ("sacred islands") would be a more exact translation. Nonetheless, Mandel'štam's epithet "holy" (*svjatoj*) is really not so "Parnassian" — regardless of where he took it from.

17. Mandel'štam accepted Makkavejskij's line without any hesitation. He may have recalled his own lines, written in 1913 ("Amerikan bar"):

> В пол оборота обернется
> Фортуны нашей колесо.

I cannot agree with Terapiano that the last two lines of "Na kamennyx otrogax" are "suše i fonetičeski bednee mandel'štamovskix" (*Vstreči*, New York, 1953, p. 15). The last two lines successfully utilize the opposition of diffuse vowels (in the syntagm *skripučij trud*) to compact. In the subsequent text all the accented vowels are compact (a-e-o-a-o); they also continue the theme of accented compact vowels from the previous two lines: a-o-e-o-o-o-o. On the synaesthethic perception of compact and diffuse vowels, see my article "The Sound Texture of Russian Verse in the Light of Distinctive Features," *IJSLP* IX, 1965, and my communication, "Zvukovaja faktura stixa i ee vosprijatie," *Proceedings of the Sixth International Congress of Phonetic Sciences* (Prague, 1970).

18.   See an analysis of this poem in D. M. Segal's article, "Mikrosemantika odnogo stixotvorenija," *Slavic Poetics: Essays in Honor of Kiril Taranovsky* (The Hague, 1973).

19.   In his polemic against symbolism (in the article "O prirode slova"), Mandel'štam chooses precisely the rose as an example of "correspondences nodding at one another"; he forgets that in his own poetry the rose is symbolic.

20.   Ivanov's poem, in its turn, echoes Tjutčev's lines:

Весна идет, весна идет!
И тихих, теплых, майских дней
Румяный, светлый хоровод
Толпится весело за ней.

21.   Irina Bušman (*Poètičeskoe iskusstvo Mandel'štama*, 1964, p. 65) interprets "Voz'mi na radost' " as a love poem, too. She finds a similarity between it and Catullus's poem "Vivamus, mea Lesbia, atque amemus." However, there are no direct reminiscences from Cattulus's poem in Mandel'štam.

22.   It should be noted that in different sonnets Bal'mont reveals other figurative meanings of these two symbols. The sun, moon, and honey symbolism of the entire book is complex and polysemantic, of course. The symbolic meanings: bee / poet and honey / poetry are also found in Bal'mont's *Sonety*. For example:

Идет к концу сонетное теченье.
Душистый и тягуче-сладкий мед
Размерными продленьями течет,
Янтарное узорчато скрепленье.

. . . . . . . . . . . . . . .

Замкнитесь пчелы в улей. Час зимы.

(«Сохраненный янтарь»)

И все пчела, и все к цветам склонен,
В звененье крыл ввожу церковный звон.

(«Вязь, 1.»)

А я? Не совершая ли влюбленье
Цветка в цветок, с зари и до зари,
Пчела лишь собирает янтари?

(«Вязь, 2.»)

23.   Currently, the word symbol is often misused. We therefore venture to remind the reader of the basic difference between symbol, metaphor and allegory.

A symbol always preserves its primary, material level. Take, for example, pink, azure and dark-blue distances, scarlet and red dawns, a violet west, a yellow sunset, wind and snowstorms, "night, a street, a lamp, a pharmacy" in Blok's poetry. In the first place, these are elements of a real landscape. They acquire further, abstract meanings only on the higher level. The metaphor, an abbreviated simile, has no concrete level. Similarly with allegory: being an extended metaphor, it has only a figurative meaning. In Krylov's fables, lions, asses and monkeys do not appear as real animals; they are conventional types which represent people. One should also make a clear distinction between a symbol and an analogy. It is true that analogies also have a concrete, material level of meaning. As was shown in Chapter Two, the "dry herbs" in Mandel'-štam's imagery, while remaining a real object, are at the same time a reference to the poetry. If in analogies the relation of material and abstract levels is simple (one to one), with symbols the figurative meaning is always polysemantic. Finally, one should bear in mind that the most complex symbols, such as religious and mythological ones, as well as symbols of poetic schools inclined toward mystical revelations (German Romanticism, Russian Symbolism) have an additional emotional level. Thus, such symbols work on three levels: (1) material, (2) emotional, and (3) spiritual. This threefold function of symbols was long ago exactly defined by Thomas Aquinas: they are outside of us, in us, and above us.

24. In this line the epithet "*v mexa obutaja* [ten']" is striking. This epithet is so unusual that the reader has a right to assume that there is an unknown reminiscence behind it. I would not be at all surprised if a subtext were found for this epithet as well. It should be noted, however, that Mandel'štam returned to the motif of inaudible steps in July 1932 ("Stixi o russkoj poèzii, II"), in the image of the soft boots of the executioner:

> И угодливо-поката
> Кажется земля пока,
> И в сапожках мягких ката
> Выступают облака.

25. *Sočinenija Deržavina s objasnitel'nymi primečanijami Ja. Grota* II, 1868, 550.

26. Mandel'štam and Arbenina used to go together to the theater (*Vtoraja kniga*, p. 70). It is true that "V Peterburge" is not a love poem: it is addressed to the poet's friends, the acmeists (the *my* in the first line). However, the image of Russian women recurs throughout the whole poem as a leitmotif (lines 7, 23, 31):

> 7. Все поют блаженных жен *родные* очи . . .
> 23. И блаженных жен *родные* руки
> 24. Легкий пепел соберут . . .
> 31. Все поют блаженных жен крутые плечи . . .

In the second version of the poem Mandel'štam changed the first quatrain of the last stanza. Lines 25–26 are read as follows:

Где-то хоры сладкие Орфея
И *родные* темные зрачки.

There is no doubt that the *"rodnye zrački"* belong to one of the "blažennye *ženy"* (lovers or wives, not mothers). One should keep in mind that lines 23–24 are a plausible reminiscence from Puškin ("Krivocovu"):

Смертный миг наш будет светел;
И *подруги* шалунов
*Соберут* их *легкий пепел*
В урны праздные пиров.

Mandel'štam has only one poem dedicated to his mother (written after her death in 1916), "Èta noč' nepopravima." As for the "rodnaja ten'" in "Koncert na vokzale," this image was discussed in Chapter One.

27. In *Tristia* the epithet *prozračnyj* is very often used in images connected with death. See Jurij Levin, "O nekotoryx čertax plana soderžanija v poètičeskix tekstax," *IJSLP* XIII, 1969, 139. See also Chapter Four, note 14.

28. In that case, the first line of the fourth tercet, "Oni šuršat v prozračnyx debrjax *noči*," might be compared with a line from "Grifel'naja oda": "I *vozduxa* prozračnyj les"; in those examples *noč'* and *vozdux* retain their real, literal meaning.

29. I assume that Vjačeslav Ivanov borrowed his image of a "necklace of starry tears" from a poem by Pečerin, published by M. Geršenzon in his book *Žizn' V. S. Pečerina*, a year before the publication of *Cor ardens*. Pečerin's poem is a part of his *poèma* "Toržestvo smerti," and it has the title of "Pis'mo Èdmunda k Èmilii (s posylkoju stixotvorenij ego)". The comparison of tears with pearls is a commonplace in poetry in general (in Russian poetry it goes back to Lermontov's "sleza — žemčužina stradan'ja"), but the metaphor necklace-poetry is not a usual one. Here is the text of Pečerin's poem:

Души моей царица! Ожерелье
Вам посылает ваш певец младой.
Быть может, вам на брачное веселье
Поспеет мой подарок дорогой.
Не правда-ль? Жемчугу богатое собранье?
Смотрите: крупно каждое зерно,
И каждое зерно — слеза, воспоминанье,
И куплено слезой кровавою оно . . .
Не плавал я среди морей опасных,
Не в пропастях сокровищ вам искал,
Не звонким золотом червонцев ясных
Вам ожерелье покупал:
Из сердца глубины, при светоча сияньи,
С слезами песнь моя лилась в полночный час –
Из этих песен, слез, живых воспоминаний
Я ожерелье набирал для вас.
Как должную вам дань, с улыбкою небрежной,

Приймите эту нить стихов и слез моих:
Так боги в небесах приемлют безмятежно
Куренье и мольбы от алтарей земных.

Vjačeslav Ivanov, even if he did not read Geršenzon's book, could have known this poem from Ogarev's collection *Potaennaja literatura XIX stoletija* (London, 1861).

The metaphor necklace-poetry is found in Puškin, too:

В прохладе сладостной фонтанов
И стен, обрызганых кругом,
Поэт бывало тешил ханов
Стихов гремучим жемчугом.

На нити праздного веселья
Низал он хитрою рукой
Прозрачной лести ожерелья
И четки мудрости златой.

Can we not trace the titles of Gumilev's and Axmatova's early collections back to Puškin? The image of "dead bees" appears in Gumilev's famous poem "Slovo" (in the collection *Ognennyj stolp*). Nils Nilsson devoted a special article to this poem, "The Dead Bees" (*Orbis Scriptus, Dmitrij Tchižewskij zum 70. Geburstag*, 1966). As Nilsson has shown in detail, this poem arose against a background of the theoretical discussions of that time about the "living" and "dead" word. It is not without interest to compare Gumilev's dead bees with Annenskij's dead flies, without, of course, insisting that Annenskij's image (borrowed from Apuxtin) was the prototype for Gumilev:

Мухи-мысли ползут, как во сне,
Вот бумагу покрыли, чернея . . .
О, как мертвые, гадки оне . . .
Разорви их, сожги их скорее . . .

The question of the interrelation of the images of the dead bees in Mandel'štam's and Gumilev's poems remains open. Mandel'štam's poem was written in November 1920. We know that Mandel'štam and Gumilev used to meet in Petrograd. Blok saw them both at an evening of poetry at the Poets' Club in Litejnaja, October 21, 1921 (*Sobranie sočinenij* VII, 1963, 371). Axmatova, too, writes about the evenings of poetry in 1920 in which Blok, Gumilev, and Mandel'štam took part. It is quite probable that Gumilev became familiar with Mandel'štam's poem soon after it was written. It is not known when Gumilev's "Slovo" dates from; it was published for the first time in the almanac *Drakon*, in May 1921. Without ruling out the possibility that the image of the dead bees arose independently in both poets, Nilsson nonetheless tends toward the supposition that Mandel'štam borrowed the image from Gumilev and that Mandel'štam's poem is, seemingly, a polemical answer to Gumilev. I do not consider the last assumption likely. In Mandel'štam's poem, the symbolism of the necklace of dead bees stemmed from the comparison of kisses to bees; it lacks the meaning which Nilsson reads into it.

30. See Cvetaeva's explanation of the origin of this poem in "Istorija odnogo posvjaščenija," *Oxford Slavonic Papers* XI, 1964.

31. Compare also Mandel'štam's line: "I Šuberta v šube zamerz *talisman*" ("Na mertvyx resnicax Isakij zamerz," 1935). The fur coat is Mandel'štam's favorite image for poetry, or art in general, as a defense from the world's coldness (in *Šum vremeni*, the end of "V ne po činu barstvennoj šube" and in several poems written in the 1930s). The image of "veer prošlyx let" is suggested by Mandel'štam's reading of Bergson; it is explained in Mandel'štam's essay "O prirode slova."

32. The poem "A nebo buduščim beremenno" formerly was a part of the cycle published in the almanac *Lët* (1923). See Chapter One, p. 6 and note 12. In this cycle the metaphor for an airplane, the honeybee (*medunica*), which belongs to the positive semantic field, is opposed to a negative image of dragonflies, a metaphor for military airplanes ("assirijskie kryl'ja strekoz" in "Veter" and "kryl'ja strekozinye" in "A nebo."

33. This poem will be discussed in Chapter Six.

34. The suggestiveness of this poem results, in part, from its skillful sound texture. It is built on strident and acute (bright) /s/ and /z/. Alternating forms with plain and sharp /s/, *os-os*', are, of course, a striking paranomasia. But they are more than that. B. L. Whorf maintains (*Language, Thought and Reality*, New York, 1956, p. 267) that acute (bright) phonemes are perceived synesthetically as being sharp (in a tactile sense), as opposed to the grave (dark) ones, which are blunt. If it is so, then the distinctive feature of sharpness intensifies the effect of synesthetical perception. Thus, if /s/ is sharp, /s'/ is still sharper. The stridency and sharpness of the consonants /s/ and /z/ excellently echo the motif of "narrow wasps sucking the Earth's axis."

35. While my book was in the process of publication, Nils Nilsson published an essay devoted to Mandel'štam's "Voz'mi na radost'" in *Russian Literature* 7–8, 1974; reprinted in his book, *Osip Mandel'štam: Five Poems* (Stockholm, 1974). This essay is a step forward toward a better understanding of the Mandel'-štam poem. In his 1963 comments Nilsson believed that the poem was addressed to an impersonal reader; now he knows that the poet's addressee was a woman with whom he was in love. In his first article the love theme was not even hinted at; now he accepts the fact that "Voz'mi" is a love poem (compare: *Scando-Slavica* XI, 47–49, and *Five Poems*, p. 75, note 1, and p. 85), but he still does not analyze it as such. In his new comments on the third tercet, Nilsson gives a number of fine examples where metaphoric bees are connected with poetic creation, but he completely ignores the other large context where bees have explicit erotic connotations. The main image in the third (central) tercet is "fluffy kisses," not bees; the bees serve only as the second part of a simile, because they are fluffy as well. As I understand it, the central tercet is very important because it puts the love theme in the forefront. I do not believe that "fluffy kisses" could simultaneously work on two levels: on the material one and as a metaphor for poetic words. If the kisses are real, then the epithet "fluffy"

can be easily explained as a result of metonymical thinking (see Chapter Two, note 24; particularly compare Puškin's "mladoj i svežyj poceluj" and Mandel'-štam's "moxnatye pocelui"). It would be much harder to explain the epithet if the kisses are a metaphor for poetic words. No wonder that Nilsson did not comment on that epithet. In one respect Nilsson is right: in "Voz'mi" the love theme is "combined with the theme of poetry." But the latter is brought forward in the last tercet: a necklace is a suggestive metaphor for poetry. Finally, I do not believe that "Voz'mi" continues the tradition of early nineteenth-century friendly epistles, such as Jazykov's, which he wrote to his friends and his brother while sending them some of his poems or modern German books (*Five Poems*, pp. 70–71). A comparison of Mandel'štam's absurd gifts, such as "ožerel'e iz mertvyx pčel," or "peresypaemyj pesok," to Puškin's wild gift in "Poslanie Del'vigu" ("Primi sej čerep, Del'vig, on / Prinadležit tebe po pravu") might have been more appropriate.

## Chapter VI: The Soil and Destiny

1. See "Istorija odnogo posvjaščenija," *Oxford Slavonic Papers* XI, 1964, 134. The following poems belong to the "Cvetaeva cycle": (1) "V raznogolosice devičeskogo xora," (2) "Na rozval'njax," (3) "Ne verja voskresen'ja čudu." See Cvetaeva's letter of July 25, 1923, to A. Baxrax, published in *Mosty* 5, 1960, 316.

2. According to information coming from Mrs. Mandel'štam, her husband converted to Lutheranism in Finland, in 1908 or 1909. It is possible that it happened later, after his return from his studies abroad, when he decided to enroll in the University of St. Petersburg. In 1911, he was twice in Finland: in March and in August (see his letters to Vjačeslav Ivanov in *Zapiski otdela rukopisej* 34, Gos. biblioteka imeni V. I. Lenina (Moscow, 1973), 273–274).

3. Pavel Florenskij's *Stolp i utverždenie istiny* was published in 1914. Unfortunately, we do not know when Mandel'štam personally met Father Florenskij. However, he read his writings before he went to Kiev in 1919 (N. Mandel'štam, *Vospominanija*, p. 248). Mandel'štam knew S. P. Kablukov before 1916 and discussed religious problems with him, according to Mrs. Mandel'štam: "Kablukov borolsja s tjagoj Mandel'štama k katoličestvu, xotel obratit' jego v pravoslavie, zastavljal sdavat' èkzameny v universitete, čego tot organičeski ne umel, i nakonec, iskrenno ogorčilsja, kogda v stixax posle romana s Marinoj Cvetaevoj vdrug prorezalsja novyj golos. Kablukovu, kak mnogim rodnym i duxovnym otcam, xotelos' soxranit' mal'čika v netronutoj junošeskoj ser'eznosti. Mandel'-štam tjanulsja k Kablukovu i, verojatno, mnogo ot nego polučil" (*Vtoraja kniga*, 33–34).

4. See Edward Gibbon, *The History of the Decline and Fall of the Roman Empire* II (London, 1929), 157–158.

5. See Lloyd B. Hoslapple, *Constantine the Great* (New York, 1942), pp. 317–319.

6. Victor Terras, "The Time Philosophy of Osip Mandel'štam," *The Slavonic and East European Review* XVII, no. 109, 1969, 351.

7. N. Gumilev, *Sobranie sočinenij* IV (Washington, 1968), 363.

8. In his 1914 review of the first edition of *Kamen'*, Gumilev also noted Mandel'štam's symbolic "Music with a capital M."

9. See Mandel'štam's description of the Wrangel jail in his essay "Men'-ševiki v Gruzii" (1923):

И мне пришлось глядеть на любимые, сухие, полынные холмы Феодосии, на киммерийское холмогорье из тюремного окна и гулять по выжженному дворику, где сбились в кучу перепуганные евреи, а крамольные офицеры искали вшей в гимнастерках, слушая дикий рев солдат, приветствующих у моря своего военачальника.

10. In this triad, *staruxa* clearly relates to *tjur'ma* with which it is joined by the sound repetition of the grave (dark) *u*. In general, the stressed vowel *u* is dominant in this stanza (five out of ten). Four stressed and one unstressed *u* are in rhyme position; moreover, the supporting consonants in all four rhymes (*m* and *b*) are also dark. Such a sound texture underlines the gloomy mood of the whole stanza.

11. The echo of the "childhood" and "jail" images is also underlined by the grammatical form of the substantives (accusative case) and by their syntactic function (direct object): "zabud' — pticu, staruxu, tjur'mu; vspomniš' — osu, penal, černiku."

12. Nevertheless, the theme of silence does not disappear from Mandel'štam's poetry of the thirties. The Voronezh poem "Naušniki, naušnicki moi" (April 1935) contains a direct quote from Tjutčev's "Silentium!"; "Nu, kak metro? *Molči*, v sebe *tai*, / Ne sprašivaj, kak nabuxajut počki" (Tjutčev: "*Molči*, skryvajsja i *tai*"). This, of course, is not Tjutčev's voluntary silence, but a compulsory one, dictated by fear: don't ask even about such a harmless thing as the coming of spring.

13. M. P. Alekseev, *Stixotvorenie Puškina "Ja pamjatnik sebe vozdvig. . ."* (Leningrad, 1967), p. 224.

14. The syntactic structure of the poem is not quite clear. The gerund *otkidyvajas'* is puzzling. Is it governed "from a distance" by the verb *tverdet'* ("Skat . . . tverdeet . . . otkidyvajas'")? Or is it a noncoordinated gerund referring directly to the subject (*skat*), as in Mandel'štam's early poem "Nevyrazimaja pečal'" (1909): "I, tonen'kij biskvit *lomaja*, tončajšix pal'cev belizna"? If we may believe Georgij Ivanov, these lines provoked an animated discussion in *Cex poètov* (see commentary in Mandel'štam's *Sobranie sočinenij*, vol. I). A similar dangling gerund is found in Pasternak's "Klevetnikam" (1917): "Ničtožnost' vozrastov kleveščet. / O junye, a nas? / O levye, – a nas levejšix, – *Rumjanjas'* i junjas'?" In contemporary prose, such noncoordinated gerunds are sometimes used by Solženicyn. Since elliptical syntax is characteristic of Mandel'štam, I would propose the following reading: (1) "skat [Krasnoj ploščadi] tverdeet, otkidyvajas' do risovyx polej"; (2) "ee skat tverdeet [i budet tverdet' do tex por], pokuda na zemle poslednij živ nevol'nik."

15.  See Puškin's poem "K morju" (1824). See also Mandel'štam's lines written in June 1935:

> На вершок бы мне синего моря, на игольное только ушко,
> Чтобы двойка конвойного времени парусами неслась хорошо.

Compare in Puškin:

> Прощай, свободная стихия!
> . . . . . . . . . . . . .
> Моей души предел желанный!
> . . . . . . . . . . . . .
> Не удалось навек оставить
> Мне скучный, неподвижный брег,
> Тебя восторгами поздравить
> И по хребтам твоим направить
> Мой поэтической побег!

16.  Mandel'štam will return to the image of the crucifixion in a Voronezh poem dated February 4, 1937: "Kak svetoteni mučenik Rembrandt," where he speaks of his "burning rib."

17.  A similar poetic interpretation of Red Square's convex surface is found in Leonid Martynov's poem "Krasnye vorota" (first publication in *Novyj mir*, 1952, no. 6):

> И вот тогда
> С обрыва тротуара
> При разноцветном знаке светофора
> Возвышенность всего земного шара
> Внезапно открывается для взора.
> . . . . . . . . . . . . . . . . .
> Земного шара
> Выпуклость тугая
> Вздымается в упругости гудрона.
> Машины, это место огибая,
> Из полумрака смотрят удивленно.
>
> А город
> Щурит искристые очи,
> Не удивляясь и прекрасно зная,
> Что с Красной площади еще гораздо четче
> Она
> Видна –
> Возвышенность земная!

It is very likely that Martynov knew Mandel'štam's poem before he wrote his own.

18.  It should be noted that in two poems written in 1916 Mandel'štam already had a negative image of the Kremlin and of Red Square. Namely, in "Vse čuždo nam v stolice nepotrebnoj":

Все чуждо нам в столице непотребной:
Ее сухая черствая земля
И буйный торг на Сухаревке хлебной
И страшный вид разбойного Кремля.

And in "O ètot vozdux":

О этот воздух, смутой пьяный
На черной площади Кремля!
Качают шаткий «мир» смутьяны,
Тревожно пахнут тополя.

19.  As is known, the original text of Puškin's poem was published in 1881. Mandel'štam's poem was published for the first time abroad, in *Vozdušnye puti* II, 1961, and, in the Soviet Union, in *Den' poèzii*, 1962.

# AUTHOR'S NOTE

The essays collected in this book were originally published with the following titles:

**Chapter One:** "The Problem of Context and Subtext in the Poetry of Osip Mandel'štam," *Slavic Forum: Essays in Linguistics and Literature.* The Hague: Mouton & Co., 1974.

**Chapter Two:** "O zamknutoj i otkrytoj interpretacii poètičeskogo teksta," *American Contributions to the Seventh International Congress of Slavists* I, Linguistics and Poetics. The Hague: Mouton & Co., 1974.

**Chapter Three:** "The Jewish Theme in the Poetry of Osip Mandel'-štam," *Russian Literature* 7–8. The Hague: Mouton & Co., 1974.

**Chapter Four:** "Razbor odnogo 'zaumnogo' stixotvorenija Mandel'-štama," *Russian Literature* 2. The Hague: Mouton & Co., 1972.

**Chapter Five:** "Pčely i osy v poèzii Mandel'štama: K voprosu o vlijanii Vjačeslava Ivanova na Mandel'štama," *To Honor Roman Jakobson* III. The Hague: Mouton & Co., 1967.

**Chapter Six:** (I) "Osip Mandel'štam: 'Na rozval'njax, uložennyx solomoj'," *Russian Literature* 7–8, 1974; (II) "Dva 'molčanija' Osipa Mandel'štama," *Russian Literature* 2, 1972; (III) "Mandel'štam's Monument Not Wrought by Hands," *California Slavic Studies* VI, 1971.

The essays published in 1967 and 1971 have been considerably reworked. Additions and changes were also made in the essays published later.

# INDEX OF NAMES

Afanas'ev, A. N., 36
Alcaeus, 90, 161
Alekseev, M. P., 169
Andronikova, Salomeja, 148
Annenskij, Innokentij, 4, 38–39, 45, 58,
    63, 96, 143, 155, 156, 166
Apuxtin, A. N., 166
Arbenina, O. N., 62, 105, 108, 152, 164
Ariosto, Lodovico, 64, 154
Aucuturier, Michel, 145
Axmatova, A. A., 3, 15, 68–69, 83, 105,
    132, 148, 151, 152, 155, 157, 160, 166

Bachelard, Gaston, 149, 160
Bal'mont, K. D., 70–71, 96, 103, 104,
    149, 163
Balzac, Honoré de, 3, 148
Baratynskij, E. A., 37, 112, 149
Barnstone, Willis, 89
Batjuškov, K. N., 1–3
Baudelaire, Charles, 148
Baxrax, Aleksandr, 168
Belyj, Andrej, 3, 5, 6, 38, 129, 136, 154,
    156
Benedict XV, 146
Bergk, Theodor, 87, 91, 162
Bergson, Henri, 167
Blok, Aleksandr, 1, 3, 6, 7, 9, 28–29, 56,
    58, 69–70, 75, 81, 90, 105, 108, 129,
    155, 166
Bobrov, Sergej, 16, 139
Bosio, Angiolina, 141
Brjusov, Valerij, 6, 150, 157
Brown, Clarence, 4
Broyde, Steven, 119, 136, 137, 152, 154
Brzostowska, Janina, 85, 89, 91, 93, 162
Bunin, I. A., 90

Burljuk, David, 15, 17, 139
Bušman, Irina, 163
Butomo-Nezvanova, O. N., 69
Buxštab, B. Ja., 142–143

Caesar, Gaius Julius, 7
Catullus, Gaius Valerius, 2, 3, 163
Chénier, André, 78
Constantine the Great, 119–120
Cruden, Alexander, 158
Cvetaeva, Marina, 4, 116–118, 120, 147,
    149, 152, 167, 168

Čaadaev, P. Ja., 118, 120
Čajkovskij, P. I., 8

Dal'nij, G. See Superfin, G. G.
Daniil Zatočnik, 86
Dante Alighieri, 3, 7, 37, 38, 46, 64, 65,
    152, 154, 155
David, King, 60, 145
Del'vig, A. A., 168
Democritus, 7
Deržavin, G. R., 3, 29–30, 32, 106–107,
    141, 158, 162, 164
Dickens, Charles, 3
Dimitrij, the Pretender, 117–118, 120
Dimitrij, Tsar Ivan's son, 118
Dymšic, A. L., 141

Edmonds, J. M., 90
Esenin, S. A., 6, 46, 80, 138
Euripides, 39, 150, 152

Feodorov, A. F., 156
Fet, A. A., 3, 22, 23, 144, 159
Filofej, starec, 120

Flaubert, Gustave, 148
Florenskij, P. A., 118, 168

Gercyk, Adelaida, 83
Gercyk, Evgenija (Adelaida's sister), 83
Geršenzon, M. O., 165–166
Gibbon, Edward, 168
Ginzburg, L. Ja., 8, 9, 26–28, 62, 117–118, 141, 143
Gnedič, N. I., 147
Goethe, Johann Wolfgang, 2, 37, 49, 135
Goetz, Johann Nikolaus, 106
Goleniščev-Kutuzov, Pavel, 92, 162
Golosovker, Ja., 144
Grot, Ja. K., 164
Gumilev, N. S., 3, 6, 39, 105, 122, 142, 150, 160, 166, 169
Gurdžiev (Gurdjieff), G. I., 6, 137

Heine, Heinrich, 33, 80
Heraclitus, 157
Hesiod, 6, 86, 90, 92, 97, 146, 161
Hill, P. Maurice, 89
Homer, 3, 42, 61 (*Iliad*), 87, 92, 93, 144, 146, 147, 157 (*Odyssey*)
Horace (Quintus Horatius Flaccus), 42, 86
Hoslaple, Lloyd B., 168
Hugo, Victor, 38

Ivan, son of Maryna Mniszek, 118
Ivan III of Russia, 120
Ivan IV of Russia, 118
Ivanov, Georgij, 169
Ivanov, Vjačeslav Ivanovič, 3, 83, 85–93, 95, 96, 98, 99, 101, 102, 104, 105, 110, 111, 146, 153, 157, 161–163, 165, 166
Ivanov, Vjačeslav Vsevolodovič, 140

Jakobson, Roman, 94, 145
Jazykov, N. M., 3, 168
Joel, the Prophet, 54
John, the Evangelist, 54, 57, 152
Jowett, B., 86, 97
Justinian the Great, 120

Kablukov, P. S., 168
Karcevskij, S. I., 85, 96
Kataev, Valentin, 79, 160
Kireevskij, I. V., 149
Komissarževskaja, V. F., 148
Krylov, I. A., 164
Kuzmin, M. A., 149

Pjast, Vladimir, 140
Lapšin, I. I., 140
Leconte de Lisle, Charles, 39
Lermontov, M. Ju., 3, 6, 15–17, 70, 75, 107, 125, 139, 141, 147
Levin, Ju. I., 4, 78, 141, 149, 152, 165
Levinton, G. A., 87, 89, 98, 154, 155, 161
Livšic, Benedikt, 3, 6, 135
Lomonosov, M. V., 159
Longus Sophista, 106

Maeterlinck, Maurice, 106
Majakovskij, V. V., 6, 7, 46, 61, 129, 149
Majkov, A. N., 97
Makkavejskij, Vladimir, 97–98, 153, 162
Mallarmé, Stéphane, 39, 63
Mandel'štam, N. Ja., 6, 19, 55, 57, 60–66, 98, 120, 135, 140, 141, 152–154, 160–162, 168
Margvelašvili, Georgij, 28, 40–41, 46–47
Mark, the Evangelist, 54
Martynov, Leonid, 170
Matthew, the Evangelist, 54, 55
Mniszek, Maryna, 117–118
Močul'skij, K. V., 85
Mozart, Wolfgang Amadeus, 2, 19–20
Munexin, Mixail, *d'jak*, 120

Nekrasov, N. A., 18, 80, 127
Nerval, Gérard de, 150
Nilsson, Nils Åke, 86, 102, 110, 145, 147, 166–168
Novalis (Friedrich von Hardenberg), 149

Odoevskij, A. I., 147
Ogarev, N. P., 166
Oleg, Prince, 150
Oleša, Ju. K., 79
Ovid (Publius Ovidius Naso), 2, 3, 44–45, 144, 146

Palestrina (Giovanni Pierluigi), 146
Parnax, Valentin, 154
Pascal, Blaise, 52
Pasternak, Boris, 6, 7, 29, 80, 81, 115, 129, 141, 145, 160, 169
Paul, the Apostle, 152
Pečerin, V. S., 165
Petrarch (Petrarca, Francesco), 136, 138
Petrovyx, Marija, 149
Pius IX, 146

Plato, 86, 87, 97, 161
Pliny the Elder, 159
Poe, Edgar Allan, 3, 19, 140, 148
Przybylski, Ryszard, 84–87, 89, 91, 92, 95, 97, 98, 143, 161, 162
Pseudo-Anacreon, 90
Puškin, A. S., 2–5, 18, 19, 31, 45, 52, 54, 62, 75, 78, 100, 116, 117, 125–128, 131–132, 138, 145–147, 151–152, 154, 165, 166, 168–171

Racine, Jean Baptiste, 3, 150
Rembrandt van Rijn, 65, 154, 170
Romanov, Pantelejmon, 80
Ronen, Omry, 6, 51, 52, 57, 143, 149–150, 161
Ronsard, Pierre de, 86
Rubinštejn, Anton, 8

Salieri, Antonio, 20
Sappho, 3, 85–93, 95–97, 110, 153, 161
Schiller, Friedrich, 49
Schubert, Franz, 2, 69, 135, 167
Segal, D. M., 32, 119, 141, 143, 144, 154, 163
Sel'vinskij, Il'ja, 114
Serov, V. A., 153
Shakespeare, William, 92, 135
Skrjabin, A. N., 17, 151–152
Solženicyn, A. I., 169
Stalin, I. V., 113
Stankiewicz, Edward, 156
Strauss, Richard 148
Struve, Gleb, 154, 155
Sumarokov, A. P., 93
Superfin, G. G., 108

Tasso, Torquato, 2, 3
Terapiano, Jurij, 97–98, 162

Terpander, 84, 87, 93, 95, 97, 162
Terras, Victor, 44, 122, 143, 153, 169
Theocritus, 161
Thomas Aquinas, 164
Tibullus, 3
Timenčik, R. D., 154
Tjutčev, F. I., 3, 16–17, 32–33, 36, 37, 43–44, 52–53, 80, 87, 121–124, 139–143, 146–147, 149, 158, 163, 169
Toddes, E. A., 37, 121, 142
Turgenev, I. S., 156
Tušinskij Vor, 118
Tynjanov, Jurij, 24–26, 141

Uspenskij (Ouspensky), P. D., 137
Ušakov, D. N., 138

Vaksel', Ol'ga, 62, 160
Valéry, Paul, 60
Vasilij III of Russia, 120
Veresaev, V. V., 85–89, 93, 161, 162
Verlaine, Paul, 45, 106
Vielé-Griffin, Francis, 111
Villon, François, 45, 144–145
Virgil (Publius Vergilius Maro), 158 (*Aeneid*), 161

Wells, H. G., 4
Whorf, B. L., 167
Wilde, Oscar, 54, 148
Wrangel, P. N., I, 105, 124, 169

Xardžiev, N. I., 4, 140, 148, 155
Xazina. *See* Mandel'štam, N. Ja.
Xlebnikov, Velimir, 4, 6, 46, 129, 135
Xomjakov, A. S., 149–150

Zieliński, Tadeusz (Zelinskij, F. F.), 146

Žukovskij, V. A., 157

# INDEX OF MANDEL'ŠTAM'S WRITINGS

"Abbat," 147
"Ajja-Sofija," 119
"Amerikan bar," 162
"A nebo buduščim beremenno," 6, 40, 112, 167
"Ariost," 64, 112
"Armenija," 12, 40, 140

"Barsučja nora," 7, 114
"Batjuškov," 2
"Bessonnica. Gomer. Tugie parusa," 61, 147

"Čerty lica iskaženy," 155
"Četvertaja proza," 14, 41, 60–61
"Čtob prijatel' i vetra i kapel'," 144
"Čto pojut časy-kuznečik," 18, 63, 68–81, 105, 140, 152, 155, 159, 160, 161
"Čut' mercaet prizračnaja scena," 141

"Da, ja ležu v zemle, gubami ševelja," 126–132
"Dajte Tjutčevu strekozu," 37
"Dano mne telo—čto mne delat' s nim," 10, 41
"Dekabrist," 66
"10 [Desjatoe] janvarja 1934," 5
"Devjatnadcatyj vek," 65
"Dombi i syn," 105
"Dušu ot vnešnix uslovij," 39, 74
"Dvorcovaja ploščad'," 57, 59, 139
"Dyxan'e veščee v stixax moix," 10, 143

*Egipetskaja marka*, 30, 34–35, 37, 59, 141, 145
"Emu kavkazskie kričali gory," 38
"Esli b menja naši vragi vzjali," 13

"Ešče daleko asfodelej," 77, 111
"Ešče daleko mne do patriarxa," 30
"Ešče ne umer ty, ešče ty ne odin," 153
"Ešče on pomnit bašmakov iznos," 38
"Ėta noč' nepopravima," 48, 51, 54–55, 165

"Feodosija" (poem), 11
"Feodosija," sketch "Staruxina ptica," 124
"Flejty grečeskoj tèta i jota," 64
"Fransua Villon," 45

"Gončarami velik ostrov sinij," 64
"Grifel'naja oda," 2, 15, 19, 31–32, 35, 46, 79, 107, 119, 140, 141, 144, 165

"I ponyne na Afone," 51
"I Šubert na vode, i Mocart v ptič'em game," 2, 38
"Iz omuta zlogo i vjazkogo," 51–53

"Ja bol'še ne rebenok. Ty, mogila," 126, 135
"Ja budu metat'sja po taboru ulicy temnoj," 79–80, 153, 160
"Ja naravne s drugimi," 27, 39, 108–109
"Ja ne iskal v cvetuščie mgnoven'ja," 69, 151, 155
"Ja ne slyxal rasskazov Ossiana," 1, 46
"Ja ne znaju, s kakix por," 11, 21–41, 47, 79, 144
"Ja nynče v pautine svetovoj," 13, 135
"Ja p'ju za voennye astry," 59
"Ja po lesenke pristavnoj," 11, 22, 41–47, 79
"Ja prošu, kak žalosti i milosti," 66
"Ja slovo pozabyl, čto ja xotel skazat'," 39, 75–78, 104, 128, 158, 159, 160, 162
"Ja vižu kamennoe nebo," 14

"Ja v xorovod tenej, toptavšix nežnyj lug," 158
"Jazyk bulyžnika mne golubja ponjatnej," 119

"Kak ètix pokryval u ètogo ubora," 150
"Kak rastet xlebov opara," 27, 35–36
"Kak svetoteni mučenik Rembrandt," 170
"Kak tel'ce malen'koe krylyškom," 137, 142
*Kamen'*, 33, 37, 48, 50, 143, 169
"Kancona," 64–65
"Kassandre." *See* "Ja ne iskal v cvetuščie mgnoven'ja"
"Kazino," 159
"K ènciklike papy Benedikta XV," 146
"K nemeckoj reči," 2, 66
"Kogda mozaik niknut travy," 55–56
"Kogda na ploščadjax i v tišine kelejnoj," 155
"Kogda Psixeja-žizn' spuskaetsja k tenjam," 75–77, 104–105, 109, 158
"Kogda usnet zemlja i žar otpyšet" (Petrarch, Sonnet 164), 12, 138
"Kogda v temnoj noči zamiraet," 151
"Koljut resnicy. V grudi prikipela sleza," 12
"Komu zima — arak i punš goluboglazyj," 31
"Koncert na vokzale," 7–11, 14–17, 138–140, 165
"Kto znaet, možet byt', ne xvatit mne sveči," 11
"Kuda mne det'sja v ètom janvare," 13
"Kuvšin," 64, 154

"Lamark," 122
"Leningrad," 59
"Lišiv menja morej, razbega i razleta," 128
"Ljublju pod svodami sedyja tišiny," 11, 48
"Ljublju pojavlenie tkani," 12, 43

"Masterica vinovatyx vzorov," 147
"Medlitel'nee snežnyj ulej," 136
"Men'ševiki v Gruzii," 169
"Mne xolodno. Prozračnaja vesna," 59
"Mne žalko, čto teper' zima," 108
"My naprjažennogo molčan'ja ne vynosim," 19
"My s toboj na kuxne posidim," 153
"My živem, pod soboju ne čuja strany," 126

"Na blednogoluboj èmali," 139

"Na kamennyx otrogax Pièrii," 61, 83–98, 153, 159, 161, 162
"Na mertvyx resnicax Isakij zamerz," 167
"Na rozval'njax, uložennyx solomoj," 115–120, 132, 152, 168
"Na strašnoj vysote bluždajuščij ogon'," 58–59
"Našedšij podkovu," 4, 12, 82, 119, 138
"Naušniki, naušnički moi," 130, 131, 169
"Ne govori nikomu," 112–113, 123–126
"Ne iskušaj čužix narečij," 57, 129
"Ne sravnivaj: živuščij nesravnim," 13, 64
"Neutolimye slova," 56–57
"Ne verja voskresen'ja čudu," 110, 168
"Nevyrazimaja pečal'," 169
"Ni o čem ne nužno govorit'," 75, 120, 147
"Notre Dame," 37

"Oboronjaet son svoju donskuju son'," 131
"O, ètot medlennyj odyšlivyj prostor," 12
"O ètot vozdux, smutoj p'janyj," 11, 171
"On dirižiroval kavkazskimi gorami," 38
"O nebo, nebo, ty mne budeš' snit'sja," 15, 143
"O prirode slova," 38, 42, 45, 48, 49, 83, 156, 163, 167
"O sobesednike," 111, 132
"Otravlen xleb i vozdux vypit," 10, 33
"Ottogo vse neudači" ("Kaščej"), 143
"O vremenax prostyx i grubyx," 144

"Paden'e neizmennyj sputnik straxa," 36
"1 [Pervoe] janvarja 1924," 39, 40, 123, 128
"Pešexod," 17
"Peterburgskie strofy," 10, 59, 116
"Petr Čaadaev," 118, 120, 146
"Pis'mo o russkoj poèzii," 135
"Pod grozovymi oblakami," 158
"Poju, kogda gortan' syra," 13
"Polnoč'' v Moskve," 153
"Privykajut k pčelovodu pčely," 112, 155
"Promčalis' dni moi, kak by olenej" (Petrarch, Sonnet 319), 136
"Puškin i Skrjabin," 49, 50, 53, 151–152
"Putešestvie v Armeniju," 125

"Rakovina," 31–32, 79, 143
*Razgovor o Dante*, 7, 37, 38, 46, 67, 152
"Razryvy kruglyx buxt, i xrjašč, i sineva," 13

"Segodnja možno snjat' dekal'komani," 12

"Senoval I–II." *See* "Ja ne znaju s kakix por" (I) and "Ja po lesenke pristavnoj" (II)

"Sestry — tjažest' i nežnost', odinakovy vaši primety," 11, 98, 151

"Silentium," 10, 121–124

"Skaži mne, čertežnik pustyni," 66–67

"Skudnyj luč xolodnoj meroju," 14, 139

"Slovo i kul'tura," 2–3, 5, 45, 48, 50, 103, 137, 156, 158, 159

"Solominka I–II," 19, 59, 140, 147–148

"Sredi svjaščennikov levitom molodym," 48, 55, 57, 58, 63

"S rozovoj penoj ustalosti u mjagkix gub," 138, 153

"Susal'nym zolotom gorjat," 14

"Slux čutkij parus naprjagaet," 14

"Soxrani moju reč' navsegda za privkus nesčast'ja i dyma," 37

"Stixi o neizvestnom soldate," 13, 15, 140

"Stixi o russkoj poèzii," 129–130, 145, 164

"Stixi o Staline," 113

*Šum vremeni*: "Muzyka v Pavlovske," 7; "Bunty i francuženki," 49, 52, 53, 60; "Knižnyj škap," 34; "Xaos iudejskij," 48, 146; "Sem'ja Sinani," 151; "V ne po činu barstvennoj šube," 44, 155, 167

"Tajnaja večerja," 63, 139

"Telefon," 19, 80–81

*Tristia*, 48, 58, 156, 165

"Tristia," 145, 157

"Tvoe čudesnoe proiznošen'e," 11, 69, 155, 160

"Tvoj zračok v nebesnoj korke," 153

"Uničtožaet plamen'," 26, 74

"Ulybnis' jagnenok gnevnyj," 12

"Umyvalsja noč'ju na dvore," 139

"Utro akmeizma," 36, 56

"Vek," 40, 131

"Vernis' v smesitel'noe lono," 48, 59, 60, 75, 152

"Veter nam utešen'e prines," 136, 137, 139, 155, 167

"V god tridcat' pervyj ot rožden'ja veka," 65

"V ogromnom omute prozračno i temno," 51–54, 147–148

"Vooružennyj zren'em uzkix os," 113–114

"Vot daronosica, kak solnce zolotoe," 50, 55

"Vozdux pasmurnyj vlažen i gulok," 14

"Voz'mi na radost' iz moix ladonej," 83, 99–110, 156, 159, 168–169

"Vozmožna li ženščine mertvoj xvala," 160

"Vozvraščenie," 144

"V Peterburge my sojdemsja snova," 108, 140, 151, 152, 164

"V Petropole prozračnom my umrem," 11

"V raznogolosice devičeskogo xora," 168

"Vse čuždo nam v stolice nepotrebnoj," 170

"V taverne vorovskaja šajka," 41, 111

*Vtoraja kniga*, 156

"V tot večer ne gudel strel'čatyj les organa," 69, 155

"Vy xotite byt' igrušečnoj," 155

"V xrustal'nom omute kakaja krutizna," 11, 145

"Xolodnoe leto," 142

"Xolodok ščekočet temja," 40, 74, 78, 81–82, 128, 141, 153, 160

"Zametki o poèzii," 46

"Zametki o Šen'e," 160

"Zamolči! Ni o čem, nikogda, nikomu," 124

"Zasnula čern'. Zijaet ploščad' arkoj," 40

"Za to, čto ja ruki tvoi ne sumel uderžat'," 26, 63, 108, 143

"Zolotistogo meda struja iz butylki tekla," 62

"Znakomstva našego na sklone," 155

"Zverinec," 10, 66

"Žizn' upala, kak zarnica," 160